A PENGUIN BOOK

ONE-WAY TICKET

JONATHAN VAUGHTERS began his cycling career in Colorado, eventually racing alongside Lance Armstrong on the infamous U.S. Postal Service team. In the wake of the doping scandals that have plagued the sport, he founded what has become the U.S.-based EF Education First Pro Cycling Team, which he still manages as it competes at cycling's highest level.

D1023632

ONE-WAY TICKET

NINE LIVES ON TWO WHEELS

JONATHAN VAUGHTERS

with JEREMY WHITTLE

PENGUIN BOOKS

PENGUIN BOOKS
An imprint of Penguin Random House LLC
penguinrandomhouse.com

First published in Great Britain by Quercus, an imprint of Hachette, 2019
Published in Penguin Books 2019

Copyright © 2019 by Jonathan Vaughters
Penguin supports copyright. Copyright fuels creativity, encourages diverse voices,
promotes free speech, and creates a vibrant culture. Thank you for buying an authorized
edition of this book and for complying with copyright laws by not reproducing, scanning,
or distributing any part of it in any form without permission. You are supporting writers
and allowing Penguin to continue to publish books for every reader.

LIBRARY OF CONGRESS CATALOGING-IN-PUBLICATION DATA
Names: Vaughters, Jonathan, 1973– author.
Title: One-way ticket : nine lives on two wheels / Jonathan Vaughters with Jeremy Whittle.
Description: New York : Penguin Books, An imprint of Penguin Random House LLC, 2019.
Identifiers: LCCN 2019020523 (print) | LCCN 2019980663 (ebook) |
ISBN 9780143134145 (paperback) | ISBN 9780525505877 (ebook)
Subjects: LCSH: Vaughters, Jonathan, 1973– | Cyclists—Colorado—Biography. | Bicycle racing.
Classification: LCC GV1051.V38 A3 2019 (print) | LCC GV1051.V38 (ebook) |
DDC 796.6092 [B]—dc23
LC record available at https://lccn.loc.gov/2019020523
LC ebook record available at https://lccn.loc.gov/2019980663

Printed in the United States of America
1   3   5   7   9   10   8   6   4   2

Set in Janson MT Pro
Designed by Gretchen Achilles

Penguin is committed to publishing works of quality and integrity. In that spirit,
we are proud to offer this book to our readers; however, the story,
the experiences, and the words are the author's alone.

DEDICATED TO THE MEMORY OF DR. DEAN H. MOSHER

While I never mention Dr. Dean H. Mosher in this memoir, he was—and is—the most influential person in my life. He was my grandfather, my very first mentor, and the man who taught me how to get back up when life pushed me down.

Dean grew up the son of a country doctor and a member of a homesteading Mennonite farming family in the breadbasket of America. He learned to hunt, fish, and cook squirrels from Native Americans living near his family farm. A prankster who let livestock loose in the local high school, and a notoriously poor student in his younger years, his father thought he would fail in life and end up on the streets.

However, my grandfather had other plans. He worked his way back into academics, and eventually graduated top of his class from dental school. He returned to his hometown to run the family farm, still with my family today, and practice dentistry throughout some of America's most challenging decades of the twentieth century.

My memories of Grampa are only from my childhood, as he passed away before my cycling career had truly started. He took it upon himself to teach me how to hunt, fish, and survive off the land. He proudly looked on when I won the Fourth of July fishing derby in Mendota, Illinois, with a catch of no less than six bullhead catfish.

However, the lessons and memories from Grampa weren't always so idyllic and nice . . .

While fishing in the far north reaches of Canada, I stuck a rather large treble hook through my hand. The barb sunk deep into my flesh and wasn't coming out. We were hundreds of miles from the nearest hospital. So when I heard him say his infamous "Let me just take a look at it" words that he used when extracting teeth, I knew I was in trouble. He held my hand hard and pushed the hook through the other side of it with pliers. He then clipped the bloody barb off and slid the hook back out. The pain was absolutely blinding for a child. Yet in a flash of decisiveness and action on his part, the problem was solved. And I was free to keep fishing the rest of the afternoon, albeit with a bandage on my hand.

The lesson he'd taught me was simple: sometimes life sticks a barb in you that won't come out easily. It's then you have a choice: deal with the pain, push it out the other side, and move on—or waste a week of your life going to the hospital having surgery to do the same damned thing.

It was the lesson that has allowed me to push through so many hard moments. Sometimes, no matter how bad it hurts, you just gotta grit your teeth and push the barb through.

Thank you, Grampa. I love you to this day.

CONTENTS

AUTHOR'S NOTE

I started bike racing in complete ignorance of the fact that, from its early days, the sport had been tainted by cheating in many forms. By the time I retired from racing, I knew all about it. It is hard to pinpoint the moment when my innocence was broken, as it was a realization that slowly dawned on me rather than a single moment when I suddenly knew. I imagine the same is true for anyone involved in the sport in the 1990s and early 2000s. Enough riders have failed drugs tests, and enough have admitted to having doped, that no one can deny that the sport was thoroughly infected by doping in one form or another for many years. That is not to say that everyone did it, or that everyone knew at the time, and nothing in this book should be taken as indicating guilt on the part of anyone who has not already been found guilty of, or confessed to, illegal use of banned materials.

All I will say is that, considering how rife doping was, anyone who succeeded in the sport without doping deserves to be hailed as honorable and exceptional. Instead, sadly, everyone involved in the professional sport of road cycling during that era has the cloud of suspicion hanging over them. One of the reasons I wrote this book is to acknowledge the part I played in the creation of that cloud, and to document the things I have done since in an effort to make amends.

ONE-WAY TICKET

PROLOGUE

One of the first things you'll see, heading west from my parents' house at the top of a hill in suburban Denver, is the enormous outcrop of Mount Evans.

Every ride to school in my dad's orange Volvo station wagon, and every training ride I ever did as a child, started with me staring straight up at this huge mountain.

It's an imposing and beautiful view to see every day. It gave me purpose, gave me motivation, and even as a kid, filled my heart with the spirit of the high mountains.

It's a gorgeous mountain to look at from the top of that little hill by Mom and Dad's house. In winter, it's a massive snow-covered giant staring back at you. In the summer, it embodies the "purple mountain majesties" of Katharine Lee Bates's song "America the Beautiful."

At 14,265 feet tall, it is one of Colorado's highest mountains, and very much the most visible from the city of Denver. What makes it special, particularly to bike racers, is that it has a paved road all the way to the top. It's the highest paved road in North America, and one of the highest paved roads in the world.

Every kid in Colorado who's ever raced a bike dreams about winning the legendary race up Mount Evans. But the lure of the race isn't just about winning, but also about setting the record up the Old Lady. For a cycling-mad teenager, owning the record up Mount Evans is like holding the key to immortality.

At 14,000 feet, nature moves fast, and if you want the record,

God needs to smile on you. The winds must be just right, the weather just stable enough. To set the record you have to never let up on the pace, yet also keep a close eye on your competition, as they may sit behind you on the shallow gradients, waiting to win and unconcerned with the record.

Bob Cook, a Colorado native and peer to three-time Tour de France winner Greg LeMond, was not only a world-class cyclist, but was also a world-class academic and engineer. Bob won the Mount Evans hill climb time after time in the 1970s and 1980s, but then, just after graduating from university, was diagnosed with a brain tumor and passed away. From there on, the race was named the Bob Cook Memorial.

I won on Mount Evans for the first time as a fourteen-year-old. It was a "technical victory," as I was racing with older kids and finished fifth, but the four kids in front of me were all seventeen or eighteen years old. Our race only went halfway to the top, so we got to watch as the professional riders came past on their trudge upward into the thin, rarefied air.

I so wanted to be one of them. I thought that maybe Bob Cook was my spirit mentor. I wanted to be just like him.

I became absolutely obsessed with Mount Evans after that victory. I wanted to become one of the legends to conquer that mountain. I wanted to be king. That was how I started a fifteen-year journey of trying to break the record up Mount Evans.

The record became my Moby Dick, reminding me of "Ahab and anguish . . . stretched together in one hammock."

I chased it to the point of insanity. Many times, when it easily should have been mine, somehow it would slip away. After failing, I would stare at that mountain all year waiting for another chance to claim the record.

I drilled holes in my bike, sought out a lighter option for every component on the bike, tried experimental diets, spent weeks at extremely high-altitude training. Now, in 2019, that's all standard stuff. However, in the early '90s, it was seen as lunacy and obsessive. Indeed, I was obsessed.

My first real crack at the record was in 1992. The year before, as a seventeen-year-old, I'd finished fifth in the professional race, so I figured with a year more of adolescent growth under my belt, I'd be ready to compete for the win. I asked my team to be let out of the normal race schedule so that I could go and train in Leadville, at 10,000 feet. They begrudgingly granted me permission to go and become a crazed hermit in the old mining town for a month.

I trained harder than I ever had and adopted a low-carbohydrate diet in pursuit of losing a few pounds. I risked getting kicked off my team by replacing all the sponsor-friendly parts on my bike with the absolute lightest components I could find.

The final product was a bike so light that it would nowadays blow a hole in the UCI's weight regulations. It really didn't have brakes that exactly worked, all the bolts were titanium or aluminum and anything that could be stripped off, was. I didn't use handlebar tape, the saddle had no padding, and the seat post weighed next to nothing.

I weighed 128 pounds, my bike didn't add much to that, and I had spent a month breathing air with very little oxygen. Like Gollum with the ring, I was ready to grab the key to immortality.

From the start of the 28-mile climb, the race was going my way. The Coors Light pro team had decided they wanted the record as well, and rode a fierce tempo at the front from the very start. Mount Evans doesn't really start to steepen up until mile 7, so a strong team is always needed to break the record, as those first seven miles must be ridden fast.

As I rode in their wake, I watched quietly as Coors Light did their thing. I was an unknown to them, and in their confidence, they never bothered to worry about the skinny little eighteen-year-old on the bike with plastic brakes.

At mile 15, when the road turns off the wider, smoothly paved road and hits the narrower state park road, the gradient also steepens. So, right after this turn and at about 11,000-feet altitude, I decided to put in a sharp acceleration.

The Coors Light guys were shocked, but responded, although it took them a few minutes to get on terms with me. At this point I'd shown my cards, but I'd shown them a bit too early. I needed to pare the lead group down further, to just myself and another Coors Light rider, not three.

I figured if I was in for a dime, I might as well be in for a dollar. I accelerated again. Then once again. Soon enough it was just me and Mike Engleman. I could feel him suffering behind me, so I kept the pressure on, thinking I could deal the final blow in the last few miles.

The day had been dead calm and warm, with maybe even a slight tailwind on the longest section of the climb, from Echo Lake to Summit Lake. The road had just been repaved and you could feel the smoothness of the surface. We were going fast, very fast.

At 13,000 feet, you reach a small descent toward Summit Lake. I coasted down the only drop in the entire race with Engleman on my wheel. He'd been suffering and his teammates were now behind, so his best chance was to just sit on me and take it to a sprint. I accelerated again, as soon as the gradient began to bite, but now the road was potholed and cracked due to the extreme weather at such a high altitude.

I looked back to see if I'd finally rid myself of Engleman, and as I did, I hit a pothole.

Snap!

My seat post broke and my saddle went tumbling onto the ground. For a few minutes, I figured I could just ride to the top, out of the saddle, but at 14,000 feet, riding out of the saddle doesn't work so well.

Eventually, exhausted, I blew and could only watch Engleman ride away and destroy the record. I finished despondent. All my risky equipment choices had bitten me in the ass. I was still determined that I would come back and win, and break the record, but that day turned out to be the closest I ever got.

After that, I kept trying to conquer Mount Evans, but there was always some bizarre mishap—a flat tire, an odd cramp, or some very strange weather. The most telling incident was in 1999, when I did win the race, but didn't get the record.

Clad in U.S. Postal Service team kit and fresh from conquering Mont Ventoux in the south of France, I was clearly much stronger than I'd been as a twerpy eighteen-year-old. But by 1999, I'd also got up to quite a bit of doping.

I rode away from the field very easily. I was flying up the mountain, on my way to the record, dancing on the pedals. Just as I started thinking about how much I would break the record by, it started getting windy. Very windy. Soon enough I was fighting into a gale force headwind and barely able to keep the bike upright. The violent gusts lasted the entire long section between Echo Lake and Summit Lake. No matter how strong I may have been that day, I wasn't going to break any records.

As soon as I crossed the finish line, the sky suddenly lightened, and the wind died. I sat after the race, in the calm sunshine, my guilty conscience gnawing at me. Was the mountain trying to tell me something? Had my wicked ways somehow turned the mountain against me?

Maybe Bob Cook himself was not at ease with seeing me claim that record. I still think that. Somehow the spirit up there needed me to understand that I couldn't just have whatever I wanted, by whatever means were necessary. I needed to respect the mountain and its purity. I hadn't done that.

The Mount Evans climb was also the last race I ever competed in. I wanted to end my career there, as it was the mountain that had inspired me for so many years. I had never conquered the Old Lady, but I had reached my peace with her.

We both knew that I didn't deserve the record, but in a nod to all my attempts and perhaps my slowly evolving path back toward being a more just and honorable person, she let me win that year. It was a soft good-bye kiss on the cheek.

PART 1
1986–1988

CHAPTER 1

DEAD LAST

'm not really sure why I signed up for my first bike race.

I was terrible at school, and terrible at sports. I had very little coordination, very small muscles, and was a good six inches shorter than the next smallest kid in my class. "Athletic" would be the last term anyone used to describe me. In short, I had the academic and athletic talent of a rain-soaked worm.

So how, or even why, at twelve years old, I decided to make bike racing my big adventure, I have no idea. But it happened. On an early July morning in 1986 my parents drove me from beige, suburban Denver up to scenic, blue-skied Boulder. I was racing in the Red Zinger Mini Classic, a week-long stage race for kids, fashioned after the famous Coors Classic stage race.

The opening stage was a time trial. I wasn't really familiar with the discipline, and wondered if just riding on a lonely road, all by myself, was really what I signed up for. Noticing how nervous and focused my competitors were, I retreated to the back of my parents' station wagon and wrestled with Angie, our cuddly Bedlington terrier. Perhaps I was more of a bike *rider* than a bike *racer*? Sure, I loved riding my bike around to visit friends and girls I had crushes on. But racing to win? These kids looked bigger, meaner, stronger. They looked like hungry wolves to me.

I timidly rolled over to the start line, honestly not understanding what I was in for. It seemed simple enough: ride five miles, from A to B, as fast as you can. Yet, as is my nature, I'd overthought the whole ordeal, and felt like sliding back to the family Oldsmobile and asking Mom and Dad to take me home. But off I went, riding into the unknown territory of a solo race against the clock on Highway 36. Very soon after the start, some other rider went zipping past me. And then, soon after that, so did another. This bike-racing deal matched the absolute lack of success at athletic exploits I'd experienced to date in my life.

I was slow. Very slow.

We had set off in alphabetical order, and a few riders behind me was Chris Wherry. Wherry was a tall, handsome legend in twelve-year-old Colorado bike racing folklore. He'd won just about every race he entered and he commanded respect, even among the other twelve-year-old "superstars" hovering in the dirt parking lot that served as the start line.

Of course, soon enough he came whizzing past me, on his way to winning another race. As he passed me, he yelled out: *"Come on, dude! You gotta try a bit harder!"* It was quite embarrassing. Duly, I did attempt to up the pace and keep up with him, for all of about a hundred feet. He left me gasping and wincing, half in shame and half in pain.

I dragged myself across the finish line. I knew I hadn't done very well, but I figured I hadn't been caught by Wherry too quickly, so maybe I'd finish somewhere in the middle of the twelve-year-old category. I was being a bit too optimistic.

My parents had brought a picnic to eat in between the morning time trial and the afternoon criterium race. We sat with all the other families patiently waiting for the results of the morning time trial to come in.

I ate a bologna and cheese sandwich and slurped down a soda, all the while secretly feeding Angie scraps of the sandwich that I wasn't fond of. Finally, they posted a sheet on the side of an outhouse in the park.

My father and I reluctantly strolled over to see how I'd fared.

Over all the craning necks and taller heads, I finally spotted my name—at the very bottom of the list.

The very last spot.

I was crushed and embarrassed to even be there. I wanted to go home. I wanted to leave, immediately.

This was just the same as everything else I'd tried. I wasn't any good at it. Just like school, just like games on the playground, just like trying to fit in. I failed at all of them, and now I was a failure at bike racing, too. I just wasn't any good—at anything.

I spoke to my mother and told her I wanted to leave, immediately. I had no business being there. She was a sympathetic ear, just listening as I recounted how poor I was at bike racing, and that maybe I just needed to leave and go home.

Angie sensed that I was upset. She came over and started giving me little doggie kisses, trying to understand what was wrong. I gave her a long hug and hoped that we'd just get going, far away from this place and these people.

Meanwhile, my mother and father were locked in conversation about something. It was clearly a heated discussion and I watched as Dad waved his arms around.

My parents were never sports-minded. My father is an attorney with an acute love for the Constitution of the United States, and a very strong sense of fairness. His love for reading and for justice was very strong and something he passed on to me. He loved helping people and going above and beyond to protect the rights of his clients.

He was well liked and respected. Often, we'd be given firewood, chicken meat, or help around the house in lieu of payment for bills that his clients couldn't afford, clients that he had opted to represent anyway. He was driven by the concept of equality for all, not by a love of money.

My mother taught children with learning disabilities and speech pathology. She had wanted to become a medical doctor, but her grandfather, an MD himself, had convinced her otherwise, saying that medicine was no place for a woman. That decision, to not pursue medicine, never stopped bothering her.

Nevertheless, she managed to be very progressive for a woman who came of age in the chauvinistic 1950s, getting her master's degree in speech pathology and focusing on her career first.

She had married a younger man late in life, and didn't have me until she was thirty-eight years old. My parents were a formidable unit of intellectual horsepower, but their kid, competing in sports—particularly such an odd niche sport as cycling—was an unknown to them.

I sat on the grass, watching them argue, until finally they agreed, which—knowing how decisive and combative my mother was—meant we were about to pack up the car and go back home.

Instead, my father walked over and firmly stated that we were staying, and I was going to start the afternoon's race. I was stunned and protested to him with all my might.

Dad is a gentle soul, not predisposed to drawing hard lines about anything. He has an uncanny ability to see both sides of any issue. He would cede mostly to the more decisive nature of my mother, or even to me.

But not on that day.

He sat me down.

"If you start something, you damn well finish it," he said firmly. "Doesn't matter if you're best or worst, you don't just quit. You're going to start the afternoon race, and you're going to try your best."

I was shocked.

"I paid a lot for you to do this damned thing, so you aren't just quitting," he said exasperatedly. "No way."

My dad was the ever-supportive bear and never pushed back on anything. It was the first time my father had ever forced me to do something. And that one decision of his changed my entire life.

Later that afternoon, I begrudgingly started stage two of the Red Zinger, assuming I would just get slaughtered and lapped very quickly. I didn't want to be there and I didn't want to race. But I did, frown and all.

That start gun fired, and I struggled to quickly get my loose foot into the toe clips and toe straps on my bike. I'd fought my way back into the peloton of puberty by the end of the first short lap. Somehow this wasn't as terrible as I had thought, and going around the corners at such speed was sort of fun. I was actually enjoying myself.

Despite the fact I was the worst bike racer there, I liked it. It was a far cry from trying to play football at recess, and just hating every moment of it. No, this was different; sure, I sucked, but I loved it.

Screaming around the corners, right on the edge of losing control, fueled my adrenaline and made my heart sing. I focused hard on the wheel in front of me, and never gave in. That task became harder and harder every lap, but I gritted my teeth and refused to let go.

One by one, I started passing kids that couldn't hang on to the back of the peloton. While they looked much better on the bike than I did and were, I'm sure, much fitter than I was, I was able to suffer—to tear my guts up just that little bit more—to hold on. Twenty minutes earlier, I didn't even want to be there; now I was having the time of my life. And that was a new experience for me.

In the period of riding just a few laps, zipping around some anonymous office park outside Boulder, I changed my mind on sports.

I wanted to be an athlete.

I wanted to be a racer.

Racing absorbed me. It combined mental, technical, tactical, and physical aspects. Somehow, the balance of carving a corner on a machine came more naturally than the hand–eye coordination of catching a ball. The circular motion of pushing the pedals made more sense to my overly cerebral brain than did the supposedly "natural" motion of running. I had fallen in love with racing a bike. I was still disgracefully slow and unfit, but I desperately wanted to be good.

That week, day by day, stage by stage, I got a little bit better at racing. I learned how to take a corner, how to draft closer, how to move up in a peloton. I wanted to fight as hard as I could to be a bit better, even though I was still very far away from winning anything.

For the first time in my life, I wasn't giving up when things got rough. In school, in other sports and in life, I had shown very little natural aptitude for anything beyond memorizing random facts about the Civil War.

Deep down I was competitive, but I had never let it show. I just wasn't that great at the stuff most parents, and most kids, wanted to be good at. Football, baseball, basketball—anything to do with a ball, I was simply shit.

I was very small and nearsighted, so most people automatically assumed I'd be a good student, but my grades were miserable, too.

But then came cycling and that all changed.

By the end of the Red Zinger, I was occasionally seeing the front of the race. I'd learned during the week that I could get ahead of many of the kids that had more physical strength than I did by being willing to push myself further.

The second to last day of the race there was another time trial, but this time it climbed a big hill. I figured this would be a perfect opportunity to put that theory to the test and see if I could actually push myself to the limit, racing against the clock.

I started the time trial off with a snap in my legs and an excitement I had not felt earlier in the week. I wanted to see how good I could be if I just let go of that perfectionist anchor.

It was so liberating to just try to be the best that I could be, without being paralyzed by the "what ifs" that had held me back until then.

"What if" I wasn't the best or "what if" I was embarrassed?

So I focused on nothing more than getting the last bit of energy out of my body.

After one mile of steep uphill, I already felt I was about to pass out, or to shit in my shorts. My body wasn't used to opening up the throttle, all the way. I had no idea how I was going to continue at such an effort for another three miles, so I focused on the next fifty feet, and then the next fifty feet after that, and so on.

Over and over, I dealt with a self-imposed agony that I'd never felt before. About halfway, I spotted the rider who had started in front of me. I was about to catch him. Once again, I played games in my head, saying I'd push myself as hard as I could until I caught him, and then take a little break.

But once I caught him, I was like a kid who'd just eaten his first Pringle.

I was addicted.

I loved catching and passing this innocent victim. I now wanted the whole can's worth. I continued, dead focused on finding more prey before the finish line. And I got my wish.

As I entered the last mile, half-animated bodies began to appear on the horizon. I caught them all before the finish.

I crossed the line and immediately started retching up whatever was left in my stomach, dry-heaving like a cat with a massive hair-ball. This was something I'd never experienced before. It may have sounded terrible but it felt great. I was finally free from not trying. I was free from giving up.

Once again, Dad and I waited patiently by the outhouse for them to post the results. Unlike at the start of the week, the crowd wasn't so thick. Most of the kids had gone home, knowing they wouldn't be getting any reward, and feeling a bit tired from the week of racing.

But I was wholly invigorated. I was enthralled and just wanted the race to keep going for the rest of summer. Finally, they posted the dot matrix printout on the back of the porta-potty. I was in tenth place, in the ever-important top ten finishers in a bike race.

I'd beaten forty other kids, and wasn't all that far behind the legends of the twelve-year-olds category.

For an odd minute or two, I felt pure elation and pride. Then, as we walked back to the car, I turned to my dad.

"Next year, I'm going to win this thing," I told him. "You watch, Dad, I'm going to win it."

From then on, I began plotting how to make an athlete out of a geek—a winner out of a loser.

In the USA in 1986, there weren't very many mentors or coaches available for kids trying to become bike racers. Colorado had a few folks here and there you could get some advice from, but there was no one that was going to take me from a cute loser to a race winner through their brilliant coaching. This would be something I'd have to figure out on my own.

The one thing I did have a natural talent for was reading. If the topic was interesting to me, I could read for hours and absorb it all like a sponge.

Reading had always been an escape for me. It helped me escape from my problems making friends, escape from trouble in school, and escape from the loneliness of being an only child. Of course, most things we were assigned to read in school did not fit the bill of "interesting," and therefore I rarely showed much of my reading horsepower in school.

However, for my newfound project of learning how to train for bike racing, I was ready to read hundreds of thousands of words. I went to the library and to many bookstores, trying to source the best books on training and cycling in general.

The first American Tour de France winner, Greg LeMond, had come out with a book; the old Polish coach of the 1984 U.S. Olympic team, Eddie Borysewicz, had written a book; a translation of five-time Tour winner Bernard Hinault's book, *Memories of the Peloton*, was now available; and my favorite was Tudor Bompa's *Periodization of Training*. But I devoured anything I could get my hands on.

And so, lying there on the couch at my parents' home, I read continuously.

I learned how to position my bike, how to choose the right gear, how to bridge to a breakaway, how to eat during a race, how much to drink, how to corner, and how to brake. I learned about strength training, interval training, endurance training, how to periodize training, and—a revolutionary concept at the time—anaerobic threshold training.

Within two months of finishing dead last in my first race, I had learned more, reading on my own, than I had in the previous six years in school. I was ready to begin my quest to conquer the 1987 Red Zinger Mini Classic, and become one of the legends of thirteen-year-old Coloradan bike-racing folklore.

I began my training the first day of school in 1986. I figured it would take me a considerable amount of time just to build up to the level of fitness most kids had already achieved, just from being generally more active in "normal" sports than I'd been. Then I could start training harder and longer.

I'd learned, in my studious readings, that I most likely had predominantly slow-twitch muscle fiber, and that if I wanted to build up the explosive power needed to actually win bike races, I'd need to increase my muscular strength, which would take a considerable amount of time. I started training for the next summer before summer had even ended.

At first, my training rides were fairly short and basic. My focus was on trying to build muscle mass in my parents' basement with a second-hand weight set my father had bought for me. Squats, leg extensions, and hamstring curls were happening in abundance in the concrete cave below our home.

Right after school, every day, I went out for bike rides, whatever the weather: heat, cold, rain, snow. Weekends, which used to be built around messing around with friends and very unsuccessfully chasing girls, became two days in the week when I could ride my bike all day.

Each weekend I would explore the roads farther and farther from my parents' house. The feeling of freedom was immense, as I was traveling to places that none of my friends could ever get to without begging their parents for a ride in the car.

I'd explore deeper into the nondescript suburbs, reaching farther and farther toward the city limits, toward the mountains and beyond, to a whole new world. I would be gone for three, four, even five hours, pounding away on the pedals and exploring.

My parents had no idea where I was, or if I was safe, but they accepted that my obsession needed to run its course for me to grow up.

So, off I went in search of my dream, in search of my goal and in search of myself. I cherished these long rides when I could dream of winning for hours on end.

But more than simply winning, I started to dream of being a professional rider. In everything I'd read, I'd started to learn about the mystical world of European professional cycling. And I loved it. I loved the heroes, the romance, the difficulty, the sacrifice, the pain, the fame, and the glory.

I was entranced by it, and searched for anything I could get my hands on about this world of legends. In addition to all the books, I found some old videotapes, such as *A Sunday in Hell* and some poorly recorded CBS recaps of the Tour de France. Those VHS tapes became my most prized possessions, and I watched them over and over again.

European professional cycling was a completely unknown quantity to suburban America in the 1980s, so my obsession appeared to be quite insane to my friends and family. I was working incredibly hard and spending all my hours dreaming of a career that my parents doubted even existed.

My friends sniggered at my little pipe-cleaner legs dangling out of my Lycra shorts. And when I'd come home telling tales of how far I'd ridden my bike, they simply didn't believe it. They'd laugh and go back to playing football. I was just an odd, nerdy little kid. They figured I'd somehow fallen off the deep end and chosen to ride my oddness away. Mine was a lonely dream to pursue.

But in truth, I had been lonely long before all of this.

I had never found friends that I truly related to in school. Being neither academic nor very sporty, I earned very little respect. I was the smallest kid in seventh grade, and I'd been pushed around, made fun of, and stuffed into my fair share of lockers and trash cans.

I didn't look forward to going to school at all, so the loneliness of the bike was a welcome relief. On the open roads, no one judged my grade point average, no one judged that I couldn't catch a ball for shit. No one cared that I wasn't in junior achievement. Nope, all that mattered out on the road was how fast you could get to the top of the hill.

I'd acquired a ton of knowledge about training and racing through reading, but one thing that was missing was any expertise on how to dress for cycling. Now this may not matter so much when training through a warm Coloradan Indian summer, but as the mountain winds began to whistle in November, my training plan was becoming more than a little uncomfortable.

As the cold set in, my paper-thin shorts weren't keeping me anywhere near warm anymore. In a well-meaning attempt to fix this, my mother bought me a pair of bulky sweatpants, thinking that might be the way forward. I tried to put my cycling shorts over the 1950s gray cotton tracksuit pants, but it wasn't working. I felt like I was sitting on a wet nappy halfway through each ride, with the legs of the track pants getting caught up on the chain. I also looked absolutely ridiculous. I needed to look like a real racer, even while just training. The sweatpants had to go.

The winter deepened. On ice-cold Colorado days, I would come home with blue and purple knees, hands stinging from the bitter wind. My toes would go numb, my fingers could no longer move, and my private parts shrank away, trying their best to hide from this harsh reality.

Finally, before any permanent nerve damage occurred due to frostbite, my parents took me to the shop where we'd bought the bike, in the hope they might have some sort of special super-thermal kit that would prevent me from dying of hypothermia.

The shop was tucked away in a corner of Middle America in a bland strip mall, next to a dry cleaner's and a Chinese restaurant. To me, it stuck out like a diamond in the rough. It was named, quite beautifully, A Bike Place, and was owned by a bike-passionate—and sometimes disturbingly manic—Italian family named the Yantornos.

When my mom brought me in to buy some winter kit, I think it was the first time they'd ever seen a thirteen-year-old who was asking about how to train in sub-zero weather. Despite his gruff, rough manner, you could see the twinkle in the eye of Frankie Yantorno, the eldest son of the family, when I revealed my crazed enthusiasm for racing. He saw a kid that was completely in love with cycling, just like he was.

But Frank could never openly admit that he even remotely cared about bikes or bike racing.

"Why the fuck you wanna go ride in this shit?" he said, pointing at the snowstorm outside and making my mother blush at the language.

"Because I need to train," I said. "Gotta train to win—right?"

"Well, you ain't gonna win shit in those stupid fucking sweatpants, kid," he snapped. "Goddamn it . . . okay, hold on a few minutes . . ." With that, he slammed the backroom door behind him.

While he was gone, I began to explore the shop a bit. It was heaven.

I was bewitched by the hand-painted gussets and lugs of Colnago frames, the polished Campagnolo crank arms, the smell of rubber and chain lube, plus the muffled arguments in Italian emanating from the backroom. It was my gateway into the romance and glamour of European bike racing. I loved this place and I wanted to become Frankie's pupil.

Finally, Frankie popped back out with a few packages of clothing.

"This ain't ever going to fit you, kid, but it's better than those ugly sweatpants—or freezing your dick off."

I sheepishly tried on all these new items. They were very exotic, Italian-labeled gloves, tights, and arm warmers.

Frankie was right: they didn't fit at all. They were quite baggy on me and slid off my skin-and-bones frame. But I didn't care—they were made in Italy, and positively reeked of European adventure.

Reluctantly, Mom and Dad had given up on the notion I might want a puppy or something a bit more normal under the Christmas tree. I'd told my parents all I wanted for Christmas was some clothing that would keep me warm while riding. Hesitantly, Mom handed her credit card to this grumpy man at the bike shop.

Before we left, I asked Frankie if I could come back and talk about racing in Italy, and maybe get a bit of advice.

"I don't know shit about racing, or bikes, but maybe I can teach you a few things, kid. Now get out of here and go ride your bike in this snowstorm, ya idiot."

That was when I knew Frankie was going to be my new best friend.

So I did. Armed with Italian clothing that made weather-related excuses obsolete, I rode in snowstorms. Once Christmas was over, it was time to double down on the hard work it was going to take for me to win. I also started to make a few new friends through the bike shop, and a few of them were guys who already raced.

Frankie, who I would soon start calling Uncle Frank, noted that the only other person insane enough to train in Colorado in January was his ex-brother-in-law, Bart Sheldrake. Bart was Frank's sister's ex, and was juggling three jobs, raising a kid, and training for racing as a top-level amateur in Colorado.

Bart had gone to the Olympic trials in 1984, and was a category-one racer. Once in a while he would sheepishly come into the shop to pick up his two-year-old kid from Frankie's sister after school. Frank figured we should meet, so he invited me down to the shop one day when Bart was on co-parent patrol.

I zipped my way through the after-school traffic and headed down to the shop to meet Bart. I had a thousand questions about what it was like to be a real bike racer. He had the look of the racers I'd seen in magazines: gaunt in the face, long, lean, and leathery.

He was highly strung and socially awkward, with this funny nasal laugh. Very reluctantly, he agreed to let me pick his brain about his experiences of bike racing for the better part of the afternoon. But more important, Bart agreed to let me go on a training ride with him.

It was made clear that if I was to join him on his Sunday morning ride, there would be no whining, no waiting up for me, no helping me if I got a flat tire, and no mercy on the pace. I agreed with a smile on my face, counting the minutes until that Sunday when I would get to ride with a real bike racer.

My mother panicked when Sunday morning came. I was going to go on a bike ride of more than sixty miles with a man she'd never met, and who would have frightened her if she had. Why would a grown man with a child be spending so much time riding his bike on the weekend in freezing-cold weather?

Bart needed to ride early, so we met at the shop at nine. That was the earliest we could go and avoid running into too many ice patches on the road. Face frozen by the cold, he briefed me.

"Listen, I have to be back to make lunch for my kid, and I'm going to get in sixty miles. I've gotta do that in three hours," he said. "If you can keep up, great. If not, tough shit."

The pace Bart set was relentless. There wasn't a moment when I was not suffering just to hold on to his back wheel. However, there was a lot riding on this outing for me.

It was my chance to earn his respect, to earn the respect of Frankie and, most important, my chance to be invited to more real training rides and to learn from a real bike racer. I couldn't get left behind.

My little hundred-pound frame squirmed in the saddle, my shoulders bounced, my arms pulled, and my legs begged me to stop. But I didn't let Bart get away from me. I think it annoyed him a bit that this pipsqueak of a thirteen-year-old was able to hang on his back wheel.

Despite leaving a little bit later in the morning, the roads were still icy and wet. As the freezing ride went on, the derailleur cables on my bike steadily became encrusted with ice and frozen into place. So did Bart's. There would be no more gear changes during the last hour of the ride.

I was nicely stuck in a 53×17 gear. I kept turning the pedals over, achingly slowly, but Bart (clearly used to this sort of thing) was dismissive and just kept riding.

"You gotta just clench your asshole a bit more and deal with it," he grunted.

That was Bart's way of life: more pain equated to more fun.

Finally, I unraveled, hypothermic and hypoglycemic, about ten miles from home. As he'd promised, Bart didn't wait, but I could hear him yell back to me as I was grinding to a halt.

"Good job, kid! See ya next Sunday!"

I knew I had earned just a smidgen of Bart's respect.

I crawled those last ten miles. I just wanted to stop and fall asleep in a dirty snowbank, and pray that someone would find me before nightfall. But I kept turning the pedals over, achingly slow and square.

I had no money to call home or buy a hot chocolate. I had one working gear. And I had ice falling off my chin. I was so hungry, so cold, and so miserable, but there was no way to get home other than to just keep going. That would be a valuable lesson to learn. Sometimes there is no better option. You just have to keep going.

The look on my mother's face when I walked through the door was priceless. You could see anger, disappointment, pride, and maternal instincts all fighting against one another in her head. She wanted to feed me, hug me, get me in a hot bath, while yelling at me for being such an idiot—all in one breath.

Normally, I don't much like baths. They just seem overly indulgent, long, and boring. But there is nothing in the world like a hot bath after a bone-chilling day on the bike. The contrast between pushing your body so hard that it almost breaks in wet and cold weather, to sliding into the warm womb of a hot bath, is intense.

CHAPTER 2

BREAKAWAY AT BUCKEYE

I rode my bike to school every morning. When I left in the afternoon, I'd hear howling laughter from the kids loading onto the school buses, or going to football practice, mocking my funny bike shorts and saucepan helmet.

It hurt to hear that, and it hurt to know that I didn't fit in, but I told myself that I was off to hang out with a much cooler guy than the kids at Cherry Creek High. His name was Frankie, a world-traveled artist, a guy who made a living in New York City as a bike messenger.

Down at the shop, Frankie would indulge me in stories of great racers with fantastical, larger-than-life names, like Fons De Wolf. He'd lecture me on his total certainty that any bicycle component made in Japan was absolute garbage, and that the only *true* bicycle was a steel Italian frame fitted with Campagnolo.

He gave me an Italian nickname, Gianni, and he offered up some brutal insights.

"Riding *Shitmano* is like fucking with a condom on, Gianni. It's safe, it works, but it fucking sucks," he said of the Japanese component giant.

The shop was becoming a refuge for me. It was a place I loved and where I felt respected and understood. It would become a second home for many of my tortured teenage years.

A few days after that first training outing with Bart, I rode down to the shop to tell Frankie about my Sunday adventure and to get my bike working again, after turning it into an icy and salty seized-up mess.

"I heard Bart kicked your ass, kid," Frankie said by way of greeting. Then he ran his eye over my crippled machine.

"This bike looks like a fucking disaster, ya idiot. You gotta take care of this shit—*Jeezus*!"

As Frankie was coaxing my bike back to health, I sat in the backroom marked "Employees Only" listening to his stories about life, bike racing, and being an adult. It tickled him to call me "Gianni." Occasionally, after an exceptionally grueling outing with Bart, I'd hear *Gianni-morto!* or "Gianni-dead!" Frank would carefully paint "Gianni" on the top tube of all my bikes for many years to come.

Frank's two sisters, Dominique and Monica—who had also been nicknamed Tiny and Priss, respectively—were often at the shop, too. Legend had it that Priss, Bart's ex-wife, used to be quite the bike racer.

At first they seemed irritated by me, this little twerp, always following Frank around the bike shop, but after some time I think they thought it was cute. To me, the whole experience was amazing; I was hanging out with a family of adults who knew everything about bikes. It was so much better than spending time with a bunch of middle-schoolers obsessed with football and makeup.

The Yantornos would get into spectacular fights. Chain rings would get thrown at heads, inventive Italian swear words would come into play, and Frank's dog, Ducco, a rather aggressive chow, would get agitated and start yanking at the chain he was tied up to, which often broke.

Every month a new Victoria's Secret catalog would arrive in the mail. I always knew roughly what time of the month it was going to arrive, and would furiously pedal to the bike shop in order to sneak a peek. Priss and Tiny would be looking at it in the office, giggling by the time I got there. They would pretend it was nothing. Eventually, they'd pull me into the office, like a little brother.

"Okay, Gianni, you can take a look," they'd say. "I mean, you need to see this sort of thing if you're ever going to have a girl-friend."

I was very, *very* far from having a girlfriend in high school. Not so many cheerleaders were interested in guys that were five inches shorter than them and wore spandex shorts and a bucket on their head. But Tiny and Priss saw potential in my future, and told me that someday I'd grow into my ears and make someone very happy. They became my big sisters.

I would open the catalog with bright, wide eyes, my imagination running wild. I'd feel my blood boiling in a way that is only familiar to kids going through puberty. Suddenly I'd realize that getting made fun of by kids my age wasn't the only problem with wearing cycling shorts.

I'd hope no one would notice. But of course, they always did.

"Hey, Gianni, nice fuckin' boner!" Frankie would yell.

Priss and Tiny would defend me.

"Fuck you, Frankie, you're just jealous he can still get a boner!"

Then the fights would start. Chain wrenches, Italian swear words, and Regina cog sets would be hurled across the workshop, yet again, as Priss and Frankie went at each other. On and on my wonderful afternoon would waste away, hanging out in the bike shop. I loved it.

Training meanwhile was clicking along quite nicely. I could feel the improvements coming week after week. I was getting stronger and stronger, and, on occasion, felt that eventually my legs might be big enough to fill out my baggy extra-small shorts.

As I trained more, I discovered a gaping hole in my abilities as a rider—my sprint. I just had absolutely zero acceleration relative to other riders. In my first races, I hadn't really noticed this weakness, but now that I was getting a bit fitter, it really showed.

Anything that required really stomping on the pedals was just not my forte. In hindsight, this shouldn't have been a surprise, as I was built like an asparagus with arms. My knees were a good few inches wider than any part of my thigh and my legs looked like two toothpicks held together with an olive.

I started sprint training. Twice a week, I would sprint over and over trying to eke out just a bit more from my toothpick legs. It wasn't pretty. To start with, anyone could beat me. Anyone. But I just kept chipping away, even if it seemed like a doomed task. Long sprints, short sprints, uphill sprints, downhill sprints, tailwind sprints, headwind sprints. Every Tuesday and Saturday, I sprinted. Over and over.

I had become obsessed with training, but the other thing that I'd become obsessed with, in my build-up to the 1987 Red Zinger Mini Classic, was equipment. I quickly found that this was a sport built for nerds. I spent hours drooling over catalogs that contained bladed spokes and drilled-out chain rings. I saved what I could to buy something that might make me just a little bit faster.

I also became totally obsessed with weight, and much to the chagrin of Frank, I bought an aluminum Vitus frame. Frank said it was crooked and, as it was built by French people, clearly garbage.

I learned quickly that the Yantornos believed that French people were the reason for all the problems in the world.

They couldn't make bike frames, cook food, fly airplanes, or build cars. They smelled bad and were snobby. Most of all they were the enemy of any self-respecting Italian bike-racing family. Worse, I had broken the code of honor by buying a French-built frame.

Frankie warmed to his task.

"Gianni, that thing looks like someone took a shit in the lugs. The glue is just hanging out. I'm not touching this fucking frame, it probably has herpes."

Eventually, I talked Frank into building up my super-light, tiny 50-centimeter Vitus. He told me it would be too flexible and break. He may have been overestimating my strength as a rider. I pointed out that Sean Kelly rode a Vitus. He still wasn't having it.

"Gianni, pro riders could ride anything and still go fast. Bernard

Thévenet won the Tour de France on a bike made for delivering newspapers. Your Vitus still sucks. And so does Sean Kelly's . . ."

Sucky or not, I loved my blue Vitus.

It felt light under my legs and fast up the hills and I really doubt I flexed it any more than the cheese-and-baguette-eating Frenchmen that designed it. I still weighed only a smidge over a hundred pounds and it started to become very clear that going uphill would become my weapon in racing. Even on my weekend pain sessions with Bart, when the road went really steeply uphill, I was now able to match him. It seemed as if I was always suffering far more than Bart, but one way or another, I didn't let him get away from me.

Soon enough, the spring weather started getting a bit warmer, and the summer races started getting a bit closer. I kept a close eye on the mail, looking for the race registration packs, almost as closely as I was looking for errant Victoria's Secret catalogs.

The races I had begrudgingly finished the year before had now become an obsession. I was counting down the days. I was excited and impatient to get racing, and was getting a bit bored with my solo training rides and the weekend rides with Bart. The previous year, I'd fallen in love with the excitement of racing. Training, it turned out, is a bit mundane, tedious, and sometimes boring. I was definitely starting to feel a bit stale.

Luckily, there was a step between training and actually racing. As soon as daylight saving time arrived, Bart introduced me to an impromptu evening event, the Meridian ride. Sixty to seventy bike riders showed up at a south Denver office park—named Meridian— every Tuesday and Thursday night and pretended to race, full gas, for one hour. The Meridian ride was, and still is, a Colorado bike-racing standard.

The Meridian was a bit of an insider proposition, though. You had to know someone who knew someone who knew when to show up. It was the Fight Club of bike racing. Nothing was official; it was underground, illegal, on open roads and you didn't talk about it—to anyone.

Bart was the king of this two-wheeled Fight Club. He'd been undefeated in many years at Fight Club, and the tales of his trouncings spread through the Coloradan bike-racing grapevine, like the legend of Paul Bunyan. Once Bart thought I was ready to know about Fight Club, he invited me out to give it a try.

I was both honored and nervous as hell, but there was no amount of fear that could get me to miss my invitation to the underground. The Meridian ride became my favorite after-school activity.

Absolutely nothing about Fight Club was a good idea. The range ability was huge. From triathletes to track riders; men, women, girls, boys; those who'd never ridden in a peloton before; those who never should have; all the way to category-one riders, like Bart. Any and all were welcome—if you were cool enough to know about it, that is.

There was no red tape, no officialdom at all. There was no official distance, no start or finish, and there were certainly no road closures or police protection. You just showed up at six p.m. and raced. We would blast through red lights, overtake traffic, and do everything in our power to give someone a ride in an ambulance. It was fast, it was dangerous, and I loved it.

It was also a great teacher. Cycling is a sport that has to be learned by racing, by experience, by trial and error. There are things that can't be learned through coaching or instruction. The way a peloton surges and bunches up; the fluid dance that happens in and out of every curve.

Fight Club may have been a lawyer's dream and a mother's nightmare, but it was an incredible teacher. It taught me how to maneuver in a peloton; it taught me how to time an attack, how to hold a wheel, how to keep momentum, and how to not crash—at least not that much.

I felt like a bloodied warrior every Tuesday and Thursday night returning home for my mother's Midwestern-style dinner. Over hamburgers and coleslaw, I would explain to my parents that I was learning how to survive battle.

I was getting impatient for school to end. It couldn't happen soon enough for me, as by now many of my classmates realized I was *that* kid, the kid they'd see everywhere, riding around in spandex. This just wasn't socially acceptable in Middle America back in 1987.

There was the occasional half-empty milkshake thrown at my head from a passing car by high schoolers with brand new driver's licenses. Then, of course, there was the name-calling: being called "faggot" or "queer" was a weekly occurrence. By this point it was long past hurting me; it just filled me with deep rage. I was going to be famous one day, and these fuckers were going to know my name.

Physically, I wasn't big enough to fight back, but the torch had been lit for me to shame these cretins. Somehow, someway, they would feel shame for doing this shit to me. If it took a decade, so be it. Being little and being picked on instilled a deep need for success, for proving people wrong, and it also fueled anger, an anger that was key to my journey of becoming a bike racer.

It was time to race a real race. We'd sent in the application, paid the entry fee, gotten the T-shirt and numbers, and signed all the liability waivers. Frankie helped me go over my precious bike as if it was the Christ child in the manger. He carefully showed me how to re-pack all the bearings, how to change the cables, how to true my wheels, and how to tune the rest. As I left the shop, he gave me some beautifully tender and encouraging words for my first race.

"I fuckin' hope you're better at racing that ugly-ass French bike than you are at fixin' it!"

I was ready and I was nervous. My parents were ready, too—ready for this odd obsession of mine to be over with. We loaded up the family station wagon with a cooler of bottles, Fig Newtons, the Bed-lington terrier, and my blue Vitus. My mother fretted over whether I'd eaten enough for breakfast, and my father fretted over whether we'd left on time. Soon enough, the laser-blue Oldsmobile lumbered northward, motoring on toward my destiny.

The Buckeye road race was my first event. Buckeye is in the mid-dle of nowhere, Colorado, tumbleweed country at its finest, and just outside of Fort Collins. As with any race in Colorado, it was an early morning start.

The years taught me that if you weren't waking up in the dark, you weren't really bike racing. We parked the blue beast in a dirt field, unloaded my bike and started pinning on numbers. It felt electric to me. Unlike the previous year, where I was a reluctant participant, this time I was on a razor's edge, my nerves on fire. I was ready to prove myself.

You could smell fear in the morning chill. The other parents scurried around with walkie-talkies, coordinating their son's race and trying to not lose smaller siblings in the chaos. Water bottles were filled, helmets were clasped, and cleated shoes were put on feet by the herd of parental supporters.

I saw the legends of the previous year, and Chris Wherry, the kingpin of them all. They would all know my name after today, I was certain of that, or so I thought, although I still didn't really know if I was any good. After all, I hadn't been the last time I raced with these guys. My insecurities of the previous year bubbled up in my head and I had to fight hard to suppress them.

The race was one lap of a mainly flat eighteen-mile loop on a bright, calm, and cool Colorado summer morning. I stood quietly, shivering with nerves, waiting to go. The crack of the gun sounded out over the barren fields and tumbleweeds, and I scrambled to clip into my loose pedal. I'd practiced clipping in, over and over, but with all my jitters I was still slow and clumsy. Already I was a little behind most of my rivals, but I quickly sprinted my way back to the front.

The attacks started immediately.

Everyone jumped after every move, and so the bunch ebbed and flowed, over and over, as pubescent warriors tried to break free from the pack. There was screaming and shouting through the chopping wheels and yelled warnings of attacks from others. The pace was still quick for most thirteen-year-olds, and fatigue began to take its toll, shrinking the peloton down, rider by rider.

The final five-mile stretch of the Buckeye loop had a few long rolling hills that gradually rose up to the finish line. I'd decided to wait until that stretch to try my chances. It felt like forever waiting for the final phase; I wanted to strut my stuff and show these guys. But I knew I needed to be patient. I waited, an archer with bow strung taut, holding his shot for the perfect moment.

We turned right onto the final stretch and straight onto the biggest hill of this mostly flat race. In a momentary pause, during which the peloton took a collective breath before the hill, I made my move.

As I was unknown to many of the other kids, I wasn't immediately chased down. Within a few seconds, I had a gap. It was then, at that very moment, that I felt a very deep primal instinct jolt into gear.

I was being hunted down and the adrenaline of fear surged up in me. It felt as if I would perish, as if in a scene out of a BBC *Planet Earth* video, a lone wildebeest chased down by a pack of rabid jackals. But this little ninety-eight-pound wildebeest would prove a challenge to the arrogant jackals. I'd never felt this way before, not when racing the previous year and not even in all my training with Bart.

The feeling was something new, something feral and intense. It was fear like I'd never felt fear before. Fear of losing, fear of failure, fear of being caught.

It was the desire to just ride off the road and pretend to crash to avoid confronting failure, and the desire to push even harder to never let the jackals win. It took everything I had to forcefully convince myself the best way forward was to give everything I had into trying, and to not let the fear of failure cripple me into hiding from the outcome.

The gap held over the top of the hill. In the far distance, I could see the finish line banners. Now I began to believe I could do it.

I wanted my mother to see me cross the line first.

I wanted Frankie to hear about me winning later that day at the shop.

I wanted to show Chris Wherry I was stronger than he was.

And I wanted to prove to all my stupid friends back home at school that I was something more, something better than they understood. I was the wildebeest worthy of leading the herd. I wanted to win.

I tucked my head down as tightly as I could and pushed on toward the banners, looking back under my arm just once to see if the others were going to catch me.

"Don't let them. *Don't let them*. Don't. Let. Them," I told myself, over and over.

My need to win had become more about the fear of getting caught than about the joy of racing or victory. I was obsessed with proving people wrong. Obsessed with conquering the negative. My fists clenched the handlebars as I fought the desire to slow down just a little bit.

I was puffing like a freight train and my legs rubbery, but I knew from my rides with Bart that if there was one thing I could count on from my weak little body, it was my ability to tolerate and overcome an intense amount of pain. So I did.

Instead of trying to ignore or minimize the pain I was feeling, I dove into it, embracing it, focusing on it—almost addicted to it. For the first time in my life, I felt in control. When my body kept telling me to back off, to slow down, I remember envisioning a giant red sign that said *no*.

No to slowing down, *no* to quitting, *no* to getting caught, *no* to failure.

I couldn't get a girl to come to the homecoming dance with me, nor could I pass my algebra final exam, but I could force my body to press through pain in a way most people couldn't, just to go a bit faster on a bike.

The pack put together a belated chase, but it was too late. I would have died rather than get caught, and I rode that way. As the line approached, I took one last look back. And I saw no one close. I could have started celebrating the win much sooner, but out of fear

I kept on the pedals at full gas until the finish line was well underneath me. Then, finally, I raised an arm in victory.

The relief was intense and flooded through me, as if I'd been wrapped in a warm woolen blanket after being rescued from a rough sea. I should have felt an intense sense of joy, or that's what they tell you. But I didn't feel a rush of pride in victory.

I was just happy I didn't let anyone down. Not Frankie, not my mother, and not Bart. And, finally, I had won.

CHAPTER 3

THE ORANGE VOLVO STATION WAGON

Victory at the Buckeye road race fueled a desire for more of this bike-racing "thing." I started looking at races in distant corners of Colorado, in other states, and even started to wonder how to qualify for the National Championships.

I am sure my parents were both half happy to see their drifter of a son finally fully engaged in some activity, but also half concerned at the level of my obsession. Meanwhile, the economy in Colorado had taken a dive and Mom and Dad had been having some financial troubles, which only added to the strain.

They were more concerned with being able to pay the mortgage and put food on the table than they were about traveling to and from bike races. My plans for these far-flung races seemed a bit far-fetched to even think about, aside from being too far to get to. Still, they supported my daydreaming, and they helped me devise cheap ways of traveling to these events.

That was essential to me. I craved getting to the next level of bike racing, but I didn't want to burden my parents with the financial load of this obsession.

At the same time, I needed to at least start going to a few regional events to maybe get some attention. I needed to turn the heads of local teams, national team coaches, and maybe a sponsor or two. If I did well I could earn a bit of prize money, which would beat a summer job, and maybe even pay for the gas money to get to the next race.

Of course I would still need to convince my parents to drive me to these events. I knew Dad had enough time to take me to them, as his practice was suffering from the blighted economy. So I figured I would pitch the idea of him driving me to a few. Enter, stage left, my dad's bright-orange 1974 Volvo station wagon.

The Volvo had well over 200,000 miles on it and smelled of pungent pipe smoke and spilled coffee. It was the car I'd been driven to school in since I was a baby.

The top achievable speed was under the speed limit and it burned so much oil that you needed to refill it every time you stopped for gas. The torn seats had sheepskin covers put over them, and were covered with ashes from Dad's pipe.

The presence and smell of my dad, smoking a pipe in the Volvo, window open, on a freezing January morning in Colorado, is one of my fondest memories. Now this great old friend on wheels was to transport me to the battlegrounds of Colorado cycling.

But there was more in store for the orange Volvo. It was to become more than just my transport to races—it was to morph into a multi-purpose cycling support vehicle. Its destiny was to motorpace me in training.

Motorpacing is the art of riding close behind a car, or a motorcycle, using the slipstream of the vehicle to reach much higher speeds than would normally be possible. From what I could tell, motorpacing was the golden gateway to becoming a great rider.

I'd read about it in Eddie Borysewicz's training book, but more important, I'd seen motorpacing in the movies. Like any cycling nut of the 1980s, I had watched *Breaking Away* and *American Flyers*. Those two films, depicting American kids breaking into road racing, embodied all of my dreams and experiences.

I saw myself, like the kids in *Breaking Away*, as a "cutter" from a poor family on the wrong side of the tracks, going to the ever-sowealthy Cherry Creek High School. I thought I was Dave Stoller, hero of *Breaking Away*, a reject finding my way in life by racing a bike and dreaming of a grand European adventure. Part of becoming Dave was learning to motorpace.

In my earliest attempts at motorpacing I would try to huddle behind the bumpers of slow, unsuspecting, and usually elderly, motorists. This proved a bit risky. All too often, the sight of a red-faced kid riding in his rearview mirror would panic the driver, causing them to slam on the brakes and sending me flying onto the trunk.

After a few such incidents, I figured I needed a solution that involved having the driver actually being aware of what was going on, rather than terrified. It really did seem the best choice for everyone. So I asked my father if he'd be willing to give motorpacing a try.

His response was very typical; he didn't answer yes or no, just started asking me more questions as to exactly what I was trying to achieve from this rather odd desire to ride my bike directly behind a station wagon. But he soon agreed.

I think he viewed it as a father–son bonding activity. Most kids played catch with their dads, got help with homework, or went fishing. Dad and I never did much of that stuff—we had different temperaments and there was a general feeling of distance from each other. But our after-school motorpacing sessions transcended our differences and became our bond.

Unexpectedly, he turned out to be the perfect motorpacer. My father is perhaps the slowest driver I've ever met, and he is not prone to quick directional changes, in any aspect of his life. He is the living definition of deliberate.

He rarely needs to use the brakes because he never goes fast enough, in doing anything in life, to use them. While this steadiness is exactly the opposite of my edgy impulsiveness, and perhaps the reason we were never terribly close, it proved absolutely perfect for motorpacing.

The orange Volvo proved to be the dream vehicle for motorpacing as well. It was a heavy lumbering beast whose best days were long since behind it. It had very little acceleration from the overused engine, and the brakes didn't work that well, either, all of which was just perfect.

I would meet Dad at Chatfield Reservoir after school every Wednesday. Chatfield was a state park, and there was very little traffic. The roads within it were mainly flat with few corners, and very few potholes. Those conditions were just what I needed to perfect the art of bumper chasing.

We started with me just riding behind the car, sitting on the bumper at around 24 miles per hour. Both of us were getting used to the various signals and communication we'd need to make this a remotely safe thing for a parent to be doing with his child. Fairly quickly, we started getting a feel for the subtle movements and nods that indicated to each other what was going on. It slowly became our common language.

Dad and I didn't speak too much in day-to-day life, but in those motorpacing sessions at Chatfield, our language was fluent. We soon learned to think of hills, corners, curves, and other traffic in the same way. A little nod and quick sideways glance were enough for us to completely understand each other. Through furtive nods back and forth in the rearview mirror of the orange Volvo, my communication with my father was the best it had ever been.

Oddly, I think we both looked forward to our Wednesday afternoon sessions. I can only imagine what the park rangers thought watching my old man, fresh from debating a case at the courthouse and dressed in a three-piece tweed suit, smoking a pipe and driving around in a beater of a vehicle, his lanky teenage cyclist son glued to the back bumper.

Our sessions became more intense and complex, as I would add intervals into the rides, where I would try and sprint past the orange behemoth. We were soon easily surpassing 37 miles per hour, which was technically illegal and beyond the speed limit. Every once in a while, we'd have to pass a truck towing a fishing boat or a camper van in the park.

This made for some excitement. Dad would go out into the left lane and begin the pass with his kid glued to the exhaust pipe. The looks and headshakes we'd get as we crept past some old fisherman driving a Ford pickup were priceless. I could see Dad was proud. His son was riding a damned bicycle faster than a Ford F-150.

It's still the only time I ever saw my father break the speed limit.

Despite inhaling the heady mix of carcinogenic oil and pipe smoke that wafted from the Volvo, the training worked for me. I started winning larger races more often.

Despite my small size, I found that I was actually pretty good at time trials, whether they were uphill or even quite flat. Time trials had a unique appeal to me, as they were all about how much pain you could tolerate. In time trials there was no rabbit to chase, no rival next to you, no external motivation, no visual cue. It was just you, your bike, and a road.

There weren't the snappy accelerations of sprinting, or the quick tactical decision-making of road races. It was just this pure effort. The ability to concentrate on one thing to the exclusion of all else was a very specific skill, separate from those required when racing at the heart of the peloton.

Having suckered my father into driving me to a few races, and brimming with newfound confidence, I signed up for the 1988 Colorado State Time Trial Championships. As it turned out, the championships would embody the lonely ethos of time-trialing. They were held in the far-eastern Colorado plains in a town called Strasburg.

Strasburg, an agricultural town that felt abandoned, was the definition of desolate, with just the wind and dust to keep you company. If it has an end-of-the-line feel, that's because it's where the last spike was driven to complete the Transcontinental Railroad.

But there was good reason in choosing such a desolate spot; bike racing in Colorado didn't have so much money in the 1980s, so the race organizers couldn't afford to close the roads. Instead, they just tried to pick the road with the least traffic and the town with the lowest population. At Strasburg, they succeeded.

A little before four a.m. on a Saturday, just after school had ended for the year, my father and I ate some soggy cornflakes in the kitchen, filled a small Coleman thermos with water—marked with a Sharpie *For Dove Hunting*—and then loaded the bike into the back of the Volvo.

After a splutter, a lurch, and a few backfires, we set off to try and become the state champion of Colorado. It was no small task, as Colorado was perhaps the cycling hotbed of U.S. racing in the 1980s. It wasn't simple to win in Colorado, and like another of Frankie's protégés, Clark Sheehan, had shown, if you could win the Colorado Championships, you could also win the National Championships. While there was absolutely nothing at stake from a prize money standpoint, there was a lot at stake in terms of pride.

My start time was seven a.m. We pulled into the parking lot a bit later than I had hoped, due to the Volvo having a bit of a rough morning, but we'd got there. I started my warm-up and Dad went and got my race numbers. It was absolutely freezing, as it always is in the early morning in Colorado.

I pulled on all the winter riding gear I'd bought from A Bike Place, which was finally, belatedly, starting to fit. Nervously, I watched the infamous teen prodigy Bobby Julich warm up across the parking lot in his red and green 7-Eleven junior team uniform.

Bobby was in the next age category up from me and was a much better rider than I was, but, every so often, I could beat him in time trials. I was so obsessed by the thought of winning that I wasn't really paying attention to the time. Dad had pinned my number on, I was all decked out in my rainbow skinsuit, and I went for one last little loop to warm up. Dad was a bit nervous about me leaving the immediate start area, but I dismissed it as being the overanxiety of a stupid parent.

I mean, I had to warm up—right?

When I got back to the start area, I could hear the race official frantically screaming someone's number, calling for them to get to the start line. Suddenly I realized it was my number they were yelling.

Dad had the red-faced, exasperated look only an extremely well-organized man can have when dealing with a space cadet son. I got to the line as quickly as I could, right as they started the final count-down for me.

"...5...4..."

I was still trying to yank my warm-up tights off my legs and get my jacket unzipped as my chances of being state champion disappeared, second by second, into the cold Colorado wind.

"...3..."

I begged Dean Crandall, the gruff and stern official, for a later start time—a do-over, basically.

"...2..."

He looked at me and Dad. "No, this will be a good lesson for you, kid."

"...1!"

I got on my bike and started, albeit dejectedly. It seemed a lost cause. What an idiot. Due to my own hubris and not listening to my old man, I'd blown my chance to win the championships.

I puttered along through the first mile of the time trial, but then, as I threw my last piece of warm-up gear onto the side of the road, I realized something very important: I might not win, but if I just gave up, I wouldn't qualify for the National Champs, either.

I panicked. For a moment, I pondered pretending I'd crashed in a ditch so I could go home. But then logic hit. I'd only lost a minute or so due to my missed start time. If I did a great ride I could maybe finish fifth and still go the Nationals. And that was enough. I started to dig into the effort, fighting to keep my chances of going to the Nationals alive.

There was a tailwind out to the turnaround and my minute man, the rider who'd started sixty seconds behind me, had passed me by the time we reached the cone in the middle of the road that marked the halfway point. However, as soon as we turned into the wind, I caught him.

Then I really started fighting and, after a few minutes racing into the headwind, I found peace in the silence and the pain. I forgot all about being the idiot who missed his start. I forgot all about not having any chance of beating Bobby Julich. I just focused on the pounding of the pedals and my steam-train breathing. My panic had gone.

I passed another rider. And another. And then yet another.

At one mile to go, I was in such a state of suffering that I felt like I was going to shit my shorts at any given moment. Drool was coming out of my mouth because I couldn't afford to close it long enough to swallow. I needed the air. But I just owned that state and continued to push.

I didn't really know what "dry heaving" was until that day. But when I crossed the line, I learned. I immediately started lurching, retching and trying to vomit. It was loud. Really loud.

The other parents looked on in disgust and amazement at the noise and convulsions. But their amazement was also at how far I'd pushed myself, how deep I'd gone. I tumbled off the bike and just sat there, trying to throw up the nonexistent food in my belly. I was glad my mother wasn't around to witness her son in such a state.

I'm sure she would have said something like: "Pushing yourself that hard can't be good for your heart."

Dad found me.

"Looks like you made the best of a bad situation," he chuckled. "Hope you learned something today."

My father was a meticulous timekeeper at these events. Using just an old wind-up wristwatch with a second hand, he knew all the times of all the kids. Today, however, he wasn't volunteering much information.

There was a pause, but eventually, ashamedly, I asked him.

"So, do you think I qualified for the Nationals?"

He looked at me, almost annoyed.

"No," he said. "I think you won."

On the drive home, I fell asleep in the tobacco-scented sheepskin seat cover of the orange Volvo station wagon, just like I had every day on the way to school. I was completely spent. But every once in a while, when I opened one eye, I'd look down and see the gold medal hanging around my neck. I couldn't wait to show Mom. Dad and I agreed we wouldn't mention the dry heaving, though.

I began training for the 1988 U.S. Cycling Championships. Of course, there were some additional races for the Volvo to shepherd us to before heading to the Nationals. The major preparatory event I wanted to race was a week-long stage race called the Casper Classic, in Casper, Wyoming. It was a hot, windswept affair in a town that had long been abandoned by the rest of the world. But it would be a tough race, and would get me ready for the Nationals.

I won the time trial early on in the race and then took the race lead. However, on a long and windy strip of road, I was given a harsh lesson in what an echelon was, and how not to ride in one.

I crashed. Hard.

I was up and on my bike very quickly, but as I chased back up to the front I felt an intense pain in my forearm. It hampered me for the rest of the stage, even though I managed to struggle home to the finish with the peloton.

After the finish, we drove over to the local hospital for X-rays. I had broken my arm, right on the growth plate above my wrist. As the doctor wrapped the enormous plaster cast around my arm, he said no bike riding for at least four weeks.

I couldn't believe it. *Four weeks?*

A month off the bike would ruin any chances of doing anything at the Nationals. This couldn't be true. Why the hell couldn't I just ride with a cast? The answer was that I could, but if I crashed again and fractured it again, it would damage my arm's growth. Plus, it was going to hurt like hell for a few weeks.

My parents knew I was sad, but tried to console me.

"Well, there's always next year," Mom said.

But as we got back in the car, all I could think was, *This is bullshit.* We were about halfway home from the hospital when I spoke.

"I'm racing tomorrow," I stated.

My parents both tried to protest, but I was resolute.

"If you guys won't drive me to the race tomorrow, then I'll just ride my bike to the start," I said stubbornly. "I'm racing. I don't care if I end up with one arm shorter than the other one. I'm racing here. And I'm racing at the nationals."

My poor parents . . .

And so I did, and I suffered like a pig in the summer sun.

I was unable to grip the handlebars while trying to manage this massive 1980s plaster cast, seemingly made out of cement. In fact, I was unable to get out of the saddle at all. My arm was so swollen in the heat it pressed hard against the cast and, in the aftermath of the crash, my whole body hurt. But I was not quitting while in the race lead. No way.

I'd read many stories of pro riders in Europe suffering through horrible injuries and illness, continuing through races with diarrhea, broken collarbones, infections, and fevers. They never gave up. It was their job, and the fact that they were so tough qualified them for that job.

That was my dream, too, to prove myself to be tough enough to withstand anything. I wasn't going to give up; I was going to be like them—the blue-collar, hard-working, tough-as-old-boots European riders. I wasn't like these overly pampered soft kids from the USA who had their parents worried at every shift in the wind direction.

Of course, as I couldn't really follow any attacks, I did lose the race lead, but I kept my pride, and I also kept my hopes alive for the Nationals. You could see other parents shaking their heads as I rode by with that huge blue cast on. They would never let their children race a bike in such a state.

Tsk tsk, tut-tut.

But then I hadn't given my parents much of a choice, so they watched, nervously, counting the laps until it would all end and we could go home.

I managed to cling on to fifth place overall, but more important, I had kept my hopes of doing well at the National Championships alive, and proved to my parents how much I really wanted this dream to be real. The drive home was, admittedly, a bit subdued, as they were both upset that I'd raced. But I could tell they were proud.

I'd shown true grit, and maybe that outweighed the risks I'd taken to finish. I'd proven I was not going to give up, and that comforted them a great deal.

The cast came off one week before the Nationals. The doctor was amazed at how fast my arm had healed. He'd never seen anything like it, he said, as he cut off the cement that had been weighing me down. With my injury troubles behind me, the family, including the dog, all made the trip out to Pennsylvania for the 1988 U.S. National Cycling Championships.

But we were forced to leave the faithful orange Volvo behind, knowing that we'd all explode from its lack of air-conditioning. Dad always said the Volvo had 4×80 air con—that was air-conditioning with four windows open at 80 miles per hour. But we all knew the Volvo couldn't go 80 miles per hour, and in the middle of the American heartland in August, this mattered. So we left my old friend behind, and took the blue Oldsmobile station wagon on the long trip across the country to race bikes against the nation's best.

In the late 1980s American cycling scene, word spread fast. I had already heard the legend of a New York kid—from Brooklyn, Queens, or somewhere—who had won everything in the fourteen-to-fifteen age category. He was said to be eight feet tall and to have a beard, the thickness of which had never been seen before on a fourteen-year-old. Apparently he was unbeatable.

Every rider from the East Coast who dared to come out west had tales of this kid's invincibility. Everyone who had raced with him was intimidated by him. Many of the tales came from Bobby Julich, who warned me against getting cocky about my Colorado State Championship. Bobby said the hairy giant from New York would crush me in the National Time Trial Championship.

That billed the confrontation as David versus Goliath. This time, most people were betting on Goliath.

Warming up for the time trial, I finally caught a glimpse of Goliath. His name was George Hincapie. He was resplendent in his gleaming white GS Mengoni skinsuit and straddling a gorgeous time trial bike, immaculately kept with shiny Campagnolo components and dual Campagnolo disk wheels.

He was handsome, too. He looked like a teenage version of Lancelot, just ridden in from Camelot. That was, except for the dark, greasy, permed, and curly mullet streaming out from underneath his helmet. That was more New Jersey than Camelot.

I told Dad that George was the man to set his Casio watch by.

Dad nodded nervously, unnerved by the relative chaos that the East Coast National Championships meeting was compared to the local bike racing scene back in Colorado. Instead of the cold and crisp Colorado mornings we were used to, it was a hot and muggy Pennsylvania afternoon, with flies and mosquitoes doing their rounds. We were in Hincapie's territory, and I was scared. But at least this time, I didn't miss my start slot.

It always felt like I was right on the verge of a panic attack in the minutes before a start. That day was the most nervous I'd ever been. Somehow, though, I overcame it, and used all my pent-up nervousness to go fast. After all, my parents had driven me all the way over there.

Plowing into the thick and humid air felt much different than racing back home at high altitude. The whole sea-level racing experience was new to me. I was pushing as hard as my little legs would go, but didn't seem to be moving very fast. I was soaked from sweating, but I wasn't breathing very hard. I felt like I might pass out from the heat and humidity, but I definitely was not going to dry heave.

I crossed the line totally spent from the effort, with my mother insistent that I was far too red in the face, and pouring ice water over me. Of course, she also wanted to feed me. My mother was always trying to feed me. I didn't want anything to eat, though: I wanted to know how I'd done compared to the legend of Long Island. Dad said he didn't know. He knew we were within a few seconds of each other, but he didn't know which way it had gone.

So we waited, impatiently, for the results to come back. When they were finally posted, it was neither George nor I who had won.

Instead we'd finished second and third, been beaten by a kid from Indiana. This seemed unthinkable, impossible, but there it was in print, in black and white.

The awards ceremony was an hour or so later, and I finally got to meet my nemesis—and the kid from Indiana. George was exceedingly shy and polite. He told me that all he'd been hearing about was this legendary kid from Colorado that no one could beat. He'd heard I only weighed eighty pounds, and that I had lungs twice the size of a giraffe's.

George said that he'd been scared of me and that everyone he'd talked to from Colorado said he had no chance of beating me. It was funny telling each other about all the tales of grandeur we'd heard about each other, all the fears we'd built up.

And here we were in a parking lot in Reading, Pennsylvania, getting silver and bronze medals, beaten by a kid from Indiana no one had ever heard of.

MOAB

As I won more races in different locations across the USA, I started to dream of racing in international competitions. One way to be sure of this happening was to qualify for the Junior World Championships. That became my focus and goal for the 1989 season.

In order to qualify, you had to do well in a series of Junior World qualifier races across the USA. The first of these was always in Moab, Utah, sometime around Easter. It was a race that attracted the best from across the nation, all of whom were trying to earn a spot on the Junior World Championship team.

Moab is in dry, high desert in a desolate and unpopulated part of eastern Utah. It has a few kitschy 1950s motor hotels and diners, complete with flickering neon lights to draw in tourists. It is also an intensely beautiful place, with giant red sandstone arches in the nearby national park and wide-open blue skies.

Moab draws people in from all over the world, just to see the enormity and grand beauty of these arches. The first stage of the Moab qualifier was a typically western and very early morning road race that ran through Arches National Park. It was hard and hilly and usually determined the overall race winner of the weekend stage race.

I knew the pattern in junior racing. Everyone rolled along rather tentatively until a few key moments or hills in the race, and then in small spurts, the winner was chosen. As our cold eight a.m. race start approached, I was expecting more of the same. We'd lollygag out to the big hills, there'd be a few attacks on the steepest pitches, the lead group would be selected, and then we'd race the last few miles to determine the winner.

This time, though, it was different. Within seconds of the start gun going off, the entire junior peloton was strung out in single file, already breaking into pieces. On a pan-flat section of road, some sixty miles from the finish, someone was driving the pace at a speed never seen before in junior racing.

We were flying, and it was as if a grenade had been thrown into the middle of a normally docile group of polite bike racers. Kids who normally might be expected to be in contention for the win were dropped before we even hit the first hill. It was as if a motorcycle was leading the peloton.

I slowly clawed my way forward through the disintegrating field, astonished at the state of the red-faced, near-dead riders I was passing on my way to the front. I finally made it up to where Bobby Julich was clinging on to the wheel in front of him.

"Who's . . . THAT . . . on . . . the . . . front . . . ??" I gasped.

Bobby, breathless and barely audible, said one word.

"Lance."

As we hit the first climb of the day, I finally made my way to the front to witness this beast, Lance, at work. He clearly cared little for the tactical nuances of cycling and was just trying to single-handedly eliminate everyone from the race through sheer brute force.

His shoulders were much wider and more muscled than any of the other kids, and his face was that of tormented determination. He wasn't here to win the race; he was here to impose his will. He was here to crush, pillage, and dominate.

I quietly slipped back a few wheels and figured I'd bide my time and see if this supernatural beast would continue to slash his way to victory, or if he might eventually run out of rage and hate and his head of steam would wear off. Bobby, a cagey and intelligent bike racer, was thinking the same thing.

Kid Lance was totally unconcerned about the few remaining competitors that desperately clung to his back wheel. He continued to smash and tear clumsily at the pedals in fits of demonic possession. His shoulders rocked back and forth as he pounded away on a gear way too big for the hill we were on. He didn't seem to care that we were saving energy on his wheel. This wasn't about winning, this was about demoralizing, squeezing, and then killing the last dregs of spirit left in his competition.

On the return leg of the race, we hit the steepest hill of the course. It was some ten miles before the finish line and was usually the definitive moment. Was everyone going to just concede victory to Lance? We certainly had all been intimidated.

In a flash, I saw Bobby jump out in front. It was an audacious attack that only served to fuel the rage. Lance pulled him back.

Then it was my turn. I accelerated away, not looking back, out of fear as much as anything. I just kept going, as if I was being chased down by a lion.

Bobby made his way up to me, with one or two other top junior riders.

"We dropped him," he blurted. "Let's go!!"

And go we did. We all knew Lance would be fighting like a wounded animal to catch back on to the group and teach us all a lesson. So we rode like the wind to escape the consequences of our insubordination.

We'd wounded the alpha dog and left him for dead. A freezing-cold sleet started to fall on the final descent and run into Moab, but I don't think any of us noticed, as we were sprinting away from our demise. We risked everything on the slick, wet corners.

Our little group worked flawlessly together until we entered the final mile. Then we sprinted for the win, with Bobby, of course, getting the better of me and another new kid, Chann McRae.

Cooling down after the race, I chatted to Bobby.

"Where did *that* come from??" I asked him.

Bobby told me more. The kid's name was Armstrong, Lance Armstrong, and he was from Texas.

He raced triathlons, but was switching to road racing and just tearing people apart. Supposedly he was best friends with the other new kid from

Texas, our fellow escapee, Chann McRae. They trained more than anyone, they knew how to hurt more than anyone, and they were going to make it big in cycling, no question.

As we stood on the podium I saw Lance out among the crowd of kids and parents, watching.

He'd ended up finishing fourth that day. He glared up at the podium with contempt and menace.

I turned to Bobby. "Well, Lance sure is strong," I said, "but man, is he stupid."

Chann, standing alongside me on the podium, heard what I'd said.

"Duuuude, I'm telling Lance you said that, and he's gonna kick your little skinny ass, motherfucker," he drawled in his Texan twang.

PART 2

1989–1995

CHAPTER 4

THE GOLDEN
GENERATION

They all—Lance Armstrong, Bobby Julich, George Hincapie, Chann McRae—went on to have careers as some of the best cyclists of their generation. These were the people who would shape professional cycling, not just in the States, but around the world, for better or for worse, for the next three decades. But back then they were just kids trying to race bikes, like me.

Bobby came to all the races in his dad's rusty camper van, with Bob Julich senior always wearing the shortest possible green Day-Glo running shorts. Lance drove a white T-top Camaro IROC-Z to the races with his mom in the passenger seat and his bike disassembled and crammed into the rear.

There were other characters that would go on to win and place in major events: "Fast" Freddie Rodriguez, Kevin Livingston, and Jeff Evanshine, to name a few. We were dysfunctional, outcast kids, pulled together by the outsider niche sport of cycling.

We all dreamed of racing in Europe and bettering multiple Tour de France winner Greg LeMond. And we were competitive, although "competitive" actually doesn't even begin to describe it. Our generation, born from 1971 to 1973, didn't just want to be good cyclists, we felt destined to dominate cycling. The issue, of course, was that we also became each other's greatest obstacles.

USA Cycling, our national federation, invited all the best and the brightest riders to various training camps at the Olympic Training Center in Colorado Springs. We would not only race with one another, but we would have to live with one another, day in, day out. We were competitive every minute of every day; 24/7 was spent trying to outdo one another.

The most infamous of these camps was December camp, where we all participated in "cross training" that was supposed to help us build up for the season ahead. Every hike, every stretching session, every workout in the gym, became a cage match. Nobody backed down—for anything. We'd do a six-hour hike to the top of Pikes Peak one day, just to do a three-a-day, running, weightlifting, and cyclo-cross workout the next.

Blisters and tendinitis, caused by overtraining, became the norm after one week of camp. Painkilling pills were secretly passed around. Drinking absurd amounts of coffee became standard, just to survive from one day to the next without crying.

The coaches, mostly from Eastern Europe, found it all quite amusing. They felt the best way to find the strongest riders was to try and crush everyone with huge training overload, and then look at who was left standing at the end of the two weeks. And, of course, we made it worse by turning every exercise into a win-at-all-costs competition.

There were a few parts of each training camp that were useful, such as VO_2 max testing, blood testing, and help in getting your bike positioned correctly. Inevitably, even some of this lapsed into the same competitive realm.

One coach decided to place a wager on the VO_2 max testing. He couldn't give an award to the highest VO_2 max, as that was partly genetic, so instead he told us that whoever got the absolute highest blood lactate reading—whoever withstood the most pain—would get to be his guest to an all-expense-paid trip to the nearby Colorado Springs strip club, Puss in Boots.

On the last day of camp, an administrator came from the main building to find me and George Hincapie. We were given separate appointment times to meet with the Olympic Training Center doctor. Neither of us had any idea what this might be about, but we both had the suspicion we were somehow in trouble.

The doctor started the meeting by handing me the results of a recent blood test that had been taken at camp.

"We'd like to bring your attention to the part of the test that says 'hematocrit and hemoglobin'," he said.

I scanned down the paper looking for these words.

Oh, no, I have cancer, was the first thing that went through my head.

The Olympic Training Center blood test had discovered cancer in my body. *My poor mother!*

"We feel these numbers are abnormally high, and we need to ask you some very direct questions," he told me.

"Okay," I responded meekly.

Then the doctor said: "Have you at any point in time received a blood transfusion to increase your performance at this camp?"

I really had no idea what they were asking me, although I did vaguely remember that there was some sort of scandal at the 1984 Olympic Games over blood. I asked them to explain what a blood transfusion was and laughed, nervously.

The doctor laid it all out for me.

"No—I didn't do that," I said. "Why would I do that . . . ?"

I'm pretty sure George got the same talk. In the end, the doctors were quite nice to us, and said they had to ask the hard questions, but that the most likely reason for these high readings were genetics. George was of Colombian descent and I lived in Denver, which maybe had something to do with it.

My father had been taking blood thinners for many years after a small stroke he had when I was a child, so perhaps he also had high hematocrit and hemoglobin. I didn't really know. Neither did George, but we were both happy to be done with these uncomfortable meetings.

The selections for the European trips that Team USA would take on were made in the aftermath of the camps and also initiated the selection process for the World Championships. The junior national team took three or four trips to Europe every year, and garnering a slot on those trips was a highly sought-after prize.

My first trip was a month in Brittany, France, the heartland of French cycling at the time. It would be my first real adventure outside the USA and my first taste of real European cycling.

The adventure started on the flight over the Atlantic, with one of my teammates sneaking a few whiskey shooters out of the drinks trolley every time it passed. By the time we arrived in Paris, he was "fighting" drunk. We had to steer him through passport control and pray that he didn't start a ruckus with someone in the airport.

Finally, we dragged him outside to our ride. The *soigneur* and mechanic that were sent to pick us up heaved our bikes into the back of the sprinter van and then threw our drunken comrade in the back on top of all the bike bags. It was a long drive out to Brittany and we had to wash the vomit off the bike bags when we arrived.

The farmhouse we stayed in looked quaint enough from the outside, but was damp and cold on the inside. We were effectively camping and were each given a pad and a sleeping bag to put on the floor. The roof leaked and we had very little hot water, which soon became an issue. After training on the first day, we figured out there was only enough hot water for one, or maybe two of us.

Being Darwinian creatures, the final kilometers of each training ride became a race to the house, a race for hot water. At first it was a bit of a joke, but it soon turned into outright warfare. Meanwhile, the coach was getting annoyed that we were sprinting full gas in what was supposed to be our cool-down period. So we decided on a shower rotation, ensuring that everyone would get a hot shower at least once every three days.

But after a few days of this, Jeff Evanshine broke ranks. As training ended, he sprinted hard toward the house and ran into the shower, laughing maniacally the whole way. The first time was funny. The second time, less so.

The third time he did it, after a particularly long, cold, and rainy training session, we all waited patiently until he was fully undressed and ready to enjoy his hot shower. We picked him up and threw him into the courtyard.

Evanshine was built the way I was: a soaking-wet, skinny little rat, about five foot nine and 120 pounds. But man, oh man, was he a beast in fighting against being thrown out into the freezing cold! He squirmed, cried, and fought like a naked hairless tiger the whole way out. It was impressive how strong he was. Finally, we got him out the door.

Then we locked him out.

No matter how loud, how whiny, and how much he begged to come back in, we left him out there, in one of those very cold rainstorms that Brittany is well known for. But he had put up a very good fight, so we respected him enough to not leave him out there all night.

We weren't bike riders. We were bike *racers*, and ruthless ones at that.

We were as cutthroat with one another as with the competition in the races we rode. It was a race among us to see who would attack first, as then the rest of the team would be obliged to sit on the chase behind. It was hardly the tactics a pro rider would use, but it worked.

We rarely lost, and quite often totally dominated, even when the field was strong and international. The USA was a force to be reckoned with. Greg LeMond was winning the Tour de France, and we were winning all the junior races in France.

There were a few riders who we didn't seem to be able to beat, though. They were the legends of junior cycling in France at the time: Philippe Gaumont (later to ride for Cofidis and then earn notoriety as a doping whistleblower) and Erwan Mentheour.

Gaumont was a beast of a man, with a protruding forehead and a beard thicker than Hincapie's. And he would win—a lot. He could sprint, he could climb, and he could power away on his own. There was no terrain that stopped him.

As we rode back to our farmhouse, following a race in which we got thoroughly trounced by Gaumont, a few French riders tagged along with us for the extra training miles. I started to attempt to chat with one of them at the back of the group. It was mainly hand gestures and snorting, but when I said the name "Gaumont" we both knew what I meant. We'd both been fileted by the man-beast that day.

Then the Frenchman gestured on his arm where the crease of the elbow lies and where veins pop up. He pushed his thumb in, mimicking a heroin addict giving himself a shot.

As he did so, he said "Gaumont!" for emphasis.

It took me a second, but then I realized he was accusing Gaumont of doping. I shook my head.

"Noooon," I replied, incredulous.

The French guy looked me in the eye.

"Mais oui!" he said.

That evening, over a fine dinner of cow tongue and green beans, we got talking about all the rumors of doping in the peloton. We each claimed to know that our favorite rider was clean and we each claimed to have zero tolerance for doping. We all agreed that dopers were cheating bastards and that Americans would never do such a thing.

These damned Frenchies and Italians would do whatever it took, but we, as Americans, were morally superior and would never resort to such behavior. Just like Greg LeMond had won the Tour clean, we all exclaimed.

Finally our Danish coach, older and more experienced, chimed in.

"In Italy, everyone thinks the Italian riders are clean and the French riders dope. In France, everyone thinks the French riders are clean and the Americans dope."

He then started telling stories about riders changing teams, and how they would either suddenly go faster or slower. I asked why one of my heroes wasn't going as fast on his new team as he had on his old one.

He chuckled.

"Maybe it's a good problem for him . . . good for his health, anyway . . ."

I refused to believe my heroes would have ever even considered doping.

"Maybe you're right," he shrugged, "but don't just assume that because someone is American that they won't ever be tempted by doping."

We all sat silently, listening to him spin a yarn about how junior riders from all over the world had the same discussion we were having. He told us how they all wanted their heroes to be clean. We had never considered that our viewpoints might be culturally biased. We'd never considered that just because someone speaks a different language or comes from a different culture, that they didn't have the same moral perspective.

"All every good racer wants is for the playing field to be level—the same rules for everyone," he said. "Because you *all* feel that if no one is cheating, that you'll win, because no one could possibly be better than you. And that's not bad, that's the way that champions think."

After Team USA got back home from those European adventures, we all immediately set out to outdo one another on home soil. Of course, this meant dispensing with junior racing and riding in all the professional races we were allowed to, at seventeen years old. If we were to succeed Greg LeMond and Andy Hampsten, we'd need to start beating all the local category-one riders and low-level pros before we reached eighteen.

I traveled with my new friend, Colby Pearce, to these local or regional races. He was a year older than I was, and owned a reliable Japanese car with enough space for bikes and luggage. It even had a bike rack. Plus we shared a love for dark alternative music and Gothic-looking women dressed in black.

Colby was the antithesis of the other bike racers I'd met. He read Nietzsche, hated all other sports, hated fraternities, hated hair that was too big, and hated a lot of life itself. He was clearly the ideal road trip partner.

We became best friends and drove all around the USA, looking for races with a lot of prize money where we felt we could beat up riders ten years our senior. If we did well in one race, we knew we'd have enough gas money to get to the next one.

Our first adventure started with a trip from Denver to Oklahoma City. Then, after collecting a few crisp green notes from the U.S. government, we drove to Bisbee, Arizona, for a five-day stage race. All this freedom and exploration came at the expense of attending school, going to senior parties, and finding our first loves in algebra class.

We were sleeping on the floors of other people's hotel rooms, driving for hours on end and then racing our bikes. We had no cell phones and no communication with home. It was just the two of us—teenagers in a white Honda with two bikes on top, on one continuous road trip, one continuous freedom ride. Colby and I became inseparable, Duran Duran–listening brothers of the road.

Colby was an interesting but troubled soul. He had lost his mother to cancer at a young age, and then lost his father to a heart attack a few years later. He was a staunch atheist, reasoning that surely no God would allow a young child to endure such pain and loss at such a tender age.

Whenever a race didn't go well or whenever his bike broke, Colby would rage at God. He would scream at the sky saying: "Why do you hate me?!"

In one such fit of rage, Colby threw an old Campagnolo bottom bracket tool straight up toward the heavens. We both lost its flight in the sun, thinking that maybe this time it actually had hit God himself. That was until, suddenly, the tool smashed down on my foot. My face turned red and my foot redder still.

"What the fuck was that for, idiot?" I asked.

Colby sat stunned.

He quickly apologized.

"My foot doesn't believe you're an atheist, so can we maybe keep the yelling at God to a minimum?" I raged.

After the incident with the wrench, there was a little less philosophical debate and a bit more listening to Depeche Mode and the

Cure. No matter what our differences might have been, we did agree on how to travel and perfected getting speeding tickets and peeing in water bottles when we didn't have time to stop before making it to the next race.

Our final stop on our month-long adventure was at the Mammoth Lakes stage race. The Soviet national team was rumored to be participating and we felt both daunted and excited.

"The Russians are coming . . . !"

It was like the scene in *Breaking Away* when Team Cinzano came to race the Bloomington 100.

The stars of the Soviet team were Vladislav Bobrik and Evgeni Berzin, both of whom went on to become very successful in European pro racing later in their careers. But even at that time they were legends in our world, as they had dominated amateur racing in Europe for the last few years. They seemed destined to become top professional riders, if their still-communist government would actually allow them to pursue such a capitalist venture.

We made the sixteen-hour drive to Mammoth Lakes, keen to show how good we were in comparison to the Russian juggernaut. We both had a lot to prove to the world and had massive, Frisbee-sized chips on our shoulders. This would be a good chance to show everyone that we, too, were pretty damned fast.

A large number of professional riders had decided to show up and test their mettle against the Soviets. There were five days and plenty of hundred-mile-plus stages over mountain passes and through deserts—it would be the hardest race either of us had ever competed in, by a long shot.

Stage one was an uphill time trial to the ski resort of Mammoth. I had no idea what to expect from myself or from the competition. It was just an honor, as a seventeen-year-old dreamer, to have been invited to such a prestigious race.

I knew I climbed well, and I knew my mind was suited to the art of time-trialing, but I'd never faced competition at such a high level. I was too nervous and too excited to eat much for breakfast. As we headed out to the start area, I saw many of my heroes warming up. There was Alexi Grewal; Bobrik; Jeff Pierce, winner of a Champs-Élysées stage of the Tour; and many more.

As I started the time trial, I figured that my goal of not getting passed from behind was enough, so despite being freaked out, I didn't feel much pressure. Nonetheless, I ended up pushing myself hard enough to revisit my old habit of dry heaving by the finish. This time, there was no Mom or Dad to comfort me as I retched in the corner.

But between bursts of bile, I heard the announcer.

"A new best time! A rider I've never heard of, but still a new best time, from Jonathan Vaughters."

I was stunned. Two race officials walked over to tell me I needed to stay around the finish area, just in case I won. Right. *In case I won . . .*

In the end, I finished second to Bobrik. But I fought valiantly with the Russians all week, through mountains, high temperatures, and crosswinds. None of my fellow junior riders could believe what I was doing, and neither could I.

Finally, I'd been the one to outperform all the rest of the riders in the "golden generation" of American cycling. The result quickly drew the attention of the national team coaches, and all but guaranteed me a place on the 1991 Junior World Championship team.

The Junior World Champs were in Colorado Springs that year, a first for the United States. The course was a hilly loop around the Garden of the Gods, at more than seven thousand feet in altitude. It would be the perfect opportunity for a climber from high altitude to win. I wanted to win. I wanted to be the first American since Greg LeMond to be Junior World champion.

Of course, there were multiple training camps in the run-up to those Worlds at the Olympic Training Center (which we had now nicknamed, quite appropriately, the Dump). During these camps, we'd occasionally overlap with the junior class just above us that had graduated into the senior ranks, which included Lance.

It was almost like high school all over again, with the older guys like Lance and Bobby acting cool and not wanting to fraternize with those of us still consigned to the junior ranks. Of course, sometimes our groups would overlap at local races in Colorado, which gave us a chance to show the guys a few years older than us that we weren't inferior.

During one of the camps, the majority of the riders went off and raced the Mount Evans hill climb. Both the junior and senior versions of Team USA were going to compete, including Armstrong. It was a short twenty-eight miles, but the air got thinner and thinner as you went higher.

The senior riders of Team USA were perhaps even more competitive with one another than the juniors, as they were already jockeying for a slot on the 1992 Olympic team. Every race counted for them, or at least every race that the coaches showed up to.

All three of the top guys for Team USA were there: Lance, Bobby, and Darren Baker. For us juniors, it marked a perfect opportunity to kick some ass, so we wouldn't get thrown into trash cans and stuffed into lockers when we got back to the training center.

I finished fifth, closely following the older and established pro riders from Coors Light and Subaru-Montgomery. Lance, who'd that year won the Settimana Bergamasca stage race in northern Italy, finished sixth. It was quite the little victory to take back to the Dump.

Another rider, a bit of an outsider named Chad Gerlach, was at the training camp, too. Chad always had the balls to take Lance on. He was the lone wolf trying to kill the alpha all the time. This was the perfect opportunity for him to get under Lance's skin. Chad would start in on Lance while we were hanging around the concrete bunker dormitory rooms we were sleeping in.

"So, Lance, whatever the race is that you won in Italy—Settimana Bergdorf Goodman, or whatever—that must not have been so hard to win," Chad mused. "I mean—you just got beaten by a 120-pound junior rider. That's gotta sting, right?"

This went on for days. You could see the annoyance building up under Lance's skin. Mind you, had the roles been reversed, Lance would have been giving this kid every bit as much shit. Then one day, Chad was gone from camp. Rumor had it that Chad had pushed

Lance too far and Lance had gotten him in a headlock and wrestled him to the ground. I even heard talk of Chad's head ending up through some drywall.

We all knew that the coaches were going to have to do something, and assumed because of the policies at the Olympic Training Center that Lance would be sent home. Words were one thing, but violence was another.

When we found out that it was Gerlach that was getting sent home, not Lance, we were all confused. The message from the coaches was pretty clear, though. Don't mess with the golden boy from Texas. The rules don't apply to him.

It was just a few weeks until the Junior Worlds and things were tense around the Dump. The final selections were being made, both for the road race and for the team time trial, and people were on edge. The fight for final selection was in high gear, and the gloves were off.

The Worlds team was divided into two parts: the team time trial selection and the road race selection. I figured I was a shoo-in for the road race, but I also thought fairly highly of my chances for the team time trial.

Colby was also keen on giving the team time trial squad a shot. So we paired up to contest the two-man team time trial competition that USA Cycling held to help determine who would be selected for Worlds.

Colby and I were convinced we deserved to be part of the team time trial squad, and thought we did a pretty good job of proving it by finishing second in the two-man team time trial. However, that event was only a precursor to the four-man team time trial, in which the coaches decided who was going to ride with whom.

It seemed inevitable: Colby and I were sure to be paired up with the other strongest kids, and that would be the time trial team for the Worlds. However, when the A, B, and C squads were announced for the final selection race, we were put on the B squad.

I was enraged. Everyone knew the coaches used the final four-man race as a way to finalize a selection that was already made. They had placed Colby and me with two other guys that weren't going to be of much help, thereby consigning us to defeat. It was utter bullshit, and quite typical of U.S. coaching in those days. They had their favorites and we were not high on that list.

So I had a chat with Colby. I told him we should boycott the kangaroo-court selection process and boycott the damned race itself. Colby was a bit more reluctant to piss off all of USA Cycling's finest coaches, and felt it might not benefit him, long term—and he was right. But after a bit more self-righteous preaching on my part, I could finally see the God-and-authority-hating fire light up in Colby's eyes. He agreed on the boycott.

I knew a boycott would risk my position on the road squad and that the coaches would see this as treacherous. But I was really resolved that it would mean much more to show other kids that they didn't have to put up with such a biased selection system.

"Set an example, dammit. Stand up for what's right, dammit. This is America!"

Plus, it felt really cool being a rebel. I felt like my biggest hero of that time: 1984 Olympic Games Gold medalist Alexi Grewal.

I loved Alexi. He spat at cameras, and ripped off his jersey while winning races to avoid giving his sponsor publicity if he felt he'd been wronged by his team. He stuck it to "The Man." He did it his way, no matter what. He was anything but the golden boy. All coaches and managers hated him, and he hated any sort of authority. I wanted to be just like him, and the exact opposite of Lance.

It turns out, however, that Eastern bloc cycling coaches are not impressed with spirited, opinionated American teenagers. It was great fun to watch the chaos we had caused, but it did, however, have its price. I was dragged into the main coaching offices at the Dump and told in no uncertain terms that they knew these shenanigans were my idea, and that if I was as much as two seconds late to any training ride or team meeting, I was getting booted off the road team for Worlds.

My whole James Dean rebel act fell apart in the meeting. I apologized and sulked my way out of the room, tail tucked and head down. For the rest of the pre-Worlds camp, I toed the line, stood up straight, said "Yes, please," and "Thank you."

The team time trial squad of George Hincapie, Fred Rodriguez, Chris Wherry, and Matt Johnson did just fine without me and finished in second place, winning the first junior world medal in a few years for the USA. The coaches made sure I knew how well they'd done without me. I kept my mouth shut, for a change, and waited for the day of the road race to arrive.

I toed the line, waiting for my chance to be world champion. I had been feeling a bit off in the build-up, and maybe fighting a bit of a head cold, but I was way too nervous to think about that. I stood at the start, shaking from nerves.

As I looked around, I saw much of the same—kids from all around the world twitching from nerves. It was an edgy morning. At the last minute they had delayed the start, as the team from Egypt had just arrived from the airport, in old 1980s-style taxicabs.

We watched as their bikes were assembled on the start line. These guys, just off a nice twenty-hour flight, were going to start the World Championships in five minutes.

They're going to last about two laps, I thought.

The start gun went off, and immediately I was in trouble. The race was fast and dangerous. Nervous junior racers were willing to risk anything at the Worlds, as it was seen as the first step to gaining a professional contract.

There were many crashes in the early laps. I dodged most of the worst ones, but kept getting caught behind, struggling to find my legs. The U.S. team was considered one of the strongest going into the race, and we all knew who the main dangers would be, with our old rival, Philippe Gaumont, topping the list.

Still, this was held on home soil, in our country, for a change, and we knew we could win. The problem was, we all wanted to be the one who would claim that victory. It was the classic conundrum in cycling. It's a team sport, where only one person gets the glory.

We all wanted the glory. But one person wanted it a bit more than the rest of us, and he wasn't struggling to find his legs that day: Jeff Evanshine.

He fought even harder to stay in front than he had to avoid being pushed out into the rain in Brittany. And when it was all said and done, it was scrawny little Jeff who won. The least favorite guy on the team, the guy who kept hogging the hot water in France.

Jeff got his revenge for being left out in the rain. Now we were the ones out in the cold, watching empty-handed as he stood atop the podium, beaming with the rainbow bands of Junior World champion emblazoned across his chest, just like Greg LeMond.

CHAPTER 5

THE GRAND ADVENTURE

L ife was an anticlimax after the Junior World Championships. It was a hot and lazy August in Colorado, and, as all my friends prepared to go to college, I took naps on the couch and tried to avoid the reality ahead.

In four short years I had clawed my way up from finishing last in my first race to representing the USA at the World Championships. I had proven myself one of the best junior riders in the world and I thought I was destined for greatness. But now the question loomed— what was next?

My parents were concerned that I wasn't taking the prospect of going to college very seriously. I was listless, just racing and training a bit to keep my time occupied, but not really knowing what the next step was.

I would no longer be able to race in the junior ranks and I would have to race with the adults and compete against professional riders—not because I chose to, but because if I wanted to keep racing, I would have to.

Could I still borrow Mom's station wagon? Did I need to get a job? Would there be a senior team that would want to support and even sponsor me? Or would I end up like the droves of twenty-four-year-old "wannabe" pro riders living in their parents' basement, envious of those who'd secured a contract on a team, yet still dreaming of one day making it big?

In my endless free time, I decided it might not be such a bad idea to enroll in a few classes at the local community college. As I needed to earn a few extra dollars for spending money, entering some local races with good prize money might not be such a bad idea, either. Luckily for me, Colby was of the same mind-set.

Like two mercenaries in search of treasure, we went off to target some local events with easily looted prize lists. The Steamboat Springs stage race was the first of these races. We both signed up for the pro category-one race, thinking we could sneak away with a few hundred dollars.

On the drive up, Colby was endlessly whining about a girl he wanted to break up with, but didn't have the courage to tell her. This was typical Colby. He was a master at attracting women, as the minute they found out he'd lost his parents, they wanted to mother and love him. He played this card often and well.

"Listen, I'll make a bet with you," I told him. "If I win this race, you have to break up with her, immediately."

He laughed at that.

"Dude, there is no way you're going to win the pro category-one race as a junior—*no way*! There are just too many good riders."

We shook hands and agreed that if I won, he would stop at the first pay phone to call her.

Neither one of us had much energy or passion left for a small race in Steamboat at the end of a long racing season. But my competitive fire was reignited by the bet.

That was the way it always was with Colby and me: there was nothing more important than winning the bet.

For three days we battled with Boulder's finest "living-in-the-basement-of-mom's-house wannabe pro riders" for top honors in the Colorado Rockies. It wasn't easy, as I hadn't been very focused on my training ever since the Junior Worlds, but I battled with everything I had. When the race ended, I'd won $5,000 in cash, a Moots titanium frameset, and most important, my bet with Colby.

After the race, I stood next to Colby at a pay phone in the parking lot of the Rabbit Ears Motel waiting for him to make his call. He protested, saying he might like her after all, and might not want to break up. I said that was fine, then he should call her now and ask her to marry him instead.

Eventually, after many awkward moments, he called her and had around a two-hour phone call. I ran around looking for more coins to stuff in the pay phone, as he endlessly circled the issue. Finally, he dropped the bomb.

It was all over: our innocence, our last junior race, our racing season, and now his relationship. We drove home, listening to the Cure, over and over again.

With the racing season over for the year, I begrudgingly started classes at the infamous Metro State College. Metro was where you went to school when your grades weren't quite good enough to get you in anywhere else.

I had decided on becoming something between a philosophy and art history major, both of which seemed like they wouldn't interfere too much with my training, should I actually find a team to ride for next year. I don't know why, but I was never terribly concerned with finding a ride. I just trusted that cycling was my destiny and that a good team would find me, somehow.

I began a back-breaking schedule of debating Aristotle and then painting Impressionism in order to keep my ever-concerned parents at bay. Technically, I was "going to college," so they couldn't complain. Despite my heavy academic schedule, I trained every day, without really any focus, but somehow thinking of it as my job.

As I'd saved more in prize money than most of my friends had made through delivering pizzas, I felt like I deserved to think of it as my job. I certainly wanted it to become my job, but someone—some team, some sponsor—had to make that happen.

That ensured a lot of time spent waiting by the phone. All day sometimes.

Some days, I felt like I was waiting for a girl I wanted to take to the homecoming dance to call me back. If I didn't get on a team, or get someone to sponsor me, it would be tough to progress in cycling. I knew that much.

I'd already won the Best All Around Rider award in the state of Colorado for category one/pro men, so there wasn't much more I was going to do regionally. The U.S. national team would take me to some races in Europe and South America, but it wouldn't sustain me financially, and I would be limited in what I could race nationally.

I was living at home, in my childhood bedroom, eating on my parents' dime. It was exactly what I was desperate to avoid. I'd watched so many promising junior riders get stuck in a rut of not quite getting noticed by the big teams in junior races, and then having to try and piece something together to keep racing.

This usually entailed living at home, begging for gas money, having a part-time job, trying to train as much as possible and looking like a complete loser compared to your friends who went off to college. I looked down on the riders that had happened to, even though I was about to become one of them.

Instead, I wanted to be like Lance or Bobby Julich. Upon graduating the junior ranks, Lance immediately went on to a big team called Subaru-Montgomery, and got a big paycheck. He didn't live at home: he had his own apartment, his own income, and his own Camaro. It was the life I dreamed of.

I sent out résumés, made calls, tried to call in favors, whatever I could do to try and get somebody's attention, to get somebody to call me. Finally, it happened.

When the call came, my mother answered the phone and called up the stairs. I picked up and heard an oddly grumbly, raspy voice.

"Hello, Jonathan, this is Warren Gibson."

Warren Gibson had run the Plymouth-Reebok team a few years earlier, and was a good friend of Greg LeMond's. He was known as a cavalier but capable dealmaker in the cycling world. He'd been responsible for helping Paul Willerton get a ride on LeMond's Z team, so he was a good contact to have in your corner.

He explained to me that he'd noticed me at the Mammoth Lakes stage race and that he'd been impressed with my ability to go head to head with the Russians. He was starting a new team for the 1992 season, and wanted me to be a part of it.

He set out my salary ($1,500 a month!), what races the team would do, and then even discussed how he'd help get me on Greg LeMond's team in Europe. I was so excited I wanted to squeal. This was it. This was the way out of my parents' basement.

The team would be sponsored by the Saturn car company, a new offshoot of General Motors, and focused around 1988 Olympic Games fourth place finisher, Bob Mionske.

Officially an amateur team—our salaries were technically "living expense reimbursement"—our goal would be to get as many people as possible on the 1992 Olympic team, especially Bob. After listening to Warren's not-so-soothing voice for an hour, I ran downstairs, excited to tell my parents I no longer had any use for them.

They were pleased I was going to be getting paid, but they were less pleased I was not going to be attending college in the spring. But there was no way around it: this was my first step toward being a real professional rider.

Just after New Year, I got my signing bonus check from Saturn in the mail, and went out and bought a rusty 1971 Porsche for $2,000. It was tricky fitting my bike inside the Porsche, but I didn't care about that. I needed a car that expressed my personality, and clearly, a barely functioning, rusty orange Porsche was just that.

As I arrived in Los Gatos, California, the next day, I spotted a portly walrus-like man with a mustache and a shiny bald head awkwardly skipping toward my car as I entered the parking lot. It was Warren.

He greeted me in a way a father greets a son returning from war after many years. He grabbed me, hugged me, kept calling me "little buddy," and excitedly showed me around the finest motor hotel Los Gatos had to offer. Man, he was excited to have his own cycling team, and his beaming enthusiasm was infectious.

Folks called Warren "the Gibbo"—or "the Walrus," but not to his face—and the Gibbo was like a kid with a very big, very new toy. I couldn't believe the excess and wealth that was being thrown around to run such an organization. There were free polo shirts embroidered with the team name, team cars plastered with sponsors' logos. Each rider was given free cycling clothing and a free helmet to boot. All our travel expenses were reimbursed. It was an eighteen-year-old's cycling nirvana. I was used to paying for gas money out of prize money and sleeping on people's couches. Now I was staying in hotels and not even having to figure out what the entry fee to the race was. And I was being paid every month! This team was fancy.

We had steak dinners out at the Chart House, we were doing photo shoots at the *Sunset* magazine home, we were being filmed for use in car commercials. We thought we were the rock stars of the California cycling scene. Soon enough, the real rock star, Bob Mionske, showed up to training camp. This was like the second coming of Jesus to us all.

Bob was the reason the team existed, as he was going to the Olympic Games, and people thought he even might get a medal. Saturn definitely believed he was going to medal in the Olympics. This belief was born from his fourth-place finish in the 1988 Seoul Olympics. That finish had also given birth to a rather funny nickname.

Bob loved to tan himself in the sun. He disliked having the tan lines most cyclists did and would sunbathe for hours. For many years people knew him as "Bronze Bob." The thing was, after he finished fourth at the Olympics, where he *almost* won the bronze medal, the nickname turned into "*Almost* Bronze Bob."

He wasn't so keen on that.

I also met my new roommates and teammates for training camp at the Los Gatos lodge. Andrew Miller was a college graduate with a degree in computer science engineering or something. He read a lot of books, did math for fun, and enjoyed telling stories of how he used to split sheets of boron with a laser back in the science lab at college.

The other was Dave McCook. Dave's favorite hobby was staring at women taking aerobics or yoga classes through the glass window of the studio. He would do this for hours on end, pointing at the ones he found most attractive.

Despite our diverse interests, we enjoyed training and traveling to the northern California races together. And we cooked together, mainly using my Crock-Pot. It was a miracle pot: we'd stuff a bunch of food in there, and by the time we'd return home from a long ride, it would be boiled into some sort of edible mush that we'd eat for dinner.

Unfortunately, one time we went up to Oregon to race in a week-long event, and we forgot that we'd left our Los Gatos palace with pinto beans cooking in the Crock-Pot. Fortunately, a hotel maid unplugged the Crock-Pot after a few days. Instead of our room being engulfed in flames due to an electrical fire, we instead returned home to a week-old, tepid, primordial ooze of pinto beans, still festering in the belly of the pot.

We raced all around the country that year, hitting the most important races, and sometimes locking horns with the bigger professional teams. But the huge focus for Team Saturn was the U.S. Olympic trials.

The Olympics were the reason Saturn had signed up for cycling. The Gibbo made it clear to us how important these races were for the team and for the sponsor. Getting "Almost Bronze" Bob on the Olympic team was the minimum we were expected to do, and the Gibbo also wanted a second rider from Saturn to go the 1992 Games in Barcelona.

This was a big ask, as there were only three riders permitted to go. Lance was already a 100 percent shoo-in, so that really left two places. But it was what the Gibbo was demanding with an urgency

I'd never seen before. Gone was the grandfatherly and warm mentor, and in his place was the high-pressure businessman.

The Olympic trials were a pretty simple affair. There would be two one-day races, both about the same distance and hilliness as the Olympic road race itself. They were to be separated by a few days, and whoever won the cumulative points from both of the days of racing would get an automatic slot on the 1992 U.S. Olympic Games team.

The first day doubled as the National Championship road race, and having the sheer numbers that we did, Team Saturn dominated. Chann McRae won the race in a coup of team tactics, which left the two pre-race favorites, Lance Armstrong and Darren Baker, isolated and unable to respond. I almost screwed the whole thing up, though, by attacking at a very inopportune time and unleashing the wrath of Lance.

My teammates were quite annoyed with me, as they should have been. It was really stupid on my part, but these were the days before radios, and information was hard to come by.

This remains one of the big reasons why I support the use of radios in races: it helps eliminate stupid racing and promotes decision-making with actual information. Anyhow, my dumbness aside, we still won the race, and were in perfect position to get two folks into the Olympic team.

I was determined to make up for my idiocy as the second Olympics trial road race started, and soon enough I found myself in the front group with another teammate, John Lieswyn. John was a bit older than the rest of the Saturn team, and was an outside bet to get on the Olympic team. He also was famously known as "Twister," as earlier in the year he had knotted his nuts during a race, and had to be rushed to the emergency room for urgent untwisting surgery.

He'd been using some extra support under his cycling shorts ever since. I liked Twister, a lot. He was an outsider and a rebel. I thought that was cool.

He wasn't one of the coach's favorites, but he was a black sheep that could still win some damned big races. So, once Twister and I, plus a few other riders, had a gap on the peloton, I pulled as hard as I could to get him away from the golden boys. And it worked.

We were well clear of the peloton with one lap remaining on the tough course. In that final lap, I closed down as many attacks from the break as I could for Twister, and then, exhausted from all the pulling and chasing, I finally got dropped from the break with just a few miles remaining.

Despite being spat out the back of the break, I was still set to finish well, in what was perhaps the most prestigious one-day race in the USA for amateur riders. It would be something to be quite proud of, and certainly look good on my CV.

But as I rolled in toward the finish, I started doing the math and realized how—if I placed in front of Almost Bronze Bob—I would steal away some of the points he needed to secure an automatic berth on the Olympic team. I knew Bob was almost sure to win the sprint from the group behind.

Knowing this, and knowing how poor a teammate I'd been in the previous trials race, I decided I needed to wait until Bob had passed before I crossed the line. I decided to wait, rolling very slowly, in fact almost stopping, and obviously losing my chance at a bragging rights position in the race.

I'm not sure what the final selection factors and points were, but Bob made the team, Twister and Chann almost did, and no one was pissed off with me anymore. The Gibbo came over to me after the race and hugged me for my unselfish act. He said I'd shown a self-lessness that was rare in cycling, but now that I'd shown such loyalty to the team, the team would certainly repay it.

These two days were the first time I'd truly understood the relationship between a sponsor, team management, and riders. The Gibbo was incredibly stressed in the weeks leading up to the Olympic trials, and he put a lot of the pressure straight onto the riders and staff.

I'm sure Saturn's marketing team was calling him asking: "How're those Olympic team berths looking?"

He was feeling that weight, which in turn landed on the team.

When we accomplished what we were supposed to, it instantly turned to joy, or at least relief for the Gibbo. It was a very small insight into what was to come in terms of understanding how commercial pressures affected sport and affected athletes.

For the moment, I was happy for the team, but it was hard to forget how these two races had turned into pressure-cooker situations with the sponsor relationship being all we worried about. The money came first, the athletic competition second.

Unfortunately, my days on the team were numbered. The Gibbo had dreams of turning the team professional the following year and didn't feel I was ready to make that step. He called in late August, letting me know that I wouldn't be asked back, and telling me that I needed to return my bike as soon as possible.

I argued with him at length, pointing out the number of great results I'd racked up in the second half of the year, but he wasn't budging. He needed more mature riders, and I'd proven to be a bit too much of a project for him to consider me turning pro. Many years later, I realized that he was right, but at that moment I hated the guy.

I sent the bike back in small pieces, not having washed it for a month. It's amazing in cycling how one can go from loving someone and seeing them as a hero, to hating them to the bone, all within a year. That's especially true when it comes to team managers. They are heroes or demons, and there's no in-between.

Whatever happened to all that fine talk about loyalty after the Olympic trials? It would be an enduring lesson for me: cycling very much has a "What have you done for me lately?" mind-set.

So there I was, back on my parents' couch again.

No matter how angry I felt about being rejected by Saturn, the stark reality was that I didn't have a team, again, for the next year. So I signed up for more art and philosophy classes, hoping to find some sort of direction in life, while also desperately hoping for a team to come knocking.

Eventually, I did get a call about doing a race in South America. It was a bit of an odd conversation with someone at the U.S. Cycling Federation, almost as if I was being lured into a trap, as opposed to being asked to compete in a bike race.

"Have you anything going on this October . . . ?" they asked, shiftily.

Apparently, if I figured out how to find some random American living in Caracas who was working for some sort of oil cartel, then I could be part of a team that represented USA Cycling in Venezuela. Who could say no?

The Vuelta a Venezuela was a fourteen-day gallop through the jungles and Andes mountains of Venezuela. I was being asked to attend the race by the U.S. national team, but it wasn't really a trip run by the U.S. Federation. In fact, it was more like the invitation was being offered in the hope that a group of insane mercenary pilgrims would take it.

This appealed greatly to me—a completely disorganized adventure in South America that would postpone my studies for yet another semester. Like a rebound relationship, it was just what I needed to heal the pain after my stinging rejection from the Gibbo.

Once we arrived in Venezuela, Colby—who had decided to tag along—and I were greeted by an enterprising cab driver who managed to convince us that our hotel was very difficult to find, and that we needed to pay him $100 each in order to reach our destination. After some discussion we conceded the point, and gave the man his money so he could drive us four miles down a very straight road to our hotel. We were off to a great start.

Soon enough after our cab ride, we found our motley crew of American teammates and our Venezuelan oil patron in the lobby of the Hotel Ejecutivo preparing for the two weeks of racing ahead.

I'd never stayed in a hotel with plastic covers on the mattresses and blue carpeting on the ceiling and walls before. Nor have I since. The Hotel Ejecutivo had the fetid scent of murder and prostitution about it, but then the air-conditioning worked really well, so I wasn't complaining about a little bit of dried body fluid in my room.

Once the team was registered and we received our race numbers, I started flipping through the race book. I found profiles of massive climbs in the Andes, and maps of roads that went to remote parts of the jungle. It made for intriguing and somewhat scary reading. It looked far more adventurous than racing in gray and boring Europe. I was totally taken by this South American racing thing; it made me feel gritty and cool, like Indiana Jones on a bike.

The start of the first stage was some hundred kilometers away from the hotel, and we were picked up by a giant rusty school bus, dating from the 1960s, to take us there. Four teams—the American, German, Italian, and Danish national squads—called this bus home for the next two weeks.

We had to pile our bikes, suitcases, and bodies into the bus, then rumble down the road each day to the start and then come back again after the finish. It was the UN General Assembly of school buses, with a bunch of very pale passengers from Europe and the USA, all having their first adventure in a place that was very different from home.

As we unloaded the bus at the start, I saw all the South American riders for the first time. They were hardened, lean, and intimidating. The meanest looking were the riders from Colombia, who were small but had a fierceness in their eyes.

I was told by our oil cartel translator that the big favorite to win was Omar Pumar, who raced for the team from Táchira, a backwoods, mountainous and lawless province of Venezuela, right on the border with Colombia. I was both daunted and fascinated by these guys in a way I never had been by the riders in France.

But despite being intimidated, I was there to race, as it might be my last opportunity to show off to a potential team or sponsor. Maybe, if it went well, I could ride for a South American team? Move to Táchira, race bikes, learn Spanish. My mother would love that idea.

The race was hot and hard—every day. When we weren't baking in the equatorial sun, we were climbing up some forty-kilometer-long climb that would take us to four thousand meters altitude. Despite the extreme difficulty of the race, the biggest toll on most of the foreign riders was from intestinal issues. I had never witnessed projectile vomiting during a bike race before, and Vuelta a Venezuela proved a baptism of fire on that front.

Repeatedly, out of nowhere, guys would just start spewing their well-intentioned breakfast all over the road. Luckily, I had prepared for such an eventuality by over-packing my duffel bag full of all kinds of energy bars, protein powders, and isotonic drinks. It was enough fake food to allow me to avoid eating some of the more interesting local cuisine.

There was, however, a side effect to this artificial diet of powders: truly breathtaking flatulence. After two or three days of eating this stuff, my body started producing a thick fog comparable to the gas the Green Goblin used to try to kill Spider-Man.

Our poor bus driver also had to deal with my odor every day, but he seemed far more understanding about my issues than the judgmental German national team. The bus driver soon greeted me every morning with a cheery *"Hola, huevos y cebolla!"* He'd very thoughtfully nicknamed me "eggs and onions," which, once understood by everyone else on the bus, became my new name.

I was the little gringo, "Huevos y Cebolla," racing through—and perhaps defoliating—the jungles of South America.

Despite the stench, our team was doing quite well in the race. We had taken the race lead on stage four with a part-time school bus driver from Minnesota named Dewey Dickey. We defended that lead like a prized melon, every day chasing down breakaways and riding the front of the peloton, just like we'd seen teams do in the Tour de France.

We began to feel pretty stud-like, patrolling for enemy attacks with our stars and stripes jerseys at the front every day. We had even earned the respect of the locals, and various teams started to work together in order to oust us. However, the race hadn't hit the most decisive stages yet and they knew we were wearing a bit thin from spending all day, every day, pounding the front of the race.

I think they figured that as soon as we hit the true Andean climbs at the end, we'd all be swept away. But before those last critical stages there was a time trial, and this set the scene for the drama to come. I had not felt great in the early stages of the race, so I shocked myself (and perhaps my teammates) by winning the time trial and moving into second place overall.

Dewey still held on to the race lead by a sliver in the time trial, but local favorite, the infamous Omar Pumar, had climbed up to third overall.

The last few stages, on Pumar's home turf in the high mountains of Táchira, were the hardest of the race. The Colombians, along with Pumar's team, were planning to give us northern hemisphere riders a lesson in pain, which they certainly did. With the rest of our team tired from all the days on the front of the peloton, protecting the lead, Dewey and I were quickly isolated when the road got steep.

Still, we were both able to match the Colombians and Pumar by steadily riding and not responding to their sharp accelerations. We made it all the way to the second-to-last stage, before finally, on the last climb, Dewey cracked.

Initially I had not noticed that he had drifted off the back of the group in the waning moments of what was the last climb of the race. He hadn't yelled or asked me to wait, but there were no radios and we didn't really have a director in the support car, either, so perhaps he was hoping to disguise his weakness by not saying anything.

I wasn't sure what to do.

If I just stayed put in the front group, I would inherit the race lead. If I waited, I might be able to heroically drag Dickey back to the front, but then again it might be that all would be lost if we didn't both catch back up.

Not for the first (or last) time in my racing days, I chose selfishness over heroism, and stuck with the lead group instead of waiting. I sat dutifully on the back of the efforts of the Táchira team, trying to discourage them by letting them know another gringo would take the race lead, even if they distanced Dickey. But I did not wait for him.

I felt guilty about this, but then justified it by telling myself that I would still win the race for the team. Plus, Dewey and I didn't even know each other before arriving in Venezuela. He wasn't a *real* teammate, just a temporary one, so what the hell did I owe him anyway?

I crossed the finish line expecting to be led up to the podium for the presentation, but oddly, I wasn't. Instead I watched as Pumar pulled on the race leader's jersey, while I anxiously questioned officials for some sort of explanation. Initially I heard nothing from anyone, and it seemed they had just arbitrarily decided the small gap between Pumar and me was in his favor.

Eventually I was told I'd been given a twenty-second penalty for not signing in on time at the start that morning, which, as it happened, was just enough to put Pumar into the race lead. I couldn't believe it. I'd never even heard of such a penalty, and certainly no one had let me know I was late during the sign-in.

Our school bus wasn't always so fast getting us around, so sometimes we would be a bit late in getting to the start area. The penalty was ridiculous, and not even in the rule book—but what was I going to do to change it in the remote jungles of Venezuela? There was no one to protest to.

Now my little bit of selfishness at the top of the climb turned into a disaster, a dick move against Dickey on my part. By not waiting to help him, and by then getting my little time "penalty," I'd lost the entire race for the team.

Colby and I decided to stay on in Venezuela, to hang out on the beach and go fishing. We'd collected enough prize money to live it up for a few days, and I needed to clear my head.

It turned into more than just a few days, and we ended up spending every last penny of our prize money on various acts of debauchery. We went marlin fishing, scuba diving, sipped piña coladas, and tipped pretty waitresses excessively.

As I sat on the beach, avoiding going back to reality, I did my best to let go of the drama of the last few days of the race. But it all made me think. At Saturn I'd been the most selfless, and in Venezuela the most selfish of bike racers, all in one year.

I couldn't quite figure out what one was really supposed to do in this strange sport, where selflessness is rewarded with hugs and pats on the back, but selfishness is rewarded with contracts, success, accolades, and money.

I was torn. I was competitive and wanted to win, to succeed and move forward with my career, but I also wanted to be liked by others in a way I never did at high school.

This paradox is the strange social experiment at the heart of professional cycling. It rewards both selflessness and selfishness at different times. The key, I guess, to being successful in cycling is figuring out when to be which one.

Eventually, the money ran out and I was forced to call time on my Venezuelan beach lifestyle. As I headed back home to Colorado, the contrasting outcomes of being unselfish at the Olympic trials by sacrificing my own aspirations for the team, yet selfish at Vuelta a Venezuela by leaving my teammate behind and focusing on my own ambitions, kept reverberating around in my head.

I returned home with a second-place overall finish in a very tough stage race on my CV. It should have been the highlight of my cycling career so far, but instead I felt like a dick. A dick without a team, a dick without a job, and a dick without any new friends from my trip to South America.

CHAPTER 6

VENTRICALLY CHALLENGED

Like any good philosophy major in his teens, I was trying to come up with a right and a wrong, a black and white about how to act in cycling—and maybe how to live my life. Yet all I saw was gray. In one of many philosophy courses that I'd acquainted myself with, I'd found the concept of cultural ethical relativism fascinating. One action that was totally ethical in one culture was an unforgivable crime against humanity in another—for example, polygamy.

Ethics seemed to depend just as much on the culture you were born into, as on notions of what constituted being a "good" person. And cycling, it seemed to me, lent itself to this type of thinking.

Here's an example. Drafting—or riding on the wheel of another rider and using someone else's hard work for your own benefit—rooted the behavior of cyclists deep in the ethical gray. As I pondered the rights and wrongs, I thought back to every moment that I'd ever been in a breakaway.

You were expected to pull on the front to help the breakaway succeed, even though your breakaway companions were the very same riders you needed to ultimately defeat. The unwritten rule was that everyone needed to do an equal amount of work on the front, keeping the pace and pushing through the wind. That was seen as fair.

You could feign weakness in a breakaway, even when feeling really strong, which, essentially, was "conning" your rivals. This con allowed you to conserve energy by spending more time drafting and less time out front riding in the wind, energy that could prove vital later, and thus giving you a greater chance of winning. This was an accepted, beloved, and taught tactic by many coaches. It was even thought of as crafty and intelligent.

Yet others in the sport thought of it as cheating. So who was right?

Well, that depended on who you spoke to after the race. There was no black or white because cycling was a sport that lived in the gray; selfishness and lying were rewarded, but so were selflessness and sacrifice. Experienced riders and coaches taught both behaviors, with no thought to how contradictory they were. Perceptions of "good" or "bad" behavior depended on circumstances and, also, who the judges were. There was one truth that I did learn, though—if you did either half-assed it was sure to end badly.

Let's remember that I was from a family that believed in the ethics of Christianity, just a few generations separated from Mennonite Quakers. Ethics and how you conducted yourself were not relative to anything other than truth we held as absolute. They were written in stone, as in the stone of the Ten Commandments.

Deceiving people was not okay. Being selfish was not okay. This was pounded into my head as a child.

Yet cycling was putting all of this into question, and during the long flight home from Caracas, I wondered if maybe cycling just wasn't for me. I wasn't very good at navigating grayness.

I wanted there to be a right and a wrong. I wanted there to be clear rules of what I was supposed to do. I wanted the sport to be different. I wanted the Gibbo to have kept me on the team for sacrificing myself in the Olympic trials, not dump me. I wished, too, that I had been a better teammate, a better person, when Dewey was struggling at that key moment in Venezuela.

I just wasn't very good at cultural relativism; I always felt like I needed to pull through whenever I was in a breakaway, no matter what the coaches told me. I was confused. I felt like my dream wasn't quite what I once thought it was. It felt dirty, compromised.

I didn't have a team for the next season, I was almost into my twenties, really hadn't made much progress in school or any other career path, and my parents were worried about me. Maybe it was time to call time?

When I got home, I started attending class again, trying to pay attention a little more, and to start reconciling what it would be like if I just walked away from cycling and moved on with life. Who would I be? Would I like it more? Would I miss cycling? Or would I feel less compromised by the grayness that enveloped it?

It was a good thing I was in a few philosophy classes, because I had pretty much decided that I needed to end the dream of being a professional bike racer. No teams wanted my services. I was vexed and confused by the unwritten rules of the sport. I just didn't *believe* any more. Deep down, however, I kept hoping this would be one of those rare moments where the saying "It's always darkest before the dawn" might actually be true.

As it turned out, it was. Right at the height of my self-doubt, in a scripted-for-Hollywood 180-degree turnaround, the phone rang at my parents' house.

I was reading some overly complex and boring paragraph by Thomas Hobbes. I guessed the call was probably Colby, wondering if I wanted to go mountain biking that weekend or something.

But it was a fellow named Mike Murray, the Missouri state representative for the U.S. Cycling Federation. He was friends with a guy in Spain who was setting up a team for the next year. Apparently, this Spanish guy had noticed my performance in Venezuela and wanted to have a chat with me about racing in Spain.

Instantly, I was jolted out of my self-pity and depression. I wasn't sure how serious this inquiry was, and I really had no idea who Mike Murray was, but nonetheless, even the thought of racing in Spain made me pulse with excitement.

Thoughts of cycling being too gray and conflicted for me were washed away by the excitement of racing for a foreign and exotic team. Racing was in my blood, I guess, and I wanted to push past the questioning and heartache that it had given me. But cycling is always heartache.

Always.

If racing bikes is in your blood, then you have to learn how to get over the heartache and move on. Which I did. The dream was alive again!

Mike proved to be a great ally. He helped me navigate all the paperwork involved with racing for a Spanish team. He reassured me that I'd fit in to Spanish-style racing, and that this team would be a good place to learn and grow.

Eventually we were able to speak on the phone with José Luis Nuñez, the manager of this upstart team. He spoke broken English, quietly and deliberately, but he seemed to make a lot of sense to me. He knew very little about me, and I knew very little about him, but he told me he wanted some American spirit in his team.

He wanted a young, ambitious rider that was a strong climber. He said he'd seen very few Americans that could climb well in South America, and even fewer whose stomachs could tolerate the food and water. He was impressed that I possessed both of those traits.

I was very flattered by what he said. The conversation seemed to fly by, much to the chagrin of my parents, who were paying about $2 a minute for me to speak with someone in Spain. We quickly came to an agreement for the next year. I would race for José Luis's amateur team, with the hope of one day turning professional. I wasn't going to get rich quick, but that didn't matter to me.

I was now committed to racing with an unproven team, run by a man I knew nothing about and had never met, in a country I knew nothing about. Nuñez had insisted I move to Spain for the entire year, which was, to be sure, a scary and intimidating prospect. I would need to be ready to go right after the new year.

It left me little time to not only try and learn about Spanish culture, but to start training again, for what would probably be more difficult races than those I'd grown used to. Also, I needed to move beyond philosophical questioning of bike racing. I would need to be ready to fight, using any means necessary, to one day be a pro rider and not to wax (and wane) poetically about the grayness of its unwritten rules. It was time to start training more and thinking less.

As I heard rumors of how hard Spanish races were, I set about training in a new, more rigorous and determined way that I felt was quite spectacular. The races over there all seemed to be well over a hundred miles long, so I would need to train for those distances in the Colorado winter to get ready. Luckily, I had a newfound friend to keep me company in my training adventures.

Jim Beasley was a law school student who lived with his parents nearby. But Jim didn't really want to be a lawyer; he wanted to be a pro bike racer. He'd traveled with me to a few races over the years, with his mother always insisting we take extra home-baked muffins with us before every road trip. Jim was the cyclist's cyclist. He just loved riding his bike as much as possible, and he loved the dream of being a professional rider.

With that in mind, he decided he'd spend the winter training with me. We'd head out most days around nine a.m. for four or five hours of training. After five hours on the road, we'd head to a local Mexican food place, Fiesta to Go, and eat a massive burrito smothered in green chili. To finish it off, we'd demolish a massive piece of cheesecake flan.

I'd then come home and take a very long cheese-induced nap on the couch in my parents' living room. Jim and I were both blissfully unaware that pro cyclists in Europe starved themselves skinny. We naively figured we could eat as much cheese as our stomachs could handle, given the five hours in the saddle we were putting in every day.

Jim helped me get my lazy, philosophical, and pensive ass out on the road each and every day that winter. He helped me revive my love for riding bikes. I could see that he would give anything to be in my shoes and have a team waiting in Spain. His eyes just lit up at the prospect of anything pro-cycling related, especially in Europe.

He loved cycling so much that he was willing to train until his fingers froze. I almost felt guilty that Jim had so much passion for cycling, given that my indulgent philosophical ponderings had almost led to me abandoning it. His love for the bike was unconditional, whereas mine seemed more like a fickle romance. I started to think that I needed to honor bike racing a bit more, if only for Jim's sake.

With each hundred-mile ride and every pile of smothered pinto beans, I felt one step closer to being ready for my Spanish adventure. I trained more miles during that December than I ever had in one month. Jim began to struggle more and more to keep up as I became fitter, but his tolerance for suffering was inspirational. He did not give up, under any circumstance. So neither could I.

Christmas and New Year's came and went and then it was time for me to begin packing for my extended stay overseas. I wasn't really sure what a team would provide and what they wouldn't, and it was far from clear from any correspondence that I'd had with them.

I knew for sure that I wanted to bring my trusty Moots titanium bike. I wanted to impress the Spanish ladies with my fashion sense, but then a suitcase full of sports coats and sweaters might not be appropriate for the Spanish climate. I wasn't really sure, and wasn't very good at folding clothing, so I just began to stuff massive duffel bags full of items that I deemed necessary.

Jim would come over at night to my parents' house, just to hang out watching me pack. We'd chat endlessly about what it would be like if one day I earned a full European pro contract and got to race with the likes of Sean Kelly, Greg LeMond, and Robert Millar. We'd both also started to read more about the best Spanish riders, like Melcior Mauri, Jesús Montoya, and of course, Miguel Induráin.

When the day came, my parents drove me to the airport in the trusty aged Oldsmobile we'd driven across the nation in. My bike was stuffed in the back with the various duffel bags. It was a quiet car ride and we barely spoke. I don't think they were very confident in what I was doing. But then, neither was I.

Information had been sparse, too. There had been just a few fifteen-minute phone calls, and some paperwork that vaguely resembled a contract. I was going to Madrid to be picked up by people I'd never met, to go and live in a place I didn't even have an address for, and to race with teammates whose names I didn't even know.

What could go wrong?

I'd purchased my plane ticket about a month earlier and, having spent most of my money on debauchery in Venezuela, I didn't really have many options. I needed the cheapest seat possible. The only ticket I could afford was one-way to Madrid. I didn't let my parents know this, as I figured it would just upset them even more.

Soon, I reasoned, I was going to be a famous bike racer who could easily afford a return ticket whenever he wanted. I would just need a few months to make that happen. No need to worry.

I felt for my parents; this wasn't what they had signed up for. Yes, most kids from my neighborhood did leave home around this age, but it wasn't like this. They went off to college in a very safe, thought-through, and controlled manner. They would get dropped off in front of some gorgeous ivy-covered dorm building, their parents beaming with pride over their academically accomplished offspring. If something went wrong, well, Mom and Dad were close by.

Instead, my parents got a son who was leaving home on a one-way ticket to a country only a decade out of a dictatorship, to try and become a bike racer, with no real information about who I was meeting nor how I would manage to take care of myself. To say the least, the likelihood of success was low.

I still can't imagine what they were feeling inside, but they didn't let on about their fears in any way.

At the very last minute, my mother hugged me, wished me good luck, and went over to the ticket counter inquiring about how much a return trip would cost. My father shook my hand and made sure I knew to call if I got into any sort of trouble. I steeled myself, and steeled my emotions, as I walked toward the boarding gates.

Later in life, this experience became a common theme for me. I was always leaving to go somewhere; I was always leaving people behind.

Sunrise lit up the endless plains of Castille as the plane landed in Madrid. The landscape reminded me of the dry plains of Colorado. It reminded me of home. I had dressed in a tweed sports coat with a nice waistcoat underneath, which I think was the reason it took my pickup party some time to find me. He probably expected a jock, wearing a tracksuit and athletic shoes. Encountering a bespectacled kid in his best Sherlock Holmes outfit may have thrown him. This would be the first of many things my new team would find odd about me.

I had no idea where we were driving to, or where I'd be living. In fact, we were heading to Valencia, which is quite a long drive from Madrid. My driver was a guy, maybe a few years older than me, who was one of the team trainers. He spoke English really well, which was the reason he was sent to pick me up.

Despite being exhausted from the long flight, I couldn't help but pepper him with question after question.

Where was I to live? Who were my teammates? What was the team name? Who were we sponsored by? What races would we be doing?

He answered some of my questions, vaguely, but certainly not all, and certainly not in any detail. Finally, he made it clear that I was expecting too much.

"We are more used to bike racers that just do what they are told, rather than ask so many questions," he said.

Right. I quietened down.

I assumed I would find out the answers soon enough. Either that or I was being driven to my murder site. Whichever it was, I didn't have much control over my fate now. I finally allowed the drone of the car and the monotony of the drive to lull me to sleep after so many hours traveling.

I was just nodding off when he spoke again.

"One thing I can let you know now is that the first thing we will do is testing," he said.

"Testing?" I asked.

"Yes," he said. "You will undergo cardiac, blood, and physiological testing to determine your potential as a rider."

It sounded rather East German to me. *Oh, well*, I thought, as I closed my eyes, *if that's what it takes* . . .

We eventually arrived at a cute little old stone hotel in a rice plain close to Sagunto. The sun was shining, and you could smell the orange groves from my hotel room. I immediately wanted to go ride my bike, and so I built up the old trusty Moots titanium and went off to explore the Spanish countryside.

Compared to the bleak dry suburban sea of brown that I'd been riding in most winters in Colorado, coastal Spain was gorgeous. There were orange groves and castles with winding little roads in between. The beach wasn't so far off, either. This Spain thing wasn't turning out to be half bad. I had a great little two-hour ride, and returned to the hotel to some tasty fish soup of some sort. Then, like the rest of Spain, I took a very long nap, lost in wonder at how cool my new life was.

The next morning I was up early, both curious and nervous about the "testing" they had planned. They told me not to eat beforehand, and to bring my cycling shoes and shorts. I guessed it would be something similar to the testing we did back at the USA Cycling "Dump." Blood test, then a VO_2 max test. That did end up being part of it, but only part.

I was driven to a clinic and greeted by a short and balding man, Dr. Carlos Barrios. He was supposedly one of the key people in identifying Miguel Induráin's talent, or so I was told. He took blood samples, and then asked me to lie flat while they ran an ultrasound of my heart.

The doctor's face changed while looking at the pictures of my heart. I wasn't really sure what was going on, and, with typical paranoia, feared that he may have discovered some sort of congenital defect. He left the room, then returned with another doctor.

They chatted away excitedly in Spanish, then told me they were going to call José Luis Nuñez, and that they would get back to me. I still had no idea what they had just found. José Luis arrived at the laboratory around an hour later and I finally met the man who was putting all of this together. He was a kind-looking man, with the type of large, tinted spectacles that the early 1980s were all about.

Like many Spanish businessmen, he had a long woolen overcoat draped around him, worn with his arms not in the sleeves. He shook my hand, calmly, and welcomed me to Spain. He then left to meet with the doctors in a conference room.

After a few minutes, they all reappeared.

"Jonathan, we would like to conduct a few more tests," José Luis said in his calm and methodical way. "Are you okay with that?"

They put me through a more familiar VO_2 max test on an ergometer. I knew how to read these tests as they were happening, so as I pushed to a higher and higher power output, I watched the numbers climb with it. I was a bit surprised, as the numbers were much higher than back in Colorado. I passed 80 VO_2 max with no problem at all, and continued. Once again, they were looking at each other excitedly.

After the tests were done, José Luis took me out to lunch with Dr. Barrios. I sat down, nervously waiting for some sort of explanation. I would learn, with time, that this was how Spanish pro teams operated. You took the tests, you did what the doctor said, you didn't ask questions, because you were a dumb bike rider that needed to focus solely on pushing pedals.

Yet, perhaps considering my different background, José Luis on this occasion made an exception.

"Jonathan, the tests were quite exceptional. You have a body built for the mountains," he said quietly, between spoonfuls of paella. I listened and then asked why, and what this meant for my racing career.

Dr. Barrios then explained to me that the left ventricle of my heart was exceptionally large, and that was one of the markers of a great cyclist. Then he went to on to discuss my *"hemogolobina,"* as he put it.

"You have very high *hemogolobina* in your blood," Barrios said. "This will be a great weapon in cycling."

As the doctor who had supposedly discovered Induráin's talent, I took his words very seriously. Yet it took me a few days to figure out the significance of this debrief.

I had a lot of red blood cells, the same characteristic they'd freaked out about back at the Dump. Barrios explained that the combination of a large left ventricle—effectively the pump—with very rich blood could mean that one day I would be a great professional cyclist. Professional racing was all about oxygen delivery, I was told, and I had a great body for doing just that.

After Barrios left, José Luis pulled some more paperwork out of his briefcase.

"We would like to change our agreement with you," he said. "We would like to move you from the amateur team onto our new professional team."

I almost fainted. Maybe it was all the testing or a lack of food, but I can remember my vision going a bit black when he said this to me.

"We are going to ride la Vuelta a España, and I need to start preparing you for it."

My jaw dropped. From broke-ass kid racing for prize money to doing a Grand Tour, all in a few months. Wow.

Wow . . .

These guys had never seen me do a single bike race; they had not even seen a single mile of me training on the open road. Yet I was being offered a pro contract based on my left ventricle and my *hemogolobina*. I quickly signed and so began a round of meetings with coaches, directors, and doctors.

Already they were discussing how I might be quite good on the stage of the Vuelta that finished on top of the Sierra Nevada mountains in Andalusia. I kept interjecting that I wasn't quite so sure I was quite ready for such a big race, but they excitedly pushed those doubts aside.

"Jonathan! You have enormous VO_2 max, enormous left ventricle, and lots of *hemogolobina*! You will have *no problem* racing la Vuelta!" they said.

I didn't believe them. I was still built like an asparagus and I wasn't so sure my spindly legs would keep up with their ambitions. But if you're barely out of your teens and everyone keeps telling you how incredible you are, eventually you begin to believe it. It wasn't long before I started to dream about winning big pro races in Europe, driving a Ferrari, and living in a mansion on the Spanish coast.

José Luis had created an interesting set-up. The personnel were half Spanish, half Russian, with me the lone American. The sponsorship dollars were coming from a Spanish businessman named Enrique Tatay, and from a sports institute in Russia in the city of Samara.

The Russian crew were effectively asylum seekers, forced abroad after perestroika had unraveled the Soviet Union and drained all the funding for athletes. Samara had agreed to some sort of loose deal with José Luis, in which they would send money to the team if Nuñez agreed to continue developing their athletes.

The Russian riders were of very high pedigree. They were Olympic and World Champions on the track, with a few big victories as amateurs on the road, too. They all were very glad to be out of Russia. They would sit around the dinner table telling stories of how perestroika may have brought freedom in some regards, but that the system had collapsed in Russia, and many of the assets and towns were now run by mafia and ex-KGB people turned mafia. To a kid from Colorado, it sounded like a very harsh existence.

Now they were in Spain, living in a rented compound with a swimming pool by the coast. They had come with their own sports directors, *soigneurs*, mechanics, and coaches. It was as if a whole Russian village had moved into one big house, and I was also given a room in the Russian mansion.

In one week I'd gone from living in suburban Denver with a father who had once worked in classified naval air intelligence at the

Pentagon, to living with a houseful of Russian expats on the beach in Spain. I'm not sure I was in culture shock, but to say my world had changed a little would be an understatement.

I was expected to train with the Russians every day, and that was also a shock. These guys did not mess around with recovery rides or heart-rate monitors. It was full gas, hammer down, straight out the door, every day, for hours and hours—and hours. The training philosophy was along the lines of what I imagined the Russian army was like—and coincidentally, many of my new teammates were also, technically, still in the Russian army.

We pounded the living crap out of one another until someone said uncle (although no one ever did). Drinking too much from your water bottle was considered weakness. Shifting into the small chain ring was also considered weakness. Eating food was considered gluttonous. The Russians, I discovered, did not fuck around.

But then they had one shot at escaping a lifetime of misery, spent digging ditches in a Russian winter, by riding their bikes fast in Spain. They were not going to lose that chance. The expression "I would give anything to win," was given a whole new meaning for me after my experiences with these guys. They *would* have given anything.

Hand over a kidney? No problem.

Sell your mother into servitude? She'll enjoy the fresh air.

Train until you're bleeding out of your ears? You don't need to hear to ride a bike fast.

One of the favored post-training activities was sitting in the laundry room and watching the washing machine. I couldn't figure out why this was so much fun, until one of my teammates explained that there were very few washing machines in certain parts of Russia, so they found the washing machine entertaining to observe.

After a few weeks of my new training regime of no rest days, no food, no quarter given, I was starting to feel a bit worn down. Eventually, much to the disgust and horror of my new Russian friends, I had to take a day off from training.

I explained to them it was just to prevent having to buy new cycling shorts so early in the season, as the ones I had would soon have holes in them from all the pedaling. They snorted in contempt and left for their training ride.

I tried to sleep all day, but by afternoon realized I had a fever. This was bad news. I had been selected by the team management to start my season a week later at the Vuelta a Valencia, and clearly, with a fever, this wasn't going to happen.

When the Russians returned from their daily death march I was in bed, coughing and wheezing. They found this to be very American and weak of me, but luckily had a solution. The boss of the Russian crew, an older director named Nicolai, came to my room with around a half-liter of clear liquid in a glass.

"Hey, Amerikanski, drink this and no more sick," Nicolai said. "Best vodka in all Russia."

Aside from the piña coladas in Venezuela, the only drinking I'd ever done was at communion at Augustana Lutheran Church, so I didn't quite know what to expect from this healthy Russian flu tonic. I'm fairly certain my Russian mentor had no idea that I had no tolerance for alcohol whatsoever. I did as he said and slowly gulped down the glassful of vodka. About an hour later, my flu seemed to have been totally cured.

I figured it might be a great time to have an in-depth discussion about upcoming race tactics for Valencia, why I felt bunny rabbits were so cute, and why I found it so interesting that some people grew hair on the top of their feet. This vodka-fueled discussion quickly moved to me declaring my undying love for my Russian teammates and then singing the U.S. national anthem to them in my pajamas. Tears of pride streamed down my face.

Yes, I felt much, *much* better. I had been cured by vodka. The flu was totally gone, along with any feeling in my lower extremities.

The next morning, however, the flu seemed to have returned with a vengeance, along with a sharp headache and vomiting. I would not be competing in the Vuelta a Valencia, as the combination of influenza and alcohol poisoning would most likely make me a very poor selection.

Instead I recovered in bed, while my Russian and Spanish team-mates went off to race. It was lonely watching them all leave. There was no sitting around the washing machine telling stories of past glories, and no getting my head kicked in on a training ride.

I was starting to become a bit homesick, along with just being sick. The team had asked the family of one of my Spanish team-mates to look after me while the rest of the riders were away. I think my sad and sick state also tugged at the maternal heartstrings of the mother of one of my teammates, Carmelo Albert.

Left alone in the house with everyone else racing, I had no trans-portation to go and get food, and wasn't really able to move around much with my fever anyway. So Carmelo's family brought some food for me to eat and, after seeing my state of loneliness, invited me to stay with them at their home for a few days. Being with a family in their home sounded a lot nicer than being dumped in a cold man-sion with no one around.

I was only supposed to stay a few days, but ended up living there for the rest of the year. I loved Carmelo's family. They treated me exactly the same as one of their sons, despite the fact we didn't speak the same language even a little bit. Somehow, they made me feel at home, and they made me feel loved.

It helped too that Carmelo was a slightly saner training buddy compared to the Russian army I'd just been with. Every morning, after a hot, home-cooked meal from Carmelo's mother, we would hit the road, riding like old friends, not Cold War enemies.

There was really only one good road in and out of Picassent, the village that Carmelo lived in, which ensured that the first and last kilometers of each training ride, leaving home and coming back, were always the same. We would end up passing the same two or three girls, sitting on lawn chairs, every morning and then again every afternoon.

As we rode by, they would yell at us. *"Manolito, quinientas!"*

I figured it was some sort of Spanish greeting. One day I happily greeted them by yelling, *"Manolito, quinientas!"* back. Carmelo looked at me in horror when I did this.

Maybe I used an incorrect verb tense? Was my grammar off? I wasn't quite sure, as I didn't really speak any Spanish.

Using some very basic, caveman-like gestures, Carmelo attempted to explain what they were saying. He started by pointing at his hand and saying *"mano."* Then he pulled out a five-hundred-peseta coin and said *"quinientas,"* clearly meaning five hundred. Again, I understood.

So, five hundred hands . . . ? What did that mean? The last and crucial part was slightly more difficult to mime, but the penny dropped pretty quickly as he mimicked a universally recognized jerking motion near his crotch, like a monkey at the zoo, while almost crashing in the process.

Now I got it! The ladies on the side of the road were advertising: five hundred pesetas for light relief. For quickly learning a foreign language and avoiding social embarrassment, I'd highly recommend the Carmelo method.

I was now focused on my first race of the year, Semana Catalana. It was a famous and mountainous five-day race in the northwest of Spain in the region of Catalonia. Maybe it's destiny—or maybe it's irony—that my very first professional race started just a few kilometers from where the team I now run is based.

Training with Carmelo had been going superbly well, or so I thought. Carmelo and I did all of the intervals and kilometers prescribed by the team trainer, we monitored our heart rates, we ate well every night, and we now spoke Spanish together. I was feeling fitter every day, enjoying Spain, and really looking forward to my first race.

REALITY BITES

The weather during February and March in Valencia was gorgeous. It was very different from the frostbite of Colorado winters. Sunny and warm every day, we'd stop to pick oranges from the groves on all our training rides. We were riding almost five hundred miles a week, every week. I was in the best shape I'd ever been in, on the bike.

I felt strong and ready for my first pro race. I daydreamed on those long training rides of how I would win the mountain stage in Semana Catalana. Okay, I might not get the overall classification—there would be some good time trial riders, like Alex Zülle, doing the race after all—but I figured I could take them in the high mountains.

I was destined to be a star, I thought. If I won, I could even afford to call home back to the USA and tell them about it.

My head full of daydreams and nerves overflowing, I lined up for the first stage of Semana Catalana. The opening stage was around 120 miles long, right along the coast near Girona. It wasn't mountainous, but it was very hilly and sinuous, all day long.

My teammates explained that the peloton would roll along at an extremely pedestrian pace for the first three hours or so, but then, as soon as television coverage started, the racing would begin, and when it began, it would be brutally fast. Steady, but fast.

I, of course, with my large left ventricle and my plentiful *hemogolobina*, would be fine with this high speed. I thought the racing pattern sounded delightful. A nice warm-up, and then a steady high-speed jaunt for the last two hours. It sounded far more enjoyable than amateur racing, which was very stop and start, and characterized by stupid jumps and attacks all day long. It was like horse racing: pro racing was for thoroughbreds, I reasoned, and I was a thoroughbred.

The race started exactly as described by my Spanish teammates, slow as a snail. We would barely be pedaling on the flat and downhill parts of the race, and then would just chug steadily up the hills with no hurry. *This is easy,* I thought, *just wait until they see my big left ventricle in full flight at the end of the day. Pro racing is a piece of cake!*

As predicted, the pace began to rise around hour three. It was nothing I couldn't handle, but we were now racing bikes, not merely touring the Spanish coastline. The rhythm was a bit uncomfortable and started to creep up on me a bit. I was actually sweating and hurting, too, even if I wasn't willing to admit that just yet. Right around the sixty-kilometers-to-go mark, the television helicopters appeared, and when that happened all hell broke loose.

I could not believe the speed difference.

We were, all at once, riding at well over any speed I'd ever experienced in any race, flying up the hills and plummeting down them. My heart-rate monitor screamed at me to slow down, as I was way, way over my threshold.

In the limited capacity for thought that I still possessed, I convinced myself that it was just a temporary blip in speed, and that the pace would slow down soon enough. Instead, it got faster. Now I was no longer racing, no longer dreaming of victory, I was just hanging on the back end of the peloton wondering when it would all end.

I slipped further and further back through the group until I was in dead last place in the peloton. My legs were burning, my heart was racing, and my big left ventricle and tons of *hemogolobina* were nowhere to be found. Finally, as we hit a steep climb with some thirty kilometers to go, I was dropped and jettisoned from the peloton. I was riding all alone, the first rider to get shot out the back.

I was not going to be the first rider across the line, like I had dreamed. Suddenly I was back where I'd started, riding my first bike race as a twelve-year-old all over again. I was the worst, suckiest, slowest, clumsiest bike rider in the pro peloton. I descended like a climber and I climbed like an out-of-shape sprinter.

Prompted by some vague sense of pride, I struggled on toward the finish, but was embarrassed every time a different team car passed me to catch up to the riders that were still actually racing. I wanted to quit, just like I wanted to quit my first bike race.

How could I be so bad? What was wrong with me?

I guess I just didn't have what it took to be a pro. I just was not as good as these guys. Not even close. Unfortunately, this time there was a big difference from my first race as a kid: this time I had trained, hard. I had put in the work, I had done my best, and yet I was nowhere close.

I limped my way in, finally catching up with one very odd-looking and angry Belgian rider on the famed ONCE team. We rode together, silently trading pulls for the last fifteen kilometers of the race. Both dejected. Both rejected. Finally, we chatted a bit, trying to make light of the situation or perhaps to find a reason for our failure.

The Belgian explained to me he was just coming back from knee surgery, and wasn't really ready for a race like this. I had no excuse like that.

He'd had his knee rebuilt, whereas I had caught a little flu bug. Mine wasn't exactly a great excuse; his was.

It was pathetic. I was the worst pro bike racer in the world, with just one pissed-off Belgian fresh from knee surgery competing for my throne. Anyhow, at least I'd made a new friend that day.

Oh yeah. My new Belgian buddy's name?

Johan Bruyneel.

PART 3
1996

CHAPTER 7

THE END OF INNOCENCE

After getting so completely crushed in Semana Catalana, I fell flat.

To work so hard at something and just not be good enough was a bitter pill for me to swallow. I also knew how gravely disappointed the team management was going to be with me. They had made a wild outside bet on an American with very little racing history in Europe. They gave me a pro contract based on my VO_2 max and my heart size. They had put a lot of faith and work into me, and here I was: the worst of the worst.

Bruyneel and I crossed the line and went our separate ways. I rolled up to the team car, which was waiting for me beyond the finish line, long after everyone else had left. I expected a *soigneur* or mechanic to drive me back to the hotel, but instead José Luis Nuñez, the big boss, was waiting for me, by himself.

This couldn't be good, I thought, nervously. I figured he'd be keen on firing me immediately and sending me back to the USA, out of sheer embarrassment at his error in ever hiring me.

Yet he calmly opened the car door for me, and then, despite his suit and tie, reached across and put the bike on the bike rack for me.

He then climbed into the driver's seat, grabbed another jacket for me to slip on to keep warm, and asked me how I was doing.

I shrugged defeatedly.

"I'm sorry," I said. "I'm sorry that I embarrassed you and the team."

He quietly started the car, and we drove away.

After a few minutes, José Luis turned to me.

"Jonathan, you have a gift given to you by God," he said. "It's like a perfect piece of fruit. But it isn't ripe yet, it isn't ready for the world to see, but it is inside you, you must have faith in that. My faith is still there, Jonathan, so please don't let your faith in yourself die."

While perhaps a little overly religious for me—I didn't think God cared much for bike racing—his words did lift my spirits a little.

It was at the same time warming and hurtful to hear him say that. Here was a guy that had placed a huge stake on me, a huge amount of his reputation and pride, and I had failed him. Yet he still believed in me. Somehow.

Then he put his arm around me.

"One day, when you make it really big in professional cycling, don't forget me, don't forget the little guy." He smiled. "That's all I ask in return."

In an odd way, history had repeated itself. I'd once been talked into continuing to race by my father and now I was being convinced to keep on trying by a new mentor, a true friend. It was incredible to have someone by your side that had such absolute, undying faith.

But it was also an incredible amount of pressure that the boss of the whole team—unlike my teammates—thought so highly of me. The rest of the team did not share that view. That evening at the dinner table, I felt a distance growing between my teammates and I. I was the runt of the litter. Again.

I knew that feeling well from middle school and high school, so I resumed my now-familiar place at the back of the line, at the back of the pack, just hoping for the scraps. During the races, I needed to keep my head down, to do everything I could just to maybe give a teammate a water bottle once in a while in the race—and to make sure I always laughed at everyone's jokes at the dinner table.

I struggled on for a few more days in the Catalan race, until finally, a day from the finish, my legs and body completely buckled. I got dropped by the peloton much too early to have any hope of making the time cut. So I unclipped, pulled over, dropped out, packed my bike up and slunk home to Carmelo's family.

Yet José Luis's words kept rolling round my head. I wanted to believe him, but my experience of racing in Europe was far from that of a "talented" rider. How could I get this fruit he was talking about to ripen a bit faster? If I really was that talented, what the hell was I doing so wrong?

I sat in Carmelo's living room, thinking about the answers to these questions. The family was quieter with me, and less forthcoming than usual. Before that first race they maybe thought they were nurturing a future star, but instead I was proving to be a bit of a dud.

I had to make a choice, find a way to get better, or cut my losses and quit. It was the same choice I would have to make over and over again in the world of cycling. So just like I'd done when I was younger, I started to plan, study, read, and plot. I chose to figure out how I was going to improve and make good on the faith José Luis had placed in me.

I began thinking more analytically about how my body had reacted during the races. It was different from racing back in Colorado or even the high Andes of Venezuela. Racing at sea level, through little towns and on narrow roads, was more about how well you could maneuver in the peloton, and how powerfully you could push on the pedals.

The accelerations were brutal and the top speed never backed off. Everyone in the European peloton could go uphill fast—*very* fast. In Stateside racing, most of the riders were a bit bigger—more big-boned, as they say. The uphill sections of any race in the USA thinned the peloton out pretty quickly.

But over in Europe, certainly in Spanish pro racing, even the very worst climbers were really fucking good. As I thought it through and analyzed some heart-rate data from the race, I realized that my lungs and heart were not really maxed out.

Instead, it was my spindly little legs and their muscles that just didn't seem to have the strength to actually turn the pedals. So perhaps the way I needed to start training would focus on power, more so than other aspects of training, like endurance or aerobic capacity.

I had recently read an article about Greg LeMond trying to make a comeback using a new device that measured power. This—the device rather than the comeback—was a wildly interesting idea to me.

I realized that I could quantitatively figure out how much power was needed to race at the front, and then could simply replicate that type of power in training. LeMond's trainer was a Dutch guy named Adrie van Diemen, who believed that even in the longest of races, the decisive action could be broken down into small chunks of crucial high-power moments.

During these high-power moments, you either had the power to follow, or you did not. The rest of the race, before and after these moments, was really just a matter of having some very basic endurance. Such endurance was easy to train for, and didn't require too many days to focus on it.

Most races contained three to four very high-power moments, lasting anything from three to twelve minutes, that very few riders were capable of following. After that the pace would settle into a rhythm that most good riders could handle.

Van Diemen's theory was to stop training for endless hours on the bike, and refocus training energies on the moments of the race that really mattered. I redesigned my entire training program based on his ideas and theories. I didn't know if that was right or wrong, but I had to change something.

So I started lifting weights in the middle of the season, started doing high-power intervals in controlled settings, and started motorpacing as much as possible. Most of my training days now were two sessions instead of one.

Gone were the days of casually rolling out of town and waving at the girls in lawn chairs. Now it was all business, all the time. All this high-intensity work needed more recovery too, so I began resting as much as I could between training sessions.

Carmelo thought I had lost my mind and, as a result, didn't ride with me so much anymore. He would go off and do long meandering rides, as we used to. He really hated pounding up and down some hill doing intervals over and over again, and he was definitely not into weightlifting.

Despite our now different training schedules, and the fact that I was the runt of the team, I continued to grow closer to Carmelo's family. Maybe they just felt sorry for me, but the warmth of the family kept me going, kept me believing, and, most important, kept me fed. Every afternoon, after training and lunch, I would sit next to the fireplace in their living room and read the J. R. R. Tolkien books I'd found in a used bookstore in Valencia.

As I drifted into the land of hobbits, they would slump in a chair, smoke cigarettes, and watch TV. The smell of smoke and the noise of the TV and grumpy chatter between the family made me feel cozy. I was at home with the Alberts, invited to big dinners and get-togethers with all the extended family members you could imagine. I got to meet new people and continue to work on my caveman Spanish.

I also had a bit of a crush on one of Carmelo's younger cousins, and when we got invited to Grandma's house for dinner, I was always a bit excited to see her. I'd been practicing my Spanish every day with Carmelo and even bought a few textbooks to brush up on my grammar.

My Spanish, like my racing, seemed to be in a static state. Dinner at Grandma's was a great place to practice. There would be at least ten relatives, Carmelo's girlfriend, a few random neighbors, and, of course, my crush around the table.

Dinner at Grandma's was a typically late Spanish dinner, served about ten p.m. After the olives and various cured pig parts were eaten, Grandma pulled a few lovely-smelling chickens, in a typical Valencian tomato-based romesco sauce, from the oven. I couldn't wait to dig in.

I was falling in love with Spanish food, which gave me even more motivation to keep pushing myself harder in training, as I didn't want to miss out on paella Sundays or the juicy roasted chickens. Sometimes it's the small things that keep you working toward your goals.

When I had mopped up the last tiny bit of sauce on my plate with bread, Grandma turned to me and asked if I had enjoyed the dinner. I proudly started to formulate a response in my beginner's Spanish.

My brain whirred.

Okay, so chicken is pollo, I thought, *but that's masculine with the "o," so maybe since these were hens, the word for female chicken must be* polla, *as that's feminine with the "a."*

"Si! Me gusta mucho comer la polla!" I announced with a beaming smile.

The room went dead quiet, briefly, before Grandma turned bright red and then fell off her chair, roaring and cackling with laughter. The rest of the room followed suit.

What was so damn funny?

Finally, after they'd all calmed down and no one else would tell me, Grandma sat back down.

She sweetly explained to me that while *pollo* did indeed mean chicken, *polla* did not mean female chicken. In fact, it was a Spanish slang word for penis.

I'd just declared to the table how much I enjoyed eating penis.

After that, I got the feeling that I would be single for a bit longer in Spain, so I figured I should stick to training.

Van Diemen and LeMond based all their newfangled training theory around power measurement. But they had access to a very expensive and brand-new SRM power meter, which cost about as much as my annual salary. I needed to find the "economy" version.

Thumbing the pages of the old Bike Nashbar catalog, I ordered a rather fancy wind trainer made by CatEye, which claimed to calculate power output. The CatEye did seem to work pretty well in keeping track of my progress, with one small issue: as it was a stationary trainer, I couldn't train on the road if I wanted to measure my power output.

I found a solution, though, and gleefully set up my new trainer on the rooftop of Carmelo's parents' house. I could still train outdoors in the Spanish sun, even if I wasn't actually going anywhere.

My new plan involved rooftop intervals on the wind trainer in the morning, then lunch and a nap. In the afternoon I'd go weight training, immediately before a motorpaced ride out on the road.

In total, I was training around four to five hours a day, but none of it was dawdling any more. It was all specific, high-power work. I plotted my power and heart rate on each ride, keeping track of improvements and fatigue. It was effective, but I was getting a bit of a reputation as a weirdo in the neighborhood, as I could be seen pounding away every morning on a rooftop in plain sight of all the village folk. I can only imagine what they thought seeing me panting like a wild animal on a stationary bike—on the roof of Carmelo's house.

The embarrassment proved worth it, though. The next races were far less catastrophic than Semana Catalana had been. I was still a long way from being able to actually finish in the main peloton at the end of a race, but there was progress nonetheless. I was hampered, though, by slight colds and fevers, limiting me more than I would have liked. It seemed that every time I rode a week-long stage race, I would get sick with some sort of cold. My high-altitude nature just did not like European viruses.

As the spring rolled on, the atmosphere within the team was getting tense. The riders were viciously fighting for a spot on the Vuelta a España line-up. Not me, though. In fact, I'd say I was hoping that I didn't get selected and, when the time came, I was relieved that I didn't make the cut. I knew that I wouldn't have made it past the first week.

Progress had come in tiny steps, rather than in the leaps and bounds I would have needed to finish the Vuelta. Instead, I watched the Vuelta on TV after lunch every day, in Carmelo's smoke-filled living room.

I was astounded by how fast the riders were riding, and doing it day after day. I was also astounded at how bad my teammates were, relative to the rest of the peloton. These guys had been Junior World champions. They ate nails for breakfast, and worked damn hard. All of the riders on the team had been accomplished and talented riders before joining Santa Clara. All of them had been VO$_2$ max–tested by the same doctors that tested Miguel Induráin, and all were deemed to have "big engines," relative to the rest of the peloton.

But somehow Santa Clara–Samara was the worst team in the 1994 Vuelta peloton. It didn't make sense to me. They were so strong. How could they be getting slaughtered so badly in the Vuelta? How could not a single one of them stay in the peloton, whenever it got thinned down to fewer than eighty guys on a hill? I was baffled.

What further fueled my confusion was that a guy on another team, who joined us on those long and dawdling training rides that Carmelo and I specialized in and who was even occasionally troubled on hills by sucky old me, was on his way to a top-ten finish overall. Meanwhile, my teammates, who were clearly stronger than him a few months earlier, were suffering just to finish the Vuelta.

I started to ask our team trainers and doctors about this. Were we doing something fundamentally wrong? Or were we just the Bad News Bears of cycling? It seemed odd that every member of one team would be so much worse than everyone else. Surely one of us would turn out not to be such a dud.

But they told me not to worry, that it was just a matter of time before we would start to see some results. I needed to be more patient. *Right, patience* . . .

The riders from our team who managed to limp across the finish line in Madrid were so exhausted, injured, or ill that they would have to be taken off the roster of any other race for at least a month. This meant that I, the "runt," would have to race extra days for the months following.

Carmelo got a call from José Luis saying that we'd need to drive up to a number of races in France. The first of these events was the Classique des Alpes, in which, excitingly, a number of my childhood heroes were lining up, including Thierry Claveyrolat, Sean Kelly, and Greg LeMond.

This mountainous one-day race was exactly the type of event I figured I might be fairly good at after my LeMond–van Diemen training program: it was short, mountainous, and intense. We packed up the team car with bikes, bags, water bottles, and Russians and began our trip north. I had high hopes and big dreams, once again, just waiting to get beaten down.

I fought for every inch on every climb that day, clinging to the back of the group, even when the peloton whittled down to half its starting size. I was suffering on the back, but I was proud to be hanging in there, when all of my teammates had long since been cut adrift.

About halfway through the race, there was a long valley section that gave me a brief chance to recover and maybe even to move up a few places in the peloton. As I clawed my way forward, I saw Greg LeMond riding right in front of me.

There he was. The Tour de France winner, the legend—the guy that I'd seen in so many magazines.

I rode up alongside.

"How are you doing?" I said nervously. "Think you can win?"

"Oh, kid, no way!" he laughed. "No way am I going to win . . . Racing is different these days. I'm just trying to survive."

I was shocked. It sounded like something I would say, not something from a guy who had won the Tour de France. I didn't get it. But sure enough, he was right, and when we hit the next climb, both he and I were shot out the back with a small *grupetto*. We limped in to finish around fiftieth or sixtieth place that day, although outside the official time cut. I still sucked, but I'd finished a race in the same group as Greg LeMond. It was something.

Our next race was a four-day event in Brittany. I was happy that the pace up in France wasn't quite so brutal as the races had been

down in Spain. There were no Italian teams or Spanish teams competing, which seemed to reduce the speed quite a bit. I'd observed
that the Italian teams and riders were the fastest, then the Spanish,
and that the French were a bit slower.

I'd also watched many a rival from the amateur ranks just a few
years earlier absolutely soar on Italian teams, whereas I was still
stuck in the mud. For example, my two rivals from that Mammoth
Lakes stage race, Vladislav Bobrik and Evgeni Berzin, were winning
Paris—Nice and the Giro d'Italia.

Remember Omar Pumar from Venezuela? He was right up there
in the mix at the Giro, too. They were actually living the dream
that I thought was going to be mine. Big houses, big salaries, and
Ferraris loomed on their horizon. Meanwhile, I hadn't even opened
a Spanish bank account.

It rained every day for the entire week of that race in Brittany.
When we got back to the hotel, we'd just step into the hot shower
with all our clothes on. At least it *was* a hot shower. In those days,
there was no washing machine to use, no team truck or luxury bus.

We washed our muddy cycling kit while we were wearing it.
Then we'd try to dry it by twisting it into a knot inside a hotel towel.
Sometimes the clothes would be dry by morning, sometimes not. It
was always *really* pleasant to put on a questionably clean and certainly damp pair of cycling shorts in the morning.

But for all the misery of the conditions during that race, I wasn't
hating it. I could hang on, and sometimes even see what the front of
the peloton looked like. I wasn't the worst rider in the race. There
were no Italian or Spanish teams to break my dreams, and that made
all the difference.

Summer finally came and I was encouraged to mooch off another
teammate's family and to give Carmelo's a bit of a break. So I packed
up all my stuff and visited Eloy Santamarta, who lived in a small
apartment with his mother in Oviedo, Asturias, near the city center.

The main motivation for moving was that the weather was now
warmer in northern Spain, the higher-altitude climbs were open,
and I could train on bigger mountains than in Valencia. Also, there

were two stage races in Asturias around that time and I wouldn't have to go far to join the team for those races.

Asturias was beautiful and green, with large mountains in every direction. The cycling culture there was rich and vibrant. You could ride up many of the legendary climbs of the Vuelta: Alto del Acebo, Cangas de Onís to Covadonga, Alto del Naranco.

Eloy and I had a marvelous time together, training every day and hanging out with his friends afterward. He had a very lively social life, with the local women calling him *"lengua de plata"* (or *silver tongue*), due to his ability to charm pretty much anyone. In contrast, I felt awkward and introverted and was in awe of Eloy. It was like hanging out with one of the really popular kids in high school, and I was the exotic American exchange student. Thoughts of Carmelo's cousin soon grew more distant.

I put in my best racing performances to date in Asturias. I was able to follow the groups much farther into the mountains than I ever had before. I almost resembled a mediocre professional cyclist by this point. I wasn't getting ill as much, either, as my body slowly adapted to European bugs.

However, despite all of Eloy's friends and fun, and despite racing a little bit better, I was also getting very homesick. I missed Colorado. Since telephone calls cost so much back then, and email didn't really exist, I hadn't been able to communicate much with my family. I missed them immensely. I really wanted to go home, but José Luis was opposed to the idea, as he felt it would soften my resolve.

In one of many kind gestures, he gave me a John Denver tape to play, hoping that might alleviate some of my homesickness. In fact it had the opposite effect, and I played it over and over and over again.

"Country rooooaads, take me hooooome, to the place, I beloooong . . ."

I'd put on my headphones and sing along out loud to anyone who would listen. Then I'd get all choked up. I missed the American West. Listening to John Denver was just making this worse. José Luis could see I wasn't doing well at all, and finally capitulated on keeping me in Spain.

After I completed the Vuelta a los Valles Mineros, the second stage race in Asturias in June, we talked some more.

"Our team doesn't do the Tour de France yet, so we don't really race in July," he told me. "If you'd like to go home and visit your family for a short while, then I understand."

I was so happy. José Luis bought me a return ticket, but before he gave it to me he made me promise that I wouldn't go home and not return to Spain.

"You have a big future ahead of you in professional cycling," he said to me, "don't abandon it."

I'm not sure if José Luis sent him to keep an eye on me, or if he really wanted to tag along, but Eloy came home with me to Colorado. They used the excuse of Eloy needing to do some altitude training, and wanting to see America. Eloy was always entertaining to hang out with, with his *lengua de plata* ensuring he was great at pickup lines, so of course he was welcome.

The flight across the Atlantic seemed endless. I couldn't wait to see my doggie, my mom, my dad, and my buddies. I couldn't wait to tell Jim and Colby all the stories from the European peloton. I couldn't wait to see the mountains of Colorado. I was even excited to see the beige Stateside suburbs again.

It had been the first time I'd been away from my parents for so long, and when they picked me up from the airport, I couldn't help but notice that there was a little more gray in their hair. I wondered if that was the stress of me being gone for so long, or just normal aging.

It was perhaps the first time I realized that my parents were actually mortal. They were clearly happy—within the context of Mennonite stoicism—to see me. We smiled and hugged. The dog meanwhile was absolutely demented, jumping and whining all over the place. It was nice to feel loved again.

We stopped and had Mexican food on the way back from the airport. The heat of spicy green chili was something I hadn't experienced in a long time. It warmed my soul as it burned my tongue.

It was good to be home.

At the same time, I didn't want to lose any of the hard-won gains I'd made in Spain. With that in mind, Eloy and I decided to enter a few American races to ensure we kept our edge.

First up was Tour of the Gila in New Mexico. Along with keeping fit, I was also curious to see how I stacked up against the American professional scene after half a year racing in Europe. The road trip down to New Mexico was fun as we marveled at the vast open spaces of the American West, ate yet more green chili and sang along again to John Denver.

Gila had grown into one of the bigger events in the USA and we knew that the competition was going to be fierce. It would be well attended, with all the top American professional teams present, including my bitter ex-employers—Team Saturn. They arrived with their trucks and cars, soigneurs and mechanics, ready for battle. I arrived in the now rusty Oldsmobile station wagon with Eloy.

Just as it has for the last thirty years, the race opened with a time trial. I set off, really in hope of holding my own before the more mountainous stages, which I was sure would suit me better. However, after a few kilometers, I had already passed the rider who'd started a minute in front of me, like he was standing still.

My confidence grew, as it seemed as if I was just flying. It was a really confusing experience, as I'd just spent the last six months being "worst bike racer in Europe", but now I was passing rivals in a time trial. Then I ripped past one of my old Saturn teammates like he was stuck in quicksand.

Wow, guess I'm having a really good day . . . I thought. Maybe it was the green chili?

Whatever it was, the more prey I passed, the more my confidence grew and the harder I pushed. I was really racing again, something I hadn't experienced in months. Instead of my head being hung low and my shoulders slumped, I felt the fire of actually competing again.

When the results came out, I'd had a great day. I'd won the time trial by almost a minute. I was amazed. Eloy was amazed. The American peloton was amazed. I'm sure José Luis was, too.

With only one teammate, wearing the leader's jersey from the first day would prove to be an interesting task, as the race would be tough to control. But Eloy did a good enough job of keeping me close enough on the flat sections so I could close up all the gaps on the uphill sections.

Whenever things got really sticky, I promised to split some of my prize money with old amateur friends if they would just take a pull or two on the front. They really needed the cash for gas. By the end of the race, I don't think I actually kept any of the prize money.

Throughout, my former Saturn teammates attacked viciously, whenever and wherever they could. The other pro teams also ganged up on me, in an effort to not be embarrassed by some weird unknown twenty-two-year-old racing for a Spanish team no one had ever heard of.

But teammates or not, by the end of the week I had won the Tour of the Gila. In fact, I had dominated the race, winning by well over two minutes. It felt so good, and I was rejuvenated by the experience. But at the same time, it was also deeply confusing to me.

How could I be so good in the USA and so absolutely shit in Europe?

Thomas Frischknecht, the former world mountain bike champion, was racing in Gila to get in shape for the forthcoming World Cup races.

"I don't get it," I told him when we spoke after the race. "In Europe, I climb worse than the fattest of sprinters, I can't do anything except make the time cut in time trials and I pretty much suck at bike racing. And here in the U.S., I just killed everyone. It makes no sense to me. I must lose power when I cross the Atlantic or something . . ."

Thomas listened for a while.

"Maybe it's not your problem," he said quietly, "but instead a problem with what is going on in European bike racing."

The little cryptic messages that kept coming from older professional riders were building. From LeMond to Frischknecht, they were trying to tell me something.

What were they getting at? What was going on that made the racing so different from what it used to be? I almost felt like Indiana Jones, entering the tomb of the pharaoh and blowing the dust off some ancient text. *"Do not pass here or ye will be cursed."*

CHAPTER 8

BURY MY BIKE IN BURGOS

When I got back to Europe, I could tell that something had changed within the team. The spirit wasn't there. The jokes were fewer and the optimism had evaporated in the dry Spanish heat.

The Russians seemed even more gray and dour than usual and the Spanish riders seemed resigned, listless. The fatigue of getting beaten to a pulp, week in, week out, was draining everyone's resolve. José Luis, too, seemed tense, worried about something. It felt like everyone wanted the racing season to end, immediately.

It was understandable. While I was perhaps the runt of the team, the team was the runt of the peloton. Our performances had been bad at best, horrible at worst. Knowing what I know now about team management, I'm sure José Luis was getting some stern words from the team sponsors.

Rumors were spreading that the Russian sponsor had never paid their part of the bill, so that Enrique Tatay was having to cover the entire funding. You could feel the pressure growing. Being patient had been the mantra of the team management all year, but now there were finally some folks at the top of the hierarchy who weren't being so patient with the management itself.

In contrast, Eloy and I were annoyingly bouncy and happy after our victorious trip to the USA. When we told everyone the stories of how we had actually won a stage race in the U.S., no one even came close to believing us.

Fat Eloy and the shitty American were winning races? Not likely.

Racing in Spain during August tended to be a bit more relaxed, as the big riders in the Spanish peloton were tired after the Tour de France. That meant that riders on little teams like ours dared not attack when the likes of Miguel Induráin wanted to have an easy day on the bike.

Instead we would roll along, in the baking hot sun, chatting away with the riders around us. I was, of course, keen to ask anyone and everyone what the Tour de France was like. Most of them would chuckle and tell me, a little condescendingly, that it was a race for grown-ups, not children.

But just occasionally, I'd find someone who would actually talk to me. José María Jiménez was one of those riders. He would ride up and ask how I was doing, how I liked Spain, and what Colorado was like.

In turn, I would pester him with endless questions about everything from training programs to how the hell he went up hills so fast. Finally, I'd get around to asking him if he was feeling good and wanting to win that day.

Based on his past exploits, I figured he could just fly away from all of us on any given hill. Jiménez was an immensely talented rider, and when the road was steep enough, he could beat anyone. Yet now he would shake his head and say he didn't feel up for much that day.

Jiménez wasn't the only big name sounding this downbeat in the late-season races. It seemed the whole peloton needed some sort of roadside gasoline refill. And sure enough, they raced like that, too.

Guys who could have danced away from me on one leg in April were now limping along, looking pale and hollowed out. There were constant complaints about being tired, about the team doctors not doing enough, about not having enough red blood cells, about being anemic.

This was so different from what I'd experienced in the Euro peloton earlier in the year. I didn't understand why everyone had just . . . *died*. It was during these long drags through the plains of Spain that a few older riders finally started to explain to me what the hell was going on.

Most teams had a team doctor that would give them some sort of "medicine," as they referred to it, that would keep a rider from getting fatigued or anemic in the big races. But after the Tour, or at the very least after a rider had signed his contract for the next year, the doctor would give them a break. It seemed that once this treatment ended, the rider would just wilt. Hence all the grumbling.

Our own team management also seemed to be discussing the role of "medicine" a lot more than they had previously. But it was clearly a divisive and contentious topic among the team brass. There also was an element of morality brought into the conversation, something that other teams didn't seem so bothered by.

Our team, as I'd slowly learned over the past eight months, was run and funded by Opus Dei. Opus Dei is a deeply religious organization, affiliated with the Catholic Church, whose members have dedicated their lives to God.

José Luis was a kind-hearted, highly intellectual man trained in geology and with a PhD. He was also a sworn and celibate member of Opus Dei. The team doctors and Enrique Tatay himself were also members, although maybe not as celibate. So, according to them, whenever our team acted, it needed to be in line with the teachings of Christianity. Filling the gas tank up with "medicine" didn't quite meet that religious litmus test.

So we ended the year with a whimper. No race wins, no pride, and no respect from the rest of the peloton. It must have been hard for José Luis to keep the morale of the sponsors and staff up. But he was a genius at making people feel good about the slightest amount of progress.

After my final race, he sat down with me for a few minutes and asked me to look back at how much progress I'd made. To me, it felt like I'd barely moved an inch forward. He encouraged me to see it otherwise.

"Jonathan, you came here with a dream and no legs to support it," he said. "Now you have begun to build your legs. And you have done it honorably. You will win a very big race one day—just don't forget about me," he said again.

I went home motivated, but also concerned about José Luis.

As the 1995 season approached, news of a new second-name sponsor came in. This would fill the void left by the Russian sponsor that had failed to pay. It was great news for the team, as it took a bit of the pressure off Tatay.

With the new sponsor also came a new crew of staff and a new head sports director for the team. This guy was definitely not intellectual, nor was he part of Opus Dei. He was a simple, gruff, old-school Spanish cycling director. Riders were to push pedals, not ask questions or have opinions. If a rider didn't win or didn't do his job helping someone else to win, it was time for a new rider. He was ruthless and he wasn't about to give up the percentage of money he was getting from the new sponsor because the team couldn't ride fast enough.

You could sense a new tension in the team's management almost immediately. After a series of poor performances, the chatter about José Luis being soft and weak grew louder and started to filter through the team. As I was José Luis's pet project, I was thrown into the same boat.

I too was soft, weak, asked too many questions, and had too many opinions. The hand-wringing and moral questioning that had gone on before about "filling up the tank" was fading. The new guy was all about getting podiums, not the "developing good riders and good humans" philosophy that the Catholic crew was taking. This guy wanted rubber-to-the-road results.

I had also finally come to understand the hard reality of all these veiled messages I kept hearing inside the peloton. It seemed that, very rapidly, what had been only rumors of EPO use had now become a reality. The entire peloton was now moving to this new way of doing things. No one referred to it as "doping," or "cheating."

Instead, doping was given more noble and gentlemanly euphemisms, such as "sports medicine" or "recovery," "being professional," and "making sure you stay healthy." I'm not sure if people actually believed this, or if the language was aimed at disguising the harsh reality, but it never once hinted that doping was somehow wrong. In Spanish and Italian cycling, doping had become normalized and there was no judgment from anyone about it.

Our new director was clearly aligned with this thinking. He thought it was very simple, and that the team doctor had two jobs: to make sure riders were healthy, and to make sure we rode fast. How that got accomplished wasn't really the business of the rider or even the manager.

"Just get it done, however it needs to be done, but don't test positive."

For most of my Russian and Spanish teammates, this worked just fine, as they didn't have any understanding of the mechanics of medicine, nor did they really care. Their job was to push pedals. This was not a moral or ethical issue to them. It was just life. You took an aspirin if you got a headache, so you took whatever the hell the doctor gave you if you got a leg ache.

Unfortunately, I knew it was doping and I knew it wasn't ethical. I also knew that it might have some nasty side effects later in life. You don't just grow new red blood cells without some sort of consequences.

My teammates would laugh and tell me to stop thinking about everything so damn much. The team doctors would never do something that got you in trouble, so why worry? It was just medicine that pro cyclists needed to stay healthy, nothing more.

But I wasn't able to switch off my conscience. I wanted to sidestep the whole issue. José Luis was very supportive of that. He didn't mind my thinking too much, as he clearly felt it was wrong, too, no matter how many times he was told he was just being soft and weak.

I knew that sidestepping the issue was going to be almost impossible, but I still thought I could figure out a way. I reasoned that I should ramp up the science in my training methods, and really optimize every last bit my body had to give.

I'd somehow saved a tiny bit of money over the previous year, and so thought I might spend it on a real coach and on a new power-measuring device. The cost of an early SRM was high, but I made the order anyway. Then I found a way to reach out to my coaching hero, Adrie van Diemen. His input was going to be costly as well.

These new costs would chew up over half of my annual income, but if I was going to make it in this sport, and do my best to avoid "taking medicine," I needed to do something different. So I paid some $5,000 for one of the very first SRMs, and I made a deal with van Diemen to train me.

I also made it my business to study endocrinology, just to get a basic idea of exactly what all of this medical talk really meant. By this time enough people had been honest with me to ensure that I knew that the three big doping products used were EPO, growth hormone, and testosterone.

I wanted to see what the side effects were and if there was a way to avoid the pressure to take them. Was there a way your body could achieve the same outcome, naturally?

I educated myself. Learning about luteinizing hormone, thyroid, cortisol, erythropoietin or EPO, human growth hormone—HGH—and all the pituitary or hypothalamic releasing factors that went along with them—really fascinated me. It appealed to my constant desire to learn.

All of the doping methods being used, back in the day, were hormone-based and naturally occurring elements already in your body. This was why nobody was getting caught by anti-doping protocols. EPO, HGH, and testosterone weren't technically drugs, but hormones already present. This kind of doping wasn't like the old days of amphetamines and such, which were clearly not produced naturally; they were chemicals and easy to find. But recombinant, or effectively engineered hormones, were just copies of what your body already had.

How would a test be able to find that?

All of the hormone levels are regulated in your body by feedback loops, meaning that if there's too much growth hormone or a surplus of erythropoietin in circulation because you injected it, your body ceases its own natural production. This shutdown is what would surely happen with the introduction of external hormones in a body that was already producing enough of these hormones on its own.

I learned that sometimes, if the feedback loops got shut down for too long, it became permanent. Failing to produce natural hormones was clearly not a healthy situation for later in life.

The second point was that more of these modern hormonal doping methods were products that boosted growth—of cells, muscle, and red blood cells. This bothered me, because obviously if something could grow more muscle, it could also grow a tumor or cancer cells.

It scared me enough to try and figure out a better way. To avoid the consequences I'd read about, I knew I needed to adjust how I was eating and how I was training, and to look into natural supplements that could stimulate some of these hormones. I was fully committed to educating myself on anything and everything I could. I threw myself, all in, on my plan, and I believed in it.

The newfangled training with van Diemen was fascinating and incredibly hard. His formula for winter training was very simple: improve the two elements of physics that actually create power, which are angular velocity (cadence) and torque (force) on the pedals. Improve those two things separately in the off-season and then slowly bring them together as the season approached.

All of our training was downloaded onto my cheap and clunky laptop and then sent to van Diemen via the newly discovered Internet. I was so excited to receive my new training program on CompuServe email. It was like waiting for a new birthday present each week.

My old training buddies felt differently. They thought I'd turned into some robot that winter, all day training according to what some weird box on my handlebars was telling me. But I didn't care. The training direction van Diemen gave me was totally in step with current training programs of the contemporary era. Reverse periodization, lactate threshold, lipid mobilization—we used all of these terms and they were integral to our training efforts.

Van Diemen was very focused on five-minute power outputs, so I threw myself into these flat-out, lung-screaming, painful intervals. All the traditionalists in Colorado thought I'd be burned out by Christmas. Van Diemen assured me otherwise.

The other big point van Diemen drove home was high pedaling frequency. This was exactly contrary to what all of the European pros I'd trained with were doing. They would push a slightly oversized gear all day long at around seventy-five revolutions per minute. The idea was that turning over the big gear would build up your leg strength.

Van Diemen thought this was ridiculous, and said we needed to optimize oxygen uptake and venous oxygen delivery by constantly practicing high pedaling frequency. This was some five years before Lance Armstrong started using this very method with Michele Ferrari. It's no exaggeration to say that van Diemen was way ahead of his time in all aspects of training.

My little red SRM became my best friend and training companion. It pushed me beyond where I had been before, and gave my training real purpose. I was convinced it would make me into a champion. However, upon returning to Europe, my teammates and directors were less convinced. A lot less convinced.

When we were reunited at training camp, they relentlessly made fun of my attempt at becoming a better cyclist through technology. To them, I was the runt, and always would be the runt. They laughed at the little red box and they laughed at me carrying a laptop around, too. When I performed specific efforts in training, they would laugh again.

The mocking got worse at the first races. At Vuelta a Mallorca, there were only two riders in the peloton with SRMs—Stefano Della Santa and I. Della Santa won many early races every season, including the Vuelta a Andalucía that year, which just made me being the butt of so many jokes feel even worse.

The Italians could not believe a shitty little rider like I would waste so much money on a training device that only big champions like Della Santa used. They would point and laugh, and then go to another friend and point and laugh again. It was worse than being made fun of for wearing Lycra shorts in high school. The teasing was more sophomoric and certainly more vicious.

Unfortunately, my racing results weren't proving anyone wrong. While I was considerably stronger than in the previous year, I was still somehow getting dropped on most climbs. It seemed that while I was now considerably faster, so was the entire peloton.

The Motorola team was also competing at Ruta del Sol and Lance Armstrong was riding for them. He was the hero of U.S. cycling at the time, as he had won the 1993 World Road Championships. He was by far the best and most successful of the generation of U.S. riders that had turned professional in recent years and had worn the world champion's jersey with some distinction the year before.

For me, racing with the Motorola team was like playing basketball against the LA Lakers. They were the team I dreamed of riding for. They were cool, well funded, and spoke English at the dinner table. They were my heroes.

But at Ruta, things were different for Lance and his Motorola team. They were getting pummeled like rank amateurs. I was quite used to my team, Santa Clara, having five riders in the *grupetto* each day, grimly grinding along to the finish, but now Motorola and Lance were in the same boat as little old us.

So all my studious, scientific training had only just allowed me to improve enough to be just as shitty—relative to the rest of the peloton—as I was before. All my numbers were so much better, but the results sheet did not reflect that. At least this time around I had a bunch of fellow English-speakers to keep me company at the back of the race, Lance being one of them.

Team Motorola were fellow runts of the peloton, and I liked having my new friends at the back. But Lance was far from happy to have me as company, and very unhappy about being at the back of the race. He would angrily rant about how fucked up cycling was and how all these guys were cheating bastards, making more money than him.

He would look disdainfully at riders that a year or two ago wouldn't have even been able to see his distant ass in the peloton. Now they were dropping him on every hill. He couldn't believe it and was angry about it in a way that only Lance could be.

He ranted about quitting cycling while he was ahead, as he wouldn't do what these rat fuckers were doing. He'd made good money already, so why not? Then he'd start up about how the UCI—the Union Cycliste Internationale—and the drug testers needed to figure something out before this problem got completely out of hand.

In the context of his later career and what we now know, this all seems ludicrous and unbelievable, but the bizarre truth is that in 1995, Lance was an incredibly talented but very angry cyclist who was having his career stolen from him by dopers. He was vocally against the use of EPO—he called it an epidemic—and wanted a test to be found to catch the cheaters who were taking it.

Lance was a strong and proud Texan. He was the indignant former world champion who was being stripped of his pride by cheats. And most important to him, they were stripping him of a better paycheck. One way or another, Lance was going to change this unfair imbalance.

The Motorola riders wore defeated and angry faces every day. By the end of the week, I was no longer happy to ride alongside my new friends at the back of the race; instead I was crushed to see my heroes, guys I'd grown up with, so beaten and defeated. If they couldn't race at the front, then how the hell was I ever going to do it?

Santa Clara was wilting under the pressure of all this, too. One season of crappy results could be written off—after all, we were only a team of neo-pros learning our trade. But by season two, the excuses were wearing thin.

José Luis was clearly battling with the new management on how to best handle the new reality of the peloton. He preached sticking to our moral convictions and sticking with the teachings of Jesus. But the new sports director felt pretty strongly that if we were going to keep our sponsors happy, we needed results, fast, and it didn't really matter how we got that done.

He'd brought a few soigneurs that had worked at the Kelme team previously along with him. These guys could not believe what José Luis and the Opus Dei doctors were telling us. They also couldn't believe how naive and innocent we were. They thought of us as stupid.

They all enthused about the doctor at Kelme, Eufemiano Fuentes, and how he was a genius that always got the best out of a rider. "Ufe" was their hero, and we heard endless stories about him and his greatness. Conversely, they grumbled and laughed at José Luis behind his back, told the riders we had an absolutely incompetent medical staff, and that now that they were in charge, things were going to change.

The battle split the team in two. I was loyal to José Luis, and believed that I needed to stick to my beliefs and not give in to the EPO epidemic that was gripping the peloton. José Luis would say that if we were patient, and prayed, then a solution would come, that a test would be invented and we would be able to race at the front.

I remember the new director coming to my room one night and calmly, and quite convincingly, talking to me about the job of a professional cyclist.

"You don't drink, you don't smoke, you don't do many of the things that hurt the body," he said. "But racing two hundred kilometers every day is very bad for the body, if you don't give it medicine to recover. I know you don't like the idea of injections, but you must be equally valiant and brave when the doctor comes to your hotel room as you are out on the road."

He painted the picture of professional cyclists as warriors in a war. And in that war, we needed the best weapons. He was convinced that doping was the right thing to do. And, in truth, he was convincing. It would be irresponsible of us to not do our jobs and let the sponsors down, he argued. They had invested in us, and now we needed to give them what they had paid for. It was only fair.

I almost believed him, but still . . .

I stood my ground, and reiterated my allegiance to José Luis's vision of the team.

My racing was still horrible, and the team wasn't doing much better. The tensions made every race unbearable, with one half not talking to the other half. I couldn't wait to go home for my little break in July.

When I came back to Europe I felt refreshed and ready to take on the second half of the season. Something had definitely changed within the "other" half of the team. I noticed a change to their attitude and their confidence, but when we raced Vuelta a Galicia, the difference became very apparent on the road.

While I was stuck suffering at the back of the race, the other half of the team was now attacking at the front. I could not believe what was happening. They were beaming with confidence. After the race, they chatted about tactics for the next day, about how they might win.

I was not part of that conversation and was alone at the dinner table. José Luis's pet project, who still couldn't hang on to the peloton over much of a hill, was still the runt. But now I didn't have any teammates for company at the back of the race. They had all moved on, and were now competing, instead of surviving. I was lonely. And I was envious.

Clearly, they didn't want me around anymore. All the riders and staff who had sided with the "priests" were now being ostracized. Pushed aside, left out. It came to a head for me right before the Vuelta a Burgos, where José Luis had insisted that I be given a place on the roster, despite a stronger teammate wanting to do the race.

The day before the race began I walked out to the hotel garage to go for a warm-up ride, only to find my bike missing. The mechanics claimed it had been stolen but, of course, like anything else in cycling, nobody could actually keep the secret. After a replacement rider was sent in, and a soigneur found me sitting on the steps of the hotel crying, I was finally told the truth.

My bike had been buried in a nearby field by one of the mechanics, on the orders of the new director.

Clearly, I was unwanted. I called José Luis and asked him to send me home. Once again, my cycling career was ending on a sour note. I wasn't good enough, just like I had never really been since my very first race.

José Luis asked me to wait a bit before giving up so I agreed to compromise. I could go home, but I would hold off on giving up on cycling entirely until December. Despite my depressive and fatalistic nature, I seem to always hold out this last little bit of hope for the future. This was no different. I didn't want to give up on cycling, but it was all getting to be far too much.

It was clear that EPO was the only way to succeed, or even to survive. Unlike previous forms of doping—cortisone, testosterone, amphetamines, whatever—EPO was a serious game changer. It wasn't the difference between first and second place, it was the different between first and last.

It couldn't be overcome by talent, hard work, or whatever else, like previous doping methods could. Even Lance, the 1993 World Road Race champion, sucked when he wasn't taking it and everyone else was. What had been a thinly veiled rumor a year earlier had become a very concrete reality. It was no longer gossip from jealous or bitter "has-been" riders. It was just a brutal fact.

You couldn't compete with already super talented and hardworking guys that now were able to process 10 percent more oxygen than they normally could because of EPO. All the inspirational words you read on posters about hard work, determination, and reaching for your dreams were just lies thought up in Hallmark offices. All the patience José Luis had preached, and all the science that van Diemen had taught me, were just wasted words.

EPO was too powerful. More red cells equated to more oxygen

and faster, much faster speeds. Gone was any human element. It was just down to math.

When I got home to Colorado, I re-enrolled in the local university. I needed something to take me away from the black hole that cycling had become. Being a normal student attending classes felt good—an escape from people who were supposed to be on your side, burying your bike.

One thing that was different from the last time I'd been in college was that this time I was a great student. After getting absolutely slaughtered racing in Europe for two years, after suffering like a pig endlessly, riding in the gutter in the rain at 37 miles per hour and getting ruthlessly eviscerated over mountain passes week in, week out, for two years—after all that suffering—getting an A+ in a chemistry course in college seemed *really fucking easy.*

I had been a lazy and uninterested student before. I'd had big dreams of being a big star, a rich pro rider driving a Ferrari around Europe. School had not mattered. School was just something to make my parents not disown me. But now school was my escape. It was my way out of the hole I had dug for myself in professional cycling.

And compared to cycling, school was easy. *So easy.*

No, I wasn't suddenly smarter than before, but I'd been given a brutal lesson in what it felt like to do something really hard. I'd gone from doing the minimum needed to pass a class, to feeling guilty if I got anything less than an A+. Now I knew what hard work really meant. Sitting on a soft, cozy couch in my parents' living room, while reading a chemistry textbook and doing calculations, was incredibly comfortable compared to what I'd gone through over in the old country.

I'd witnessed teammates who had no options other than professional cycling suffer endlessly, because they had no other way forward in life. It didn't matter whether they still loved cycling. It was all they had.

Now that I'd seen at least some of the world, I realized that all the mundane things I had worked hard to escape were actually blessings to be grateful for. I just hadn't known that before.

I was blessed to have grown up in beige suburbia, I was blessed to have parents that supported me, I was blessed that I had a hometown not being ripped apart by the Russian mafia, and I was blessed to have a mind that could actually do the schoolwork.

I owed it to all the guys I'd met in the last few years that didn't have as many options to not waste my time in school. Anything less than an A+ was an insult to them and to everything they had been through.

I'm sure my parents were feeling quite relieved during that fall. I could see they were happy and more relaxed. They didn't have to bear the worry of having a son living overseas doing something incredibly dangerous for very little pay and very little hope of a solid future. They could smile when their friends asked about me.

"Jonathan is doing quite well in school and seems to have finally settled down . . ."

But then José Luis called me.

Apparently, the new director and new sponsor were gone. With the team buckling under the weight of the new sponsor's performance expectations, they had decided to discontinue their investment. Not enough race wins, not enough TV time, too many promises, not enough meat.

Sure, the new "enhanced" version of the team had raced much better than before, but the director had sold it too high and now the very sponsor he had brought to the table was going to up and walk away. And with the sponsor went any of the leverage that he had over José Luis and the rest of the team. His influence was gone. He was gone. There was a lesson in watching that implosion that I would hold on to into my managerial days.

In the meantime, José Luis had convinced Enrique Tatay to fund the void left by the departed sponsor, and so the team would be back entirely in his control. It was all really great news for José Luis. Except for one thing: we were going to get killed at the races. José Luis's idealism was going to keep us firmly planted as the worst team in the peloton.

Was I really going to go back just to get slaughtered once again? I was now a great student with happy parents, and a warm dog sitting in my lap on the soft living room couch. Why the hell would I go back to getting the living shit beaten out of me in each and every race? The situation wasn't going to change. What was the point?

I can't say why, I guess just a compulsion of some sort, but I jumped at the chance to give it one more shot. In truth, it never entered my mind to say no. But now I had a few scars and was a skeptic. And I knew just a little too much.

I would go back, but it would be different. This time I knew what my choices really were.

CHAPTER 9

"VIVA LA QUIMICA!"

The 1996 season was my last real chance to make it as a pro. My dreams were wearing thin. I finally knew the harsh reality of the sport and how long a road it was to get to the top. So I took a new mind-set with me.

I felt that twenty-three was old enough to know whether I could keep progressing in the sport or whether it was time to go and get a real job. I knew I could go home, go back to school, and that, unlike many of my peers, my parents would be waiting with open arms to support me. Unlike the Russians, I had choices. But I also knew in my soul that I wasn't going to be happy walking away—quitting—just yet.

I'd given the whole of myself to the sport for the last decade. I'd missed going to the prom, I'd missed endless birthdays and parties, I'd missed many of the milestones my friends back home had passed. I'd put everything I had into the sport. Success or failure, I needed to know there was absolutely nothing more I could have done to make it.

As a third-year professional I knew my way around the block. I knew what would work for me in training and what wouldn't. I knew how to keep myself healthier than I used to. I also had become a lot more skeptical, too.

I began the 1996 season with the mentality of a mercenary. I needed either to achieve success or closure to this dream of mine, and I had one year to get that clarity. The focus had shifted for me—now it was less about learning and dreaming and much more about doing. There was no more time for "development," no more time for excusing poor performances because I was young.

Mentally, I had become much harder than I had been a few years earlier, and my body had grown stronger, too. I'd grown up, matured, and had a little more chest hair and muscle. Van Diemen's training was working, too, and it just took a while to have the full effect. Physically, in every training ride that winter, I sensed that I was more robust, readier to be a professional.

Unfortunately, listening to the crew and sports director that had been kicked out of the team by José Luis had also changed me profoundly. I think it had impacted on José Luis, too. Our worries regarding EPO were no longer just rumors in the press or in the peloton. EPO use was commonplace in every race.

The disciples of Eufemiano Fuentes, who had worked for the team the year before, had made that abundantly clear to me and to José Luis. Plus, most of the staff members, directors, or riders who came to us from another team would say exactly the same thing. By 1996, EPO use was all-encompassing. Unless a rider was a first-year professional, by 1996, if you raced a Grand Tour, you were almost certain to be using EPO.

José Luis desperately tried to hold on to his idealism. He began to discuss the situation with other doctors, and tried to look for some sort of acceptable middle ground, a way forward that would allow him to be faithful to his beliefs but also not kill the team he'd fought so hard to keep.

He became more philosophical about the topic, wondering where the line was between vitamins, recovery helpers and hardened, intentional doping. Was it health based? Was it what was written in the rule book? Was there some direction the Catholic Church could give? He was struggling over what was right and wrong.

It was wrong to dope, but was it right to let some of the most talented cyclists in Spain and Russia have their careers die because he was unwilling to fall in line with what was now the cycling norm? Why would you steal careers from people who had few options in life? Why would you shatter the dream of being a successful pro away from a talented and worthy rider? Was that any better than doping?

I could see this internal battle raging in José Luis from the first day of our first training camp.

He had hired a new doctor, one that was kind, intelligent, and compassionate, but wasn't part of Opus Dei. He was, instead, a bit more open to "bending" the rules without breaking them, as José Luis would say to me.

"We aren't going to dope anyone, that would be immoral, but we aren't going to let anyone become anemic or run-down either," said the new doctor.

He very firmly felt that training and racing at the level we were competing at was unhealthy, and that helping the body recover from such intensity was not only preferable, but was a moral obligation for a doctor who had taken an oath to care for his patients.

This logic soothed my inner debate, allowing me to justify the decision to turn my rear end into a pincushion. He also appealed to my newfound knowledge of endocrinology, in that he really didn't want to place exogenous hormones in the athlete's body, saying instead that he preferred to find a way to get the body to produce a little bit more of those hormones by itself.

He and José Luis were trying to tread some gray area in between obvious and blatant doping and getting your ass handed to you in every race. It was a tricky—and impossible—tightrope to walk.

Nonetheless, I wanted to try. I was dead tired of racing at the back, watching riders I was much better than as an amateur or a junior, fly away from me in every race. Some of my buddies in suffering at Motorola had turned a corner, too. They went from being *grupetto* fodder in 1995 to absolutely ripping races apart in 1996.

Lance waltzed onto the scene that year looking like he was auditioning for the X-Men. He had no body fat at all and muscles just bulging out of every seam. He'd clearly directed his anger over the injustices of doping into extreme bodybuilding that winter. Along with Frenchman Laurent Jalabert, he ripped the entire peloton to pieces at my first race of the season, the Vuelta a Valencia in eastern Spain. His performance was a long, long way from those of 1995's early-season Lance.

Lance was the least of my concerns though. It was demoralizing to watch riders I'd raced with and sometimes beaten succeeding while I was still clinging to the back end of the group. It hollowed out my soul, and made me horrendously envious and brooding. I was giving the dream one last chance, and while I didn't want to do anything that would make my mother sad, I also refused to go home, yet again, with my tail tucked between my legs.

So I agreed to testing some new "medicines" that, I convinced myself, "weren't doping." These included things like injectable L-Ornithine, an amino acid that supposedly stimulated growth hormone, and all kinds of injectable iron, vitamin B12 and folic acid. It was all totally legal, but when you're injecting yourself three or four times a week—legal or not—it makes you feel pretty dirty.

But I had felt pretty dark about things for a while. Two years of getting my head kicked in when racing, and then breaking up with my girlfriend, Carrie, had just made me nihilistic and black. I cared less about risks, less about life, less about the morality I'd been brought up with. If I was to succeed here, I needed to be ruthless and not care so much about being a good guy.

So instead of feeling guilty about injecting myself, I felt empowered. I felt like I was finally doing something to give myself a chance. I was fighting back, not just letting myself get pushed into a corner. I was feeling the same anger I'd seen in Lance the year before. My career as a pro cyclist was close to being stolen from me by all these dopers.

I had some talent, yet I was the one getting laughed at in every race?

Fuck that. It was time to end that dance.

I wanted to be a warrior. Real warriors need weapons. Real

warriors don't fight friendly, they fight to win. Real warriors don't make excuses, they make shit happen. Now I was going to make shit happen.

Our new doctor didn't want to start punching too many holes in us until we were actually worn down a bit though, so the early races that year were done without much medical help. This pissed off part of the team, as they had experienced the luxury—or curse—of feeling how much more fun it was to race when you were near the front.

For me, I was content with it, as I hadn't opened the Pandora's box of "enhanced recovery" or "medicine" or "doping" or whatever else we were calling it, just yet. In fact, I was racing much better than I had in the past, and that was after only poking a few holes in me. I was able to make the front groups of fifty to sixty guys over the top of climbs, meaning there were often eighty to a hundred guys behind me.

Of course, I would be hanging on for dear life to the fifty-to-sixty rider group in front, but I was there. The exhilaration of actually being a tiny bit in the race was addictive. I could see the various strategies of teams unfolding. I felt important, as I was often the only rider from our team in the front group, so I needed to fly the flag for everyone.

The climax of the Spanish early season was the three-week period that started with Semana Catalana and ended with Vuelta al País Vasco. We trained like absolute fiends to be good for these races. Grinding six-hour rides in the mountains of Asturias, motorpacing for hours on end, time trial simulations.

I would come back to my apartment completely spent and exhausted every day, but it felt good. I was becoming a warrior. But I now realize I was only starting to get a glimpse into what that really meant. On one of our big seven-hour mountain rides, one of my teammates was just eviscerating the rest of us, all day long. On every climb, he would pound us into the hurt locker, never seeming to feel any of it himself. He was oddly euphoric and glazed over the entire time, and just loving the hard training, feeling no pain.

Yet, after the death-march ride through the mountains, our director was really upset with him. It was confusing, as the guy had just shown us he was clearly the strongest. I thought he'd be getting a pat on the back instead of a dressing down.

At dinner that night, the director stood up and asked everyone how we felt about the rider in question. Most of us responded with a shrug and a "he's damn strong" type answer.

There was a pause.

Then the director turned to the rider.

"Why don't you tell everyone why you were so strong today?"

He was pale and exhausted and could barely stand up.

But the director didn't care.

"What's wrong? You don't feel well? Why don't you explain that?"

No response. Finally, our director told us.

"This kid was taking amphetamines all day long, so he could show how strong he was. I recognized it, because that's what I used to do."

We all sat in silence, wondering what was coming next.

"Let me tell you from experience, it's a fucking stupid choice. It messes with your body, your brain, and it puts the whole team at risk," he said angrily.

"If this kid goes to a race and the shit hasn't cleared his system, he'll test positive. And then the whole team is fucked. So don't be an idiot, like this guy. And by the way, he's not coming to any races anytime soon."

We ate the rest of dinner in silence.

I sat there, thinking about how confusing this all was. On one hand, we were being told certain "medicine" was okay to take, and on the other hand, we'd just watched a teammate be berated and kicked off the team because he'd decided to take matters into his own hands.

I realized that the unwritten rule of the peloton was "cheat, just not too much."

I was testing and riding better than I ever had in my short pro career. When the doc tested me in his lab, the VO$_2$ max results blew him away.

"I think you hit 90 VO$_2$ max there for a bit. That is exceptional, Jonathan. Now you must race just as well."

So when Semana and País Vasco arrived, I was determined to do that 90 VO$_2$ some sort of justice.

I managed to finish thirty-fourth on the big mountain stage of Semana Catalana. That doesn't sound like much, but it meant I could see the front of the race, all the way through to just a few kilometers from the mountaintop finish. I proudly looked at the results, noting that I'd finished ahead of some riders who were quite famous at the time, guys who could finish in the top ten of the Tour de France.

I was told not to get too excited, as the A-listers were "preparing for the Tour" and, obviously, wouldn't be riding very fast just yet, as it was only the end of March. While that may have been true, I still felt proud of my placing. It was a long, long way from where I'd been when I'd started in the race three years ago.

The major form swings of almost all the successful riders were something you had to get used to racing in the "Generation EPO" era. If you look at racing today or even racing in the 1980s, a top rider is a top rider, all season long.

Sure, there were still fluctuations, and maybe some will be a bit better in April or July, but as a whole, if you are good, you stay. This was not the case in the 1990s. You could never compare yourself with a top rider aiming for the Tour de France in the month of March, as he wasn't really the same rider as he would be in July.

Of course, all riders have peaks and troughs in a season, but when EPO entered the equation, the peaks and troughs became as extreme as the Himalayas. When a guy was "on form" and was taking significant doses of EPO, his performance level would be incredibly high, untouchable by rivals not taking EPO.

But when guys stopped taking EPO, giving a body that was accustomed to being oversaturated with oxygen a rest, and were suddenly having to fight for every last breath, the backlash was immense. Guys who were outright race winners in March could be unrecognizable, stuck to the road and limping along in August, after they'd ended their EPO cycle.

With every year that these guys put themselves on this roller coaster, the peaks and troughs would get more and more severe. When doping controls became stricter later on, a lot of them could just never get their bodies to respond in the same way.

I was pretty damn chipper about how I rode in Semana, and my morale was quite high. A week later, I lined up for the infamous Vuelta al País Vasco. This was the first year that Team Santa Clara had been allowed into this race, but we'd heard the legends from all the others in the peloton.

It wasn't a race that riders rode as "preparation" for some other race. It wasn't a race that they went to, without EPO, looking to get a workout for some other race a few months later. No, it was a race done by guys who were ready to kill for the upcoming Spring Classics or the Giro d'Italia. The big-name riders were here to win. It was a whole level up from what I had just, finally, got used to.

From the first stage, I was struggling to hang on. My whole team was in the same boat. Every day we'd get dropped, one by one, and then fight our way back to smaller groups also struggling to the finish. I wasn't really racing, just surviving, but I found motivation in creating a little rivalry with two contemporaries of mine on the Motorola team, Kevin Livingston and Bobby Julich.

Kevin, my teammate at Junior World Championships and noted as one of the most talented climbers in the world, and Bobby, my old Colorado rival, had both been snapped up by Motorola. But here at País Vasco, they were just as fucked as Team Santa Clara.

Every day, I'd focus on being able to hang on just a bit longer than Kevin and Bobby. It was a race, in my head, to win the Best American in the Vuelta al País Vasco classification—a race of three people. The winner would end up somewhere in the one hundreds in the real results, but no matter, it was still "best American." This was all quite ridiculous, and I knew it, but I needed something to motivate me.

I was also taking pride in being the last of the Santa Clara team jettisoned from the peloton every day. Along with the internal cage match I had going on with Bobby and Kevin, I also was fighting to be the best of the worst team in the peloton. The faster the pace, the thinner my team became.

On the hardest day of the race, right as we were all slowly getting cut from the herd, I heard a car honking behind me. It was our director waving at me to come talk. Was the man crazy? I was breathing as hard as an elephant in labor, trying desperately to cling on to the back of the peloton.

All my teammates had already been shelled, so why the hell was he bothering me, instead of trying to nurse them in to the finish? I dropped back to the car and listened.

"Jonathan, I'm sorry," he said, "but I need you to get dropped, and wait for your teammates."

Clearly, the man had lost his mind. I wasn't going to just let myself get cut adrift and wait for my teammates so that we could all miss the time cut and get sent home.

Exasperated, I said no. He implored me, and asked that I trust him. Finally, in protest, and because I felt guilty, I let the peloton go and started drifting back through the team cars. Soon, one of my teammates caught me, and then our director asked him to wait, too. We kept rolling along, until finally there were six Santa Clara riders. The director asked us to just keep a steady pace to the top of the climb, where he explained his plan.

"We're going to just let ourselves get dropped, but stay together. And then we are going to do a team time trial all the way to the finish."

This had to be the most embarrassing moment for a supposed "professional" cycling team. We had our entire team out the back, time-trialing by itself, just to be able to start the next day, not because of a crash or a flat tire befalling its leader, not because of an illness that hit the team. No, this was just because we stunk. It was humiliating.

It was an embarrassing tactic but at the same time it was unconventional and brilliant. It worked, too, as every day from then on, we'd wait for one another, allow ourselves to get dropped with the weakest rider, and then team time-trial our way right past many riders who had held on for grim death as they in turn exploded.

Every day, around ten kilometers before the finish line, our whole team would come steamrolling past the little group that Kevin and Bobby were in. It wasn't much, but I'm pretty sure I won "Best American" classification in the Vuelta al País Vasco that year—plus I salvaged the honor of not being at the rear of the field in triple digits on the results page, on a few lucky stages.

Nonetheless, we ended País Vasco exhausted, demoralized, and with our self-respect crushed. For all the pride I felt in finally having improved a little from the previous year, this race had slammed me back down on the ground. I wasn't going to keep struggling in every race, keep beating myself up, all to finish 103rd and get paid $1,500 a month.

For all the long talks with José Luis about being patient, and for all the times our team doctors talked about my big VO$_2$ max, big heart, and plentiful red cells, it just didn't matter anymore.

I simply wasn't good enough.

GOODFELLAS

We had about a month before we were going to participate in the Tour DuPont, which was the largest race in the USA, and the only one in the USA where professional teams from Europe would come over and compete. My parents were going to come and watch me compete, for the first time, at the international level. If there was one race I wanted to do well in all year, it was DuPont.

When the team doctor came into my room after País Vasco, seeing I was exhausted, seeing I was demoralized, and knowing that the one event I wanted to do well in was coming up, he and I had a long talk.

"Jonathan, the blood tests we got back for you show that you're tired from all the training and racing. Your body is used up and you cannot compete like this."

I knew this already. I was expecting him to repeat the usual mantra—"we know how hard you have worked, we know your talent, just be patient"—but this time, it didn't come.

This time he paused and looked at me, like a caring doctor would.

"I think we need to help your body recover and get healthy again for Tour DuPont."

I agreed.

"So, I would like to give you a small amount of testosterone and a few other things to help you regain your strength."

Although I had trouble imagining how José Luis had finally convinced himself that the pope was going to be okay with allowing this, I was also so very ready to finally hear it. The words came as a relief. A blessing.

I was finished getting slaughtered by a peloton that openly spoke of doping. I was done with training harder, smarter, and still getting killed. I was done with being told I was talented by team doctors and trainers, and then being laughed at and made fun of every single day in the peloton.

By this stage, I hated being told I was talented. If I couldn't actually ride as fast as these guys, what use was the talent? I was over it. I was done with being on the team that was the laughingstock of the peloton. I was done with the other riders calling us "monks" and "priests" due to our puritanical ways. And I wasn't going to lose my dream.

I didn't want to give that up over some moralistic stance. I wanted to live the dream I'd fought so hard for. The way I felt at that time, defeated and exhausted, a testosterone shot sounded wonderful to me.

Absolutely fucking wonderful.

The doctor told me that he would never give me a dose beyond my normal natural levels, that he was protecting my health by returning me to the way my body should be, that he was not hurting me.

"Don't worry, Jonathan," he said, "we are only going to do a very small amount, much less than the other teams. This isn't cheating—it's simply surviving. This is letting your talent finally be realized, nothing more."

It was a very compelling argument, and it soothed my conscience. And, for a brief moment, I almost believed him. But by this point, he didn't need to say anything to convince me that it was okay to dope. I had moved so far beyond that.

My sense of morals, ethics, and even of self had been steadily eroded, twisted, and darkened. My naivety, innocence, and conscience had turned black after so many years of being the laughingstock of the peloton. They laughed not only because I was slow, but because they knew exactly why they were fast, and didn't understand why anyone would continue to try and race against them without doing the same.

It was all made clear to me by a famous rider during Vuelta al País Vasco. Halfway up a steep climb in the middle of the race, right as I was truly starting to suffer, this rider sat up, took his hands off the handlebars, flexed his bicep, and yelled as loudly as he could.

"Viva la quimica!" he bellowed. *"Estoy tan fuerte o la quimica me ha hecho asi?! Ha! Viva la quimica!"*

"Long live chemistry! Am I really this strong or did the chemicals make me this way!?"

The entire peloton laughed and cheered—all except the Santa Clara team. We didn't laugh, because we were all breathing too hard to laugh. By this point, I was finished. I was done with being the doormat of guys like this.

Give me the damned chemicals, doctor—give me all of them.

PART 4

1997–2000

PART 4
1997–2009

CHAPTER 10

HELLO, EDGAR

In the end, the testosterone shot was a bit anticlimactic, compared to the drama that had built up in my head. I dropped my pants, the doctor gave me the shot, and I went to dinner. I kept waiting for some side effects—an endless boner or legs that felt like titanium. Just something. I wanted some damned side effects. Losing your virginity isn't always a landmark event, I guess.

After País Vasco I returned home to Colorado for a few weeks, mixing rest and training. Just like always, the dog licked me and jumped around excitedly. Just like always, my mother made whatever I wanted for dinner. Just like always, Dad asked if I wanted to go do some motorpacing.

But unlike always, this time I was packing a bunch of needles, syringes, and "medicines" in my suitcase. My fear of getting caught with them was much smaller than my fear of not succeeding. That's how far I'd traveled.

As the doctor had hoped, I recovered from País Vasco and the rather intense spring racing program very quickly. I was able to start training quite hard again within a week. The Tour DuPont had been my focus all year long, and I was determined to show some of those guys who'd been laughing at me over in Spain that I could actually race, and that I was getting stronger.

At ten days long, DuPont was my longest ever professional race, with plenty of steep climbs as it meandered its way down the eastern coast of the States. Lance and the Motorola team were there in full force, with their best squad. He had won the Flèche Wallonne Classic a few weeks earlier and would clearly be the leader. Grand Tour winner Tony Rominger and his Mapei team guardians were also present, along with a very feisty and competitive Festina team.

My goal was to place in the top ten overall. This seemed like an absurd aspiration for a rider who had never been in the top fifty on GC—the General Classification—in any top-level professional race in Europe. However, I was now one of "them." I had injected a banned substance into my body. My confidence was chemically boosted and I felt that now that I was on an equal playing field with the competition, why wouldn't I be just as good as they were?

My newfound mind-set proved almost merited. In the two hardest mountain stages, I managed to climb in the front group of fifteen or so riders, which only included Lance, a few of his Motorola lieutenants, Rominger and his boys, and then a flock of Festina riders. A few of the bullies from Spain made the group every day, and then would comment to me after the race how impressed they were with how well I was riding. Hearing them say that was odd.

Of course, it felt good to hear a compliment from a peer, but it was worth more than that personally. I felt accepted. I'd fought for acceptance my whole life and usually had struggled to achieve it. I was always the person just outside the group of friends, trying to somehow join in, to somehow fit. I was always just a bit too awkward, a bit too shy, and a bit too stiff.

I had to gain my acceptance through accomplishment, or so I thought. If I was strong enough, successful enough, and famous enough, then I could force my way into the cool circles. This desire drove everything I did. Respect from my peloton peers, because I was racing at the front, made me feel something I'd been searching for my entire life: acceptance. Doping suddenly seemed the right choice.

Unfortunately, I caught a nasty cold during the last few days of the race. The doctor did everything he could to keep me racing.

And it worked to a degree. If I'd been this sick in a race in the past, I would have had to drop out, but I was able to get out there and compete, despite hacking up a lung every day. I finished sixteenth overall, by far my best result ever in pro racing, even if it wasn't the top-ten finish that I craved.

I returned to Europe confident and content. We raced Volta a Catalunya in June, watching many top riders finalize their preparations for the Tour de France. At this level, right before the Tour, I was a bit further away from the top riders than I was at DuPont.

After the hardest mountain stage, the team doctor came into my room. He was supportive and kind as ever, telling me how I was going to be a champion one day. He'd cheered me up through my illness in DuPont. We'd chat about what was going on, about my ex-girlfriend, about the difficulties of living this strange nomadic life.

He sat down on my bed next to me and said he wanted to talk about starting to prepare for the Vuelta a España. The Vuelta had moved to September, so for our team it was the grand finale of the season. He told me how proud he was of all the improvements that I'd made and how I was becoming a better rider with each passing race.

Then he pulled out a stack of papers. They were my blood test results from the past two years. He showed me that with the combination of hard racing and training, my red blood cell count, and my infamous *hemogolobina* were slowly dropping as I became more fatigued.

I'd been told for the previous two years that my extra-high *hemogolobina* was my secret weapon, my ticket to winning a big race, and I was bemused to hear it was falling away because I'd been training hard. The doctor explained that this was quite normal, and that I shouldn't worry too much. That said, he wanted to discuss with me a way for us to make sure that my red cell count was what it would normally be, if I were well rested, by the start of the Vuelta.

"Of course, we will not be cheating or anything like that," he said, "just making sure your body is functioning within the parameters that it normally would be." I'd heard this whole song and dance before, and I knew exactly what he was suggesting.

It was time to dark-dope, to really be competitive. It was time for EPO.

By this point, my moral compass was directionless. I knew EPO was getting in even deeper—doping in the worst sense—but my sense of right and wrong had been worn down to the point that it was, yet again, just a sense of relief to finally be offered such a simple solution.

I would have given anything to regain the pride I'd once held as a real bike racer, anything to regain the joy of actually racing, to be the scrappy kid fighting for a first victory.

I wanted to be the kid who had won so many races back in the USA, the kid who everyone talked about as being super talented, the kid who doctors swooned over after seeing his test results. I wanted to be focused and purposeful, not constantly angry and resentful. And I could now see very clearly how all of that was possible. EPO could give that back to me.

Injecting EPO was quite anticlimactic, too, compared to even a B-12 shot. It was just a tiny little needle under your skin, not some massive needle in your ass. I could do it myself with zero fear. It didn't hurt at all. Just a little pinprick.

The doctor told me I wouldn't really feel any performance effects for a few weeks, that we were going to monitor everything and make sure I didn't surpass my natural rested level of red blood cells. We started out by using 1,000 IU of EPO every third day. I would later learn this was a miniscule dose, but to me it felt like I was pouring jet fuel into my tank. I think the doctor wanted to avoid giving that impression, which was (relatively) very responsible of him.

Just like he said, the effect wasn't very noticeable for two or three weeks, but then there came a point where almost imperceptibly, I was riding just a little faster in every training ride. The SRM power measurements didn't lie, either, and my power up any long climb was slowly increasing. It didn't feel like a magic bullet in training, just something that made you feel like you could train a little bit harder every day.

My first race after using EPO was the Vuelta a Burgos. I was excited to give my new engine a try, to finally see what it was like to be one of the battle-hardened professionals of the peloton.

Each day I was just a bit less fatigued than usual, and I was able to stay in the front group on all the early stages. Stage four finished up with the famed climb to Lagunas de Neila and was likely to determine the outcome of the race. I had real ambition at the start that day.

We would be out on the plains of northern Spain for nearly two hundred kilometers, and it seemed like it might be a bit windy. This would usually be a disaster for me, as I rode poorly in crosswinds, but now I felt ready for battle. Ready for anything, in fact.

The crosswinds hit around fifty kilometers from the finish and, in the ensuing chaos, the peloton fell to pieces. Normally I would have been 150 riders back, drifting in and out of the following cars, using anyone and any vehicle I could find for a draft to keep me close to the peloton for long enough to ensure that I didn't miss the time cut.

But today I was up front, with the first thirty to forty riders, bumping handlebars, throwing elbows, and not backing off for anyone. Miguel Induráin was right next to me, as were his teammates guarding him. The ONCE team was ripping the race up, as they so often did in this era, but I was staying with them, fearless and confident. EPO worked so much better than all of the other garbage combined.

The difference in how I was viewing the race was a stark contrast to how I'd seen every other race for the last three years. I had my ambition again. I had competitive fire again. I felt happy again.

Unfortunately, around three or four kilometers before the base of the final climb, I punctured, and with the peloton scattered along the road, the support car was quite a way behind. By the time I got a wheel change, the race was long since gone. I was bummed to have missed an opportunity to finally get to race up a hill, but all the same I felt something different that day.

It was the first day I thought: *I think I can make it as a professional cyclist.* It was the first day that my thoughts didn't drift between continuing racing and finally calling time and dedicating myself to university life back in Colorado.

Maybe one day I can win a big one, a proper race, I thought. My dream was back.

The team continued to get ready for the Vuelta a España and I continued taking EPO. I was excited about my first Grand Tour and excited about a second chance at showing the peloton how fast I could climb.

However, most of the team had not been paid in some time. While the riders were focused on performing in the Vuelta so they could get new contracts with other teams, the staff wasn't so excited about not getting paid, and one by one they started leaving for other jobs or other teams.

I would call José Luis, as a friend, and ask him about what was going on. In his usual calm way, he would ask me to have faith in him, as he had had faith in me for the last few years. I owed him that, but he would never really give me an explanation as to what was going on. He kept his cards close to his chest. Something was definitely afoot, however, and we rarely saw José Luis at the races anymore.

The other issue was the doping plan. While I felt quite energized by the whole experience, some of the guys who had friends on other teams did not. They said our regimen of 1,000 IUs of EPO every third day was absurd, and that most of the other teams were using 4,000 IUs every third day.

The consensus among the riders and directors was that, okay, we were doping, but that we weren't doping enough. There were two obstacles to that changing anytime soon. First, our doctor felt it was irresponsible and dangerous to use such high doses, and second, the team couldn't actually afford to buy any more EPO. At this point, the team was totally lacking funding—it was questionable if we were going to be able to buy gas for the team cars, let alone EPO.

José Luis came to our pre-Vuelta training camp to reassure us that we'd all get paid. Nonetheless, the team was in a sad state at the start of the Vuelta. The few bikes we had were more than a year old, with old chains and cables still being used to the point of being threadbare. The team truck kept breaking down and my seat post had somehow rusted into place, so I was unable to raise or lower my saddle anymore.

We were running rusty, squeaky, and bare. The staff that had remained loyal were frustrated and scared of what the future held. The riders who were there were keen to race, not for José Luis or Santa Clara, but instead to find new teams.

Ironically—or maybe not, given the level of desperation—the team was riding better than we ever had. Despite the grumblings of "not enough doping" and having bikes with rusty, worn-out chains, we were riding quickly. It's one of the odd and immutable rules of cycling: there's never a team that rides better than one that's about to go bankrupt.

In this case, however, bankruptcy hit faster that any of us expected. On the opening day of the Vuelta, we were informed that the team's financial backer had been detained by Spanish customs. The details were vague, but the seemingly persistent rumor was that he'd returned from Venezuela with some twenty kilograms of cocaine stuffed in his suitcase. Half of our vehicles and equipment were repossessed from the parking lot and José Luis was nowhere to be found. I'm sure he didn't know drugs were the source of our funding, either. No one knew if we'd be able to start the Vuelta.

Almost immediately, my morale went from sky high to bottom of the barrel. I called the airline, made a plane reservation, and packed up my stuff. I had no interest in the Vuelta, in my cocaine-funded team, in Spain, in cycling. I was a broken man once again. Despite all my training, all my sacrifice, and now all my doping, it just wasn't meant to be. I was out on the next flight home.

So I was reeled back into agonizing over my future in this insane sport. Every professional cyclist suffers self-doubt and goes through many a moment wondering if they should continue. Even riders who have won the Tour de France can tell you a few stories about the day they almost hung up the bike and never touched it again. But it seemed like I was hitting this wall each and every year, no matter how many ethical or moral compromises I made. I was exhausted and tired of contemplating quitting.

While it seemed like the easy road and hurt my pride, one option that had been kicking around my head ever since I'd won Tour of the Gila was to race for a domestic U.S. professional team. It was something I could do and go to school at the same time, something Mom and Dad would like. It'd be sort of like a high-paying part-time job.

It was an appealing prospect. Make some money, not train as hard, do easier races, and forget about doping.

It wasn't the dream I'd had at all, it wasn't racing with the most talented riders in the world, it wasn't challenging, but I guess it would allow me to buy a nice car and rent a cool apartment. That was the upside. So it felt nice and comfortable, but very hollow.

During the autumn of 1996, news broke that Lance Armstrong had very severe testicular cancer, requiring surgery and chemotherapy. It was quite a shock to everyone in cycling. In public, everyone wished Lance well, yet behind closed doors there was quite a different conversation.

Many in professional cycling instantly had the same thought.

"Was it the doping? Am I going to get cancer, too?"

I was scared—very scared—and I wasn't alone in feeling that way. I remember many long phone calls that autumn with old teammates and others in cycling, all of whom were a little freaked out. Of course, we all tried to persuade ourselves that clearly, Lance had overdone his doping, and that was the reason that he would get cancer and the rest of us wouldn't.

But it was enough of a shock to make me reevaluate my ambitions of being a top rider in Europe. I had been glad to take as much dope as the doctor would give me, and I was lucky the doctor kept me from giving myself cancer. I figured it was maybe a sign, time to cut that crap out, and to not kill myself. Time to come back home, go to school, do some easier races, and enjoy life a bit.

I signed up for a new American pro team called Comptel–Colorado Cyclist, run by a rather odd man named John Wordin. I was going to be paid twice what I was making at Santa Clara for doing races that were half the length and a quarter the difficulty. While that sounded good, it still felt a bit like giving up. I was re-signing myself to racing in the minor leagues.

I spent the fall studying and doing a bit of training. I'd given the SRM a rest, and I'd given the training techniques of van Diemen a rest, too. I just didn't care enough to put my body through all of that again. I rode mountain bikes that winter, did some skiing, and began to enjoy riding bikes once again.

The team met up for the first time outside Visalia, California, for a series of races and some training. In spirit, it was as far as you could possibly get from a European team training camp. No overcooked pasta, no gray hotels, no guys starving themselves, no doctors with needles, no two-hundred-kilometer death marches. Instead, we stayed in little log cabins and ate hamburgers and baked beans for dinner each night.

All of the riders had outside hobbies and interests, and were racing bikes because they loved it, rather than because it was a way out of having to work in a salt mine in Siberia. Dinner conversation was intelligent, training rides were playful, and the races were actually fun. While it would seem my dream of being a top professional rider in Europe was lost, at least I wasn't the beaten and jaded guy begging for more doping that I had been just a year before.

We raced well, too. From the start of the season onward, we were winning most of the biggest races. In some events, like the Redlands Cycling Classic, I was able to knock heads with a few genuine European professionals on the new upstart team, U.S. Postal Service.

We stayed at people's houses instead of hotels, and we all chipped in cooking dinner each night. As opposed to the militaristic mindset of a European team, it was more like an extended road trip with a bunch of your best friends. We ate ice cream, we raced bikes, and we won—a lot.

By the middle of the year, I had won the National Race Calendar series, which made me very proud as I was now ranked the best rider in the USA. Because of that, I was almost certain to be allocated a spot to represent the United States at the World Championships. This was quite an honor, yet despite my success on the U.S. scene, I knew I would be useless pack fodder at a race like the World Championships.

That was unless, of course, I chose to dope once again. I struggled with the idea, thinking about Lance's battle with cancer and pondering if doping had caused it. I'd already crossed the line and I knew that if I performed well at Worlds, it would be my ticket back into the big leagues. A top performance could get me a contract offer from a real European team, not the ramshackle, knockabout mess I'd just been a part of. I also knew that the U.S. Postal Service would need a few more Americans on its team in order to keep the sponsor happy.

This window of opportunity revived the dream once more, as well as my inner warrior. It was my chance to get away from the dead-end minor leagues, and get back toward Tour de France–level racing. I had enjoyed my time back in the U.S. Racing without pressure and winning races was a lot of fun, but it wasn't what made me get up in the morning.

I was pretty sure Wordin wasn't going to give me a new contract. I knew, too, that it would be unrealistic for me to perform well in the road race at the Worlds, as I wouldn't have done any races that long all season, and no matter how much EPO I took, I wasn't going to be competitive with guys coming off the Tour or Vuelta.

But the time trial was different. I could train for that in Colorado, do the shorter U.S. races and be reasonably competitive. I started to see the World Championships time trial as my last chance.

I contacted my old team doctor from Santa Clara, and asked if he'd be willing to help out. He set about designing a medical program to prepare me for the World Championships. First though, I'd need to meet up with him in Spain to pick up the supplies, and that needed to happen well in advance, as the week before the Worlds wouldn't be a long enough lead time for EPO to take effect.

Comptel had decided to do a block of European racing earlier in the year, so we arranged to meet at the Madrid airport. The doctor was carrying a cardboard box full of syringes, EPO, testosterone, and hCG. I didn't have room for all of this stuff in my luggage, so I just had to check the box at the gate.

I was meeting my teammates a few hours later in Brussels, and the thought of the thin cardboard box exploding from some rough baggage handling, syringes falling all over the baggage claim belt in front of my teammates, did worry me a bit.

Luckily that didn't happen, and for two weeks I toted the cardboard box around Europe, telling my teammates that it was simply "vitamins." The trip back to the U.S. was a bit worrying, as well, as I wondered exactly what would happen if U.S. customs decided to open up the box. But I had learned to numb myself to these concerns. It was just part of the business of being a bike racer.

The doctor had given me a more aggressive program than at Santa Clara. He was now working for a different team, and saw how most of his peers in pro racing functioned. The thoughtful and careful morality of José Luis was gone, and just like the riders, he was expected to produce results.

My build-up to the World Championships required me to be very precise with my dosing, my timing, and my knowledge of how the drugs worked. The doctor wasn't going to be with me in Colorado, and could only note down for me what he thought the program should be and trust me to do it correctly.

I'd read the stories about how riders in the early 1990s had died from cardiac arrest after taking too much EPO, so briefly wondered if unsupervised tinkering like this was how that had happened. I quickly pushed such thoughts out of my mind. I had got good at doing that.

Anyway, you had to take proper risks every time you did a bike race. Wet corners in the mountains, drafting cars in the caravan, training in open traffic, bashing elbows in crosswinds. People died in this game—it was part of its compelling appeal.

So I followed the doctor's instructions closely. The one issue I had was that it wasn't quite as simple getting blood tests in the U.S. as it was in Europe, which meant that my red cell count was a little unmonitored for most of my build-up. I finally did get an appointment to get tested just a few days before I flew over to Europe for the Worlds. The results were scary.

Apparently, the 2,000 IU of EPO twice a week was too much for my body, and I'd been cranking out red cells like a Ford factory. My hematocrit was at 54 percent and my famed hemoglobin at over 18 g/dl. Given that the UCI had recently implemented the 50 percent limit on hematocrit, if I were to be tested before Worlds, I wouldn't be allowed to race.

I called the doctor. He told me to stop taking EPO and that I needed to stay very hydrated, not only by drinking water, but by eating plenty of salt, too. So, for the week before the World Championships, I was constantly drinking water, peeing three times a night and pouring salt over everything from breakfast cereal to slices of smoked ham.

I also let the Team USA doctor know that I might have an issue. He remembered my blood tests from all those years ago at the Olympic Training Center, and recalled that I had a high red cell count. Somehow, he trusted that it was not suspicious on my part. Maybe I sounded convincing, or maybe he was just naive.

"If the UCI come knocking, I'll give you a saline IV drip," he assured me.

That would lower my hematocrit enough to pass a UCI test. It was enough to let me sleep again.

When the day of the time trial came, I was ready.

I don't think anyone inside the Team USA camp expected me to finish in the top fifty. They thought it was cute that I'd done well in the little races in the U.S., but didn't think I was going to do much now that I was up against the big boys. I needed to prove them wrong.

I started my time trial effort very fast, maybe a bit too fast for the full fifty kilometers, but I needed to be bold if I was to get the attention of a European team or the new U.S. Postal Service outfit. Plus my anger was back with a vengeance.

As I raced, all the memories of being made fun of inside the peloton, all the times other riders laughed at me, all the people who doubted me, came flooding back into my mind. Today was going to be the day I silenced them. At the midway time check I was the fastest of the early starters, in seventh place, by the time all the favorites had come through. This shocked all of those watching.

That little turd of a bike rider from that crappy Santa Clara team was putting up one of the fastest times at the World Championships?

Eyebrows were raised, but so, as I had hoped, was interest. I faltered a little in the waning kilometers, but in the final standings I had finished twelfth at the World Championships. I was the twelfth best time trialist in the world.

The head sports director from U.S. Postal Service, Johnny Weltz, came over and shook my hand. He said they would be happy to have me on the team, and that he would contact the management immediately about finalizing a contract.

I'd sold my soul to doping once again, but it didn't matter to me then. I'd found a way back into the show.

CHAPTER 11

GOING POSTAL

The U.S. Postal Service cycling team, vintage 1998, was hardly a world-crushing powerhouse. It was one of the smallest and least-funded teams, desperate for a spot in the Tour de France. In 1997, the results the team had been most proud of were fifteenth place overall by Jean-Cyril Robin in the Tour, a stage win by Adriano Baffi in Paris–Nice, and a few days in the leader's jersey from Viatcheslav Ekimov at the Dauphiné Libéré. Postal was trying to fill a big hole with limited resources.

Of course, in order to fill the Motorola hole, you needed an American champion hitting the heights, not French or Russian guys getting your results. That is why, in the winter between 1997 and 1998, the team signed Lance Armstrong.

There's no doubting that this was seen as a massive risk on their part, as Lance was still recovering from an almost fatal bout of cancer. He had been left for dead by his old team, Cofidis, and written off by the rest of the cycling world. It reflected how ruthless cycling could be that he was seen as damaged goods, plus an uncomfortable reminder to many in cycling that the risks of this new era of hormone-based doping could be life-threatening.

Years later, in my sworn affidavit in 2012 as part of the USADA investigation, I recalled how Lance had told me that the UCI should have detected a high level of hCG in his doping controls, but had failed to do so. Effectively (in his eyes, at least), the UCI was at fault for the extent of his cancer.

"If I ever have a doping problem I have this card to play," he told me.

Even so, USPS took what was seen by many as a leap of faith. Perhaps it was a publicity based move on their part, trying to draw on the goodwill Lance had received surrounding his comeback. His story had drawn more press coverage in the U.S. media than any other cycling story ever had, including Greg LeMond's three Tour wins. Now Lance and I were set to be teammates for the 1998 season—two "leftover" Americans on a brand-new American team.

After the World Championships, I'd spent excited off-season hours in contact with the USPS staff and directors throughout the winter. Clothing sizes, new bikes, training programs—it all seemed so organized and smooth compared to what I'd been used to. There were people taking care of every last detail, something we never had the luxury of on Santa Clara. By today's lavish standards, the USPS infrastructure was the equivalent of a garage start-up, but by 1998 standards it was the lap of luxury.

Our first training camp was in exotic Ramona, California, in a small motel base next to a Sizzler steakhouse. On my flight out, I struck up a conversation with an absolutely gorgeous flight attendant in transit. Thinking I was really something special as a new member of the USPS cycling team, I must have been exuding confident pheromones, as she gave me her phone number and we agreed to meet up after training camp was done. I could not have been more pleased with myself as I walked off the flight that day to be picked up by a staff member of the USPS team.

A cheery, chatty, and effusive Irish lady named Emma O'Reilly found me at baggage claim, and off we headed toward Ramona. She was an adventurer in the world herself and her wit and intelligence were immediately apparent.

I soon started asking her for romantic advice on how soon I should call this young lady that I'd just met on the flight. I didn't want to seem overly keen or desperate. She advised that I should wait a bit and remain cool. I'd never had a big sister to run such questions by so Emma began to play this role in my life. We talked incessantly on the one-hour drive north. It was a great start to camp: I'd made a new friend.

It felt great doing a training camp in the USA. Somehow it was lighter and cheerier than the training camps I'd done in Europe. The team language was English, but there were plenty of Spanish staff, which enabled me to keep up with my Spanish. It felt like I'd finally found the perfect home.

Yet from day one, there was a palpable competitive tension. This is fairly normal for January training camps on professional teams, as everyone is fresh and keen to prove themselves. It's also the start of an odd, almost Darwinian process of selecting who would be a leader on the team.

Of course, Ekimov and Robin were respected and seen as the guys we'd be working for during the year, but still, on a small team there was ample room for someone to come in and show themselves to be a leader as well. All of this usually leads to some very quick training rides in the first week of camp. No one backs down, no one says uncle.

Then, to really complicate the scenario, there was Lance. Lance was clearly the most alpha of alpha males, but, of course, he wasn't really quite sure of his form since recovering from cancer.

Would he still be the great champion that had burst onto the scene by winning the World Championships Road Race in 1993, or would he be a guy whose body never quite worked the same way again? No one knew the answer, including Lance.

He seemed insecure about his role in the team from day one, constantly pushing the pace on the training rides and questioning every decision that the management made. He clearly wanted to assert himself, to have instant respect. It was clear, too, and from the start, that he wanted to piss on Robin, although Ekimov shied away from this struggle for male dominance.

Our director, Johnny Weltz, did not sidestep Lance's need for domination, however. Things became tense very quickly between the two of them.

On one long training ride, we came to a literal and metaphorical fork in the road. Johnny had planned a ride that went left, but Lance had been poring over maps and decided that he'd rather we went right. Johnny instructed us to go left, but Lance wouldn't budge. He insisted on the opposite direction.

The entire group hesitated. Who were we supposed to follow? Who was really in charge?

Technically, the answer was Weltz, but Lance was making his stand on a desert road in southern California. He would either alienate himself from his new team, or he would become king. Time stood still as the tension among us all grew.

In the end, the team wasn't quite ready for a monarch just yet. Ekimov and Robin went left with Weltz, as did half the team. But in a sign of what was to come, Frankie Andreu and George Hincapie chose to remain loyal to their old boss, Lance, and went right.

In a moment that has perhaps defined the last twenty years of friendship with my then-roommate Christian Vande Velde, he, too, chose to follow Lance. I did not. On the road home, we could see the anger in Weltz's face. I'm sure Lance felt the same. The "Lord of the Flies" power struggle had begun. It would be that way for the rest of the year, until eventually, Lance took a firm hold on the conch.

As camp came to an end, we learned about our various race programs. Lance and his crew were to head to Ruta del Sol, while Christian and I were to remain Stateside for a while longer.

Meanwhile, I'd finally called Alisa Metcalf, the lovely lady I'd met on the flight to San Diego. Somehow, I convinced her to come and pick me up at the hotel in Ramona and take me to my next locale, in return for a nice sushi dinner. I guess I should have known she liked me back.

Alisa showed up in a tiny red Toyota Tercel, while also carrying a giant early version of a cell phone—it may have weighed twenty pounds—just in case I proved to be more dangerous than I appeared.

I wasn't sure if she was going to call the police with the phone or just bludgeon me over the head with it, if things went awry.

It took Christian and I quite a while to figure out how to stuff all my newly acquired USPS gear, bike bag, bike, bucket of protein powder, and suitcases into her poor little car. There's nothing like a glamorous first date, sitting on top of a suitcase in the front seat, neck crooked to the side, with all the windows open for valuable extra storage space. We looked like we just got evicted from our apartment and were driving to move in with Mom and Dad in Toledo.

Luckily, the date went much better than that. We feasted on sushi at a place called Japengo in San Diego, with me proudly picking up the tab. I was getting paid a pretty good wage and I quite enjoyed being able to spring for a fancy dinner with a beautiful woman.

Alisa was based in Tokyo, but her family lived in San Diego, so she was back and forth on flights all the time. I think she viewed our date as a one-off. Of course, she was right; it wasn't realistic, but I just took that as a challenge. I really liked Alisa.

The season started out strongly for me that year, winning Redlands and then heading over to Europe for Semana Catalana and Critérium International. The racing in Europe seemed a bit easier than when I left in 1996, and my old Spanish and Russian friends who had moved on to other teams agreed that the racing was considerably slower since the introduction of 50 percent hematocrit blood test.

When I'd left Europe, half the peloton was racing at close to 60 percent hematocrit, taking blood thinners to keep their blood from stopping mid-artery and provoking cardiac issues. I thought the 50 percent limit was great news for pretty much everyone. But quite a few in the peloton were not happy about it at all.

Many of the guys who would absolutely rip my legs off in 1996 seemed mere shadows of themselves now. Some of them were also having trouble controlling their hematocrit enough to stay below the 50 percent limit. It seemed every few weeks, someone was getting caught above the threshold, provoking an automatic two-week "health check" suspension from racing, courtesy of the UCI's doctors.

Hematocrit—the percentage of red cells in blood—can fall due to fewer red cells or dilution of the blood. A 50 percent hematocrit reading equates to 50 percent red cells, and 50 percent everything else (water, salt, white cells, albumin, alcohol). Hematocrit can be elevated because of more red cells or because of less water in the blood.

If you don't drink water for a few days, hematocrit goes up; in contrast, if you drink like a fish and dump a liter of saline in your vein, it goes down. Take EPO and, with time, they all go up. If you stop taking EPO, the reverse occurs. To be clear, a high hematocrit due to less water won't make you ride any faster, it just means you're dehydrated.

Hemoglobin is the little protein that red cells have inside them that carry oxygen. More red cells equate to more hemoglobin, normally, and increased red cells usually equates to higher hematocrit. Crucially, for a bike rider, all of these equate to higher speeds racing up hills.

The team doctor on USPS, Pedro Celaya, and the team's directors were all curious about exactly what I knew and didn't know about doping. Santa Clara had been known as the idealistic team trying to race clean, so once I moved to Postal, they were unsure if I'd had any exposure to doping.

Once I arrived in Europe, the topic immediately came to the forefront. My first blood test with USPS showed I was nudging the UCI limit, at around 50 percent hematocrit. I knew this was pretty normal for me coming from a long winter mainly spent at altitude, but for Pedro, it was not normal at all.

My natural hematocrit wasn't always over 50 percent, although it usually was when I was well rested and had been at altitude. However, with hard stage racing and months at sea level, it could drop as low as 46 percent. This was still much higher than most of my teammates, even when they were taking EPO.

At first, I think Pedro assumed I'd just been doping on my own.

When I explained to him that wasn't the case, he didn't believe me—I had to call my mother and have her fax over blood tests from when I was a child, showing that my hematocrit was always over 50 percent, from the age of two onward. He looked at all the values in more detail and finally, almost grudgingly, believed my story.

But, because of the UCI's 50 percent limit, he said I would not really be able to dope at all. Maybe I could take a little testosterone or growth hormone, but no EPO, as I was already so close to the threshold. This wasn't good news. You could take enough growth hormone and testosterone to kill an elephant and it wouldn't make you ride that much faster, but the impact of EPO was different, very different.

My natural level meant that even on EPO, due to the 50 percent limit, I wouldn't have much margin for improvement. Guys with a 40 percent hematocrit could take much higher doses of EPO, and thus improve their performance a lot. I hadn't really thought about a naturally high hematocrit as a disadvantage until that moment, but it was clear by the look on Pedro's face that this was a problem.

By this stage, cycling had become completely and totally obsessed with hematocrit. I had become totally obsessed with it, too. Among the riders, there were various theories of how it related to performance. Some liked to view it as an absolute measure, as in 48 percent was always better than 44, but that simplistic attitude was never based on much truth.

Every person has a red cell count, individual to them, that is almost like a fingerprint. So, while 44 percent in some people might equate to a dope-fueled raging-bull gas tank, in others it could be fatigued, slow, and almost anemic. It depended a lot on what your body was like and how your individual endocrine system was set up.

Others in cycling deviously looked at hematocrit as an absolute. Many coaches and talent scouts looked for riders that were racing fairly well in the amateur ranks, but had very low hematocrits. They knew that if they pulled them up to pro racing, they would get a bigger boost once they started taking EPO. That mind-set was, the bigger the margin below 50 percent, the better—the exact opposite of what Darwin was thinking.

It was a bitter irony. The widespread use of EPO and the introduction of the 50 percent limit ensured that the more naturally gifted you were, in terms of your hematocrit, the more at a disadvantage you became. I'd accrued SRM power data from many years, both doped and undoped. The difference EPO made to performance was crystal clear.

Those who had lower natural hematocrits could boost their levels in much greater amounts, percentage wise, than those with naturally high hematocrits. The math would always work in their favor, in comparison with someone with a higher natural hematocrit. It was a simple oxygen-carrying calculus.

I can't tell you, with certainty, if testosterone, cortisone, or growth hormone made me faster. But from a numerical standpoint, I can tell you that EPO definitely did, and I can tell you exactly how much faster. On thirty-minute test climbs, I could see the improvement clear as day on my SRM.

If, for example, your hematocrit went up from 46 percent to 50 percent after taking EPO for a month or so, it would correlate almost exactly to a four percent power increase during a thirty-minute, or maximum aerobic, effort. At elite level, a four percent improvement is a lot.

The increase in red cells meant more oxygen could be transported, meaning the muscles would stay well oxygenated and fueled beyond the point at which they would normally start to fatigue and fail. The lure of EPO wasn't based on an anecdotal story: it was down to math, pure and simple.

I needed to apply for a dispensation for naturally high hematocrit if I was ever going to be able to take any EPO. There were a few riders around—mainly Colombian riders or others from high altitude— who had these dispensations.

During the 1980s and prior to the growth of EPO use, Colombian riders had been the best climbers in the sport, but by 1998 there were very few that won much of anything. I wondered if it was because they were facing the same issue I was. Maybe, like me, their naturally high hematocrit left them with no room to "grow" their performance.

I submitted the dispensation application to the UCI and was summoned to Switzerland for additional testing to determine if indeed my hematocrit was high naturally, or if I'd just boosted it with EPO. While you couldn't suspend someone based on the finding of these screenings, you could refuse them a dispensation that allowed them to race at over 50 percent.

The UCI's hematocrit-testing machines were also notoriously unreliable, so a little miscalibration and bingo—a natural 47 percent hematocrit could easily read over 50 percent and get you suspended. Pedro was a very conservative doctor. He definitely didn't want to risk a positive test. He reminded me a little of Santa Clara's doctors.

Still, I needed the math to work a bit more in my favor. I needed a few more percentage points' margin in my direction, or that equation was always going to work against me. The irony of going to the anti-doping laboratories of the governing body of cycling in order to prove that my hematocrit was naturally high, so that I could then start doping and using EPO—well, that was pretty overwhelming.

After going through a few days of testing, my application was approved. I wouldn't be suspended unless my hematocrit surpassed 52 percent. It wasn't much, but it was enough to give me a bit of a margin. Now I could take some EPO and get back in the damned arms race. Just in time, too, as by this time the Tour de France was looming.

A week before that June's Dauphiné Libéré, Pedro and I sat down and went through all the procedures. Unlike on Santa Clara, on USPS the riders were responsible for keeping their EPO at the races. I bought a little Coleman thermos that I'd carry around, full of ice and EPO. Pedro showed me how to inject, thinking I'd never done it before.

I figured I'd just let him keep thinking that and didn't say much. But I was disappointed when, despite my new 52 percent dispensation, Pedro said I needed to take a very limited dose and never surpass 50 percent.

"We always want a margin of error," he told me. I grudgingly agreed.

I started building up for the Tour by building up my red cells. That year's Dauphiné was a mixed bag for me. The effects of the EPO hadn't really hit yet, as my exemption slip from the UCI didn't arrive until a week before the Dauphiné. Still, I finished seventh in the time trial and was reasonable in the mountains.

However, in the next race, in Germany, I could feel the effects starting to hit home. Lance was racing in Germany, too, and while he wasn't doing the Tour de France that year, he was determined to win. The tactics were pretty simple: on each and every hill, Lance would have me try and rip the peloton to pieces. I was having quite a good time riding on the front of the race, powering up the hills like a rabid dog chasing a bunny rabbit.

It felt wonderful making other people's legs hurt, as opposed to always being pounded on myself. The combination of taking EPO, while the rest of the peloton had to take a lot less than they were in 1996, was intoxicating for me. I could race, I could win, or help someone else win; I could attack, I could chase. I could do all the things I'd done as an amateur. I could feel like a bike racer. I could pretend to feel proud of myself.

Unfortunately, about halfway through the race in Germany, I went wide on a switchback and off the road for a split second. I didn't think much of it, as I hadn't really crashed, but I had brushed up against a fence or something as I flirted with disaster. I chased back up to the small lead group, Lance already yelling on the radio asking where the hell I was.

After a minute or two of resting at the back, I started the sprint up the side of the group to get up to the front. As I stood on the pedals, my foot felt wet and squishy. It was a dry day, so I couldn't understand why the hell my foot was wet. It didn't make any sense.

Then I looked down and almost passed out.

Blood was gushing out of my left lower leg. When I say gushing, I mean spraying like a garden hose. It was splattering all over my bike, my shoe, the road. As soon as the race doctor saw the wound, he stopped me, wrapped it as tight as he could and got an ambulance to the scene.

I was rushed to the hospital, where they determined I must have brushed up against razor or barbed wire at high speed. It looked like someone had tried to cut my leg in half with a straight blade. Bones, arteries, muscle, fascia, were all very visible.

The crash forced me to rest for a couple of weeks and ended my chances of going to the 1998 Tour de France, so I was sent back to Colorado to rest up and get ready for the Vuelta. To keep in shape, Christian, Lance, and I decided to race the Cascade Classic during the month of July.

I thought it would be fun to race back in the USA for a change and see some of my old friends from the year before. It was nice to be back home, but Cascade would be the first experience I'd ever had with my hematocrit plummeting after stopping EPO (and in this case losing some blood in a crash).

My hematocrit had dropped all the way to 44 percent, which was the lowest I'd ever seen it. It still wasn't that bad compared to most guys I raced with, but man, oh, man, it felt like I had no power at all. The combination of having extra red cells and getting used to it, and then having your hematocrit go down so quickly, was like riding with a flat tire.

I now understood why all the guys riding at 60 percent in 1996 rode like such garbage at 50 percent after blood tests were introduced, even though 50 percent was still more than they'd naturally achieve. It was urban legend in the peloton that there was nothing worse than a falling hematocrit, and wow, were they right. During Cascade, I sucked.

My performance aside, the week at Cascade proved an interesting one, as the race was scheduled right when the 1998 Festina affair doping scandal erupted at the Tour. Lance, Christian, and I were stunned by what we were seeing in the news. We called some friends in the race to find out what was really happening, but most of all we thanked God we weren't over there, competing in the Tour.

The scandal focused on Festina, the world's number one team. One of their soigneurs, Willy Voet, had been caught driving to the race start in Ireland with a trunk full of dope. After he'd been arrested it took a few days for the shit to fully hit the fan, but by the second week of the 1998 Tour, arrests, raids, and rider sit-downs dominated the news. The Tour was completely slammed by the French media. The race just about limped to Paris but the aftermath left everybody running scared.

Watching from the States, we were thankful that it wasn't our team getting caught up in the mess. But, of course, quite a few journalists were wondering what our opinion was of what was happening. Dan Osipow, then director of communications for USPS, asked if I would do a few interviews on the topic.

"JV, you're well spoken and grounded," Dan said. "Just tell these journalists the truth of the situation."

If he'd known what he was advising me to do, he would have shit himself. But I obliged and stayed on message, as it was now an integral part of the job to lie. I sat down with a reporter from *Outside* magazine and told him all about how Americans would never do such a thing as dope and how it was tragic for the sport to be put through such torture.

I felt like I was standing up for the reputation of the entire sport, and that I was doing the right thing by defending cycling, by pointing to other sports, by showing him we were good people. I thought I was being loyal. Perhaps all those things were true—I was comfortable doing interviews—but it was grim. I spent an hour bullshitting the guy, and I felt like a defender of our poisoned sport.

Lance, of course, won Cascade easily, starting his march toward the Vuelta a España. Unlike the Tour de France team, where things were a bit open on strategy and opportunity, the team that was going to compete in the Vuelta was all about Lance. We weren't going to be as strong as the Tour team, but we were primed to do everything we could to help him out.

Once I got back to Europe, Pedro was once again pretty hesitant to get me going on EPO. He felt that, even with my 52 percent dispensation, after the Festina scandal we needed to steer well clear of even a hint of doping.

But I wasn't riding great, either. Somehow the crash before the Tour (and perhaps the loss of blood) had really slowed my progress to a crawl. With Festina at the forefront of our minds, we didn't start taking EPO until the actual start of the Vuelta, meaning I didn't feel any effects until at least ten days into the race.

That made the first week miserable for me. I was struggling at the very back, just like during the bad old days of Santa Clara. Our director started calling me "the emissions tester," as I was spending so much time drafting the chase cars. It was embarrassing.

I wasn't much use in helping Lance, either, which was annoying to him, but then he'd never even considered trying to ride for a podium finish in a three-week race. He was there to get ready for the World Championships and to see about a stage win.

In fact, Pedro was playing it very conservatively with the whole team. He was clearly pretty rattled by the events of the Festina scandal, and vowed never to be a part of that sort of mess. I think his sources for supply of EPO were a bit scared, too.

Who could blame them? We were all scared. We'd been watching bike racers being dragged into prison throughout July. While my old Russian teammates found that sort of thing funny, and knew it was nothing compared to what a Russian prison would be like, for middle-class kids from the USA and a Spanish "doctor" trained in psychiatry, it was scary shit.

But I can tell you, the other teams could not have given a rat's ass about the Festina scandal. The race was faster than ever, right from stage one. Of a group of seventy-five riders, Lance was the only one on our team to make the front group. Ekimov, Robin, Christian, and I were all in the big *grupetto*.

Luckily, Pedro felt pity for me and started doling out EPO and growth hormone as the race progressed. He got a bit more comfortable with the fact he wasn't getting arrested—and in truth, cultural differences ensured that it was a much less stressful environment down in Spain than France.

By halfway through the race, I was going up the climbs quite quickly, or at least quickly enough to give Lance a water bottle here and there when no one else was around. Lance, too, got better and better as the race progressed, and by the last few days was perhaps the strongest rider in the race.

He wasn't going to win, but he showed a progression and capability for recovery and adaptation to an extreme workload that no one expected of a guy recently in remission. It was impressive. By the last week of the race, Lance clawed his way all the way to fourth overall.

One night in the last week of the Vuelta, I needed to borrow a laptop, as I didn't have one with me because I was trying to save a bit of space and weight in my suitcase. Lance obliged in letting me borrow his, but wanted to keep an eye on me while using it, so he made me come to his room.

I started typing out a few emails to folks back home who hadn't heard from me in a while. Lance was going through his bedtime routine, shaving his legs, brushing his teeth, and the like. While I was mid-sentence writing home, he popped out of the bathroom, pulled a vial of EPO from his thermos and filled a syringe with its contents.

I tried not to notice. He already knew I was doing the same thing, and vice-versa, but openly injecting in front of a teammate was a bit brash and not really done.

He jabbed himself while humming some Pearl Jam tune. He spat in the sink, finished with the syringe and turned to me.

"You're one of us now, JV," he said. "This is the boys' club—we all have dirt on each other, so don't go write a book about this shit or something."

I guess in some respects Lance now knew me better than I knew myself.

———————

After the Vuelta finished, USA Cycling called up and asked if I wanted to ride the World Road Championships in Holland. I felt totally exhausted, but I was still riding really fast, so I agreed to compete.

It was a new sensation to feel like utter crap every day, to not have enough energy to lift a spoon, yet to have the ability to really push hard on the pedals. The effects from the EPO program during the Vuelta were in full flow now, but even though my hematocrit was nowhere near 52 percent, Pedro was still stressed.

Lance and I were the two Americans riding in the time trial, but I really had no idea how I would fare. The U.S. team were all staying in a tiny little bed and breakfast in Valkenburg, one of those places where it felt like you were staying in someone's bedroom, and everyone watches TV together in the living room.

Lance's room was right off the living room, so when the TV didn't get shut off early enough in the evening, he'd open the door and yell at the under-twenty-three riders and junior riders to go to bed.

Early on the morning of the time trial, Pedro came rushing into my room in a giant trench coat, looking as bulky as a heavily pregnant woman. He pulled off the coat to reveal a huge bag of saline.

"Jonathan, quick—get this into your vein," he snapped. "The UCI are here! We need to get your hematocrit lower, quickly."

I did as he said. He duct-taped the bag of saline on the wall over my head and kept cussing and swearing in Spanish when it wouldn't stick to the wallpaper.

I was still a little bemused and bleary-eyed.

"How do you know they are here, Pedro?" I asked.

"How do I know . . . ?!" he said. "They're setting up all their testing equipment in the living room, that's how I know! Incredible!"

He stayed with me, peeking around the door now and then, until the bag was almost empty.

"Okay, now I must do Lance," he said breathlessly. "Good luck with the test, and remember, show them your other arm, not the one we just punctured." He rushed off.

I finished the saline and wandered out into the hall to get some breakfast before my blood test. As I sat down, I watched Pedro come back into the hotel with the same trench coat on, clearly hiding an enormous bag of saline solution under it.

By this time, the UCI doctors had all their testing equipment set up and were busy chatting over some chocolate croissants and coffee before they began their work. There was no other way for him to get to Lance's room, so he nervously walked right past the team of UCI doctors, saying "hello" and "good morning," a huge bag of saline drip under his coat, as he made his way to Lance's room.

After fifteen minutes or so, Lance emerged from his room, with no Pedro, and casually asked the UCI medics when they were going to test him.

"Oh, right now is fine, if you want?" said the doctor.

Lance agreed, and he sat down to get his blood drawn. All this time Pedro was stuck in the tiny room with Lance's wife, waiting for the coast to clear, in order to come out and get rid of all the "trash."

After the UCI had left, we laughed our heads off at the situation. Pedro was a bit annoyed with us finding it so funny. Lance and I went on to finish fourth and seventh in the time trial, respectively. I was ecstatic, Lance less so.

Much has been written about the UCI being complicit, of deals being made to cover up tests or of them turning a blind eye. I can't say I ever saw any of that myself, but I can say that many times I saw doping occurring right under their noses. So I'm not sure there was quite as much behind-the-scenes collusion going on as people would like to think, but there sure was a hell of a lot of incompetence.

CHAPTER 12

THE PUPPET SHOW

All throughout that 1998 Vuelta, Lance had been complaining about Pedro and Johnny. Johnny's free-form management style didn't jibe with Lance's militaristic approach.

Pedro's problem, though, was different. What Lance didn't like about Pedro was that he wasn't aggressive enough with doping.

Pedro didn't really like being the guy that handled the doping part of the operation, but he did it anyway. Lance wanted a guy who would bring the team to the next level, who wouldn't take such a chickenshit approach to doping, and would make sure guys were always ready to race.

You could feel the entire atmosphere of the team change after Lance got fourth overall in that year's Vuelta. Now the U.S. Postal Service team management and sponsors had a Grand Tour contender with an incredible backstory of a cancer comeback to tell. Lance knew they loved it all, knew the leverage he had, and he used it to take full control of the team. Pedro and Johnny were soon gone. Being the little underdog American team that tried its very best was gone. The new era of USPS—the Lance Armstrong era—had begun.

So as the 1999 season began, the energy had shifted within the team. We also had a new head sports director—the same guy who finished dead last with me in my first bike race—former Belgian pro, Johan Bruyneel.

As a rider, Bruyneel had forged a reputation for being very intelligent. He was completely different from Johnny in terms of organization and analytics. The team's new medical support was led by Luis García del Moral, who definitely had a different feel to him than Pedro.

There was no longer any beating around the bush regarding doping. It was planned out on spreadsheets at the camp in January and it was anything but conservative. Del Moral had the raspy voice of a man who'd smoked two packs a day for most of his life. His skin was leathery and he wore glasses with a greasy tint to them. To me he had the look of a Tarantino character.

I can't say I liked Johan or del Moral as much as I had Johnny and Pedro, but by this point in my career, the team you picked wasn't about liking someone. It was about getting results, winning races, and making money.

To be honest, I'm not sure if I even liked riding my bike anymore, but it paid well, and I was finally good at it. I'd bought my first house, had a mortgage, a few bills, and some responsibility. I knew, too, that there were only so many years left in my career as a professional rider, and that it was time to start making hay and saving some dough for a rainy day. I told myself to turn a blind eye, and not to worry about strange new doctors coming on to the team.

There were no disputes about which way to go on training rides anymore, just alpha-male chest beating and pace pushing. This was now Lance's team, and everyone knew it. The rules were simple, largely because there was only one of them: Do Not Fuck with the King. Do as you're told, and don't ask questions.

My season started out a little underwhelming, as I'd probably taken a bit too much time off after riding the Vuelta the previous autumn. Christian won Redlands, and I'd helped out a bit in getting that done, while winning a stage myself.

Beyond that though, I was somewhat unenthusiastically trudging through the spring races. Although my doping program hadn't been scheduled to begin yet, it was still possible to cling on to the peloton without doping, thanks to the introduction of the speed-inhibiting hematocrit limit. I wasn't too concerned: I knew I'd go faster later on.

After Liège–Bastogne–Liège in Belgium, I headed back to Colorado for a brief break before starting into the May and June races. I'd been dating a woman over the winter, and we'd started to get serious as the race season started. I liked her very much, but after getting home, she sat me down for the dreaded "talk."

She wasn't dealing well with me being away all the time and didn't really feel like it was much of a relationship. Once again, I fell victim to the demands of my job. I got dumped. I took it hard, and whenever I get like that I stop eating very much.

Back in Europe, it was time to chat with del Moral about doping for the races ahead. He was much less squeamish than Pedro about running things close to the limit. He also didn't really understand how quickly and strongly my bone marrow would start shooting out new red bloods cells. I think he was more used to guys who'd burned out their system "back in the '60s," as we used to say. We came up with a plan of how to "prepare" for the Dauphiné Libéré, as it was then known, and the Tour. The only missing element was exactly how he was going to get the EPO to me.

Due to the 1998 Tour's doping scandal, everyone racing in 1999 was a bit on edge. Traveling with EPO in your suitcase or sending EPO in the mail, like we used to do back in the old days, was no longer a safe option. Instead, del Moral had to drive the EPO up to me and make the handover somewhere no one would suspect.

Luckily, he was on his way up to Nice, in the south of France, to make a delivery to some other guys on the team, and Girona was on his route north. We agreed to meet at the parking area after the highway toll station, as he didn't want to drive into town and didn't want to be seen. I didn't have a car in Spain, so I had to ride my bike over to the tollbooth. Neither did I want to be seen wearing a USPS uniform, or be identifiable as a pro bike rider for such an auspicious event, so I rode over in street clothes and flip-flops.

I hung around for a few minutes and then del Moral pulled up in a white car, unmarked and with no team logos. He hurriedly started digging through a large cooler in the trunk, crammed with goodies. As I stood and watched, my curiosity got the better of me and I started digging around, too.

"What's all this stuff?" I asked. "Who's getting this?"

He slapped my hand away.

"It's not for you!" he snapped.

Damn, I thought. *I guess all the special stuff goes up to Nice.*

He handed me my EPO, some B12, and a wad of syringes, and then said he needed to get going. It had started raining, and I wanted to get out of the wet as quickly as possible, too, so I stuffed all my rocket fuel in my backpack and rode off back to town. Once back into Girona, the real farce began.

As I stopped at a red light, just a few blocks from my house, the flip-flops I was wearing slipped on the greasy wet road, and I fell off my bike at the intersection. As I fell, the backpack popped open and syringes and vials of EPO went rolling all over the crossing.

I scrambled to my feet and frantically started picking up all my gear. As it turns out, EPO vials really can roll quite some distance on wet asphalt, but luckily a kind old lady walking home from the supermarket stopped and helped me pick up all my drugs off the street. I thanked her profusely and rode off. It was a banner moment in my life, no doubt.

Del Moral had told me we would boost our hematocrit while at home in Spain, but that we'd never take anything to races in France as, in the post-Festina climate of suspicion and fear, it was just too risky. It was a bit of a tricky doping strategy, as it required going into races really hot, and then waiting for the blood cell count to slowly drift down a bit.

I voiced my concerns about this.

"There are ways to lower your hematocrit with a few minutes' notice," he told me, cryptically.

"Ways?" I asked him. "What ways?"

He told me to keep quiet. Again.

I showed up to the start of the Dauphiné well trained, light-weight (a post-breakup-starved weight of 130 pounds) and with my hematocrit hovering around 51 percent. Del Moral would fire up a massive and noisy blood centrifuge every morning to check our blood. He'd scribble the outcome down on a scrap piece of paper, and then go around telling everyone their results.

You could always glimpse the other riders' results on the scrap of paper, so you always knew exactly what everyone was up to. For the Dauphiné, I was definitely winning the team classification when it came to hematocrit. I was as ready as I'd ever been for a bike race. Lance won the prologue, with the rest of the team all pretty much finishing in the top thirty.

No longer was this a team stumbling its way through the Vuelta like the year before—we were the best team in the race. We defended Lance's leader's jersey fairly easily on stage one, but stage two became a bit trickier, as it climaxed with a sharp hill climb. There were numerous attempts at getting a big breakaway group established, although Lance was pretty relaxed about it all, as he was focused on the Tour de France, not the Dauphiné. I ended up getting in one of the big groups, which became the one that rolled away for the remainder of the day.

In a big breakaway, the group is constantly accelerating and decelerating, and breaking apart. It's never smooth, like it might look on TV, but instead a constant fight and sprint, as rivals try and take advantage of each other's efforts.

It's like riding in a giant Slinky that gets stretched and stretched before violently snapping back into shape. The new, skinnier me didn't have much snap at all to hold the wheel when those whiplash moments came, so instead, I tried to remain in the front half of the breakaway and conserve energy.

Unfortunately, on TV this looked like I was pulling the break along and trying to flick my own team leader, King Lance. This definitely wasn't the case, but at the end of the day, after Lance lost the overall lead, Alexandre Vinokourov had won, and I finished fourth. Johan was not happy with me.

Not at all.

After the race, when we got back to the hotel, Johan came to see me during my massage. He told me that what I had done was shitty and wrong. I tried to explain my perspective, but it just came off as an excuse. There was only one way to redeem myself with Johan and Lance, and that would be to take the race lead back the next day in the twenty-two-kilometer uphill time trial to the summit of the notorious Mont Ventoux.

Until this point, there had been nothing really in my career that would indicate I'd be able to win such a brutal and prestigious uphill time trial against a world-class field. Sure, I'd done well in some time trials and some mountain stages here and there, but I'd never achieved a win of this stature. But things were different now.

I wasn't riding on a poor little team trying to be clean or with a doctor that was scared of his own shadow. I was now on a team that had a very aggressive doctor, and I knew that for the first time in my career, I was truly on the program, with many of the other big names in the race. But the rift with Bruyneel and Lance bothered me.

I called my mom the night before the Ventoux stage, upset that I'd caused such issues inside the team. As we talked, her competitive side came out.

"Don't worry about them," she told me. "You go win up that mountain, and there will be no more questions." It was what I needed to hear.

I woke on the morning of the Ventoux stage ready for battle, and also relieved that the UCI blood testers hadn't shown up, because I was even more on the limit than I had been on the first day of the race. My focus was now hardened, my back was against the wall with the team, and I'd firmly staked everything, from my health to my honor, on being a successful bike racer. Now I needed to win.

I rolled off the start ramp under the plane trees in Bédoin and set off up the mountain with adrenaline killing all the pain for the first few minutes. My mind was quiet, entirely centered on one thing and one thing only. There was no sports director in a car behind me; Johan didn't see the value in that after my treachery of the day before. Which was fine by me. It was quiet and peaceful.

My body craved hitting its athletic ceiling. The feeling wasn't one of comfort, but one of accepting the intense suffering necessary to ride so fast, of using the pain to further drive my focus. I'd re-moved the water bottle cage from my bike at the last minute, instead choosing to down a full bottle right before the start. One of the mechanics, confused, asked why I'd done that, considering that Ventoux was such a long and hot climb.

"I'll be breathing too hard to be able to take a drink," I told him. And I was right.

This is what I was best at, turning my mind off and digging, going well beyond what my body was normally capable of. I was a master of pacing, too, able to mete out my energy in a precise way, so there would be absolutely nothing left of me at the finish. I counted down the kilometers, then the minutes, and once in the final kilometers, the seconds until this Zen-induced hell would finally end.

As I entered the final kilometer of the climb to the top of the Ventoux, I could hear the mechanic assigned to follow me—not really that much of a fan of Johan—yelling at the top of his lungs that I was going to win. I didn't dare think about that, as I was about to collapse. There was no energy—nothing—left, but with eight hundred meters of climbing still to go, I kept my legs turning.

It was just sheer will that kept me upright and that kept me moving toward the finish line. With four hundred meters to go, I tried to lift up out of the saddle and stand on the pedals, but my legs collapsed underneath me, buckling like those of a baby giraffe. Still, I persisted, keeping the pedals turning around.

Finally, I hit the line, in a state that I can only describe as feeling fairly close to death. I wobbled and fell. Emma O'Reilly caught me, and I lay gasping on the asphalt.

As I came to, Emma whispered: "Jonathan, you won. You won!"

After I'd recovered, I changed in the waiting camper van for the podium awards ceremony, and then produced a pee sample for the still occasional doping control. Lance had already left to go down the hill, somewhat annoyed by my victory, but Johan stayed to drive me down the mountain to the hotel.

It should have been the moment where all those years of work, sacrifice, and suffering all became worthwhile. I had broken the record for the Ventoux, with the fastest ascent ever. I'd won the stage, and I'd taken over the race lead. It should have been the greatest moment of my career, when everything seemed right, just for a minute.

Yet when I stepped up on the top step of that podium, I didn't feel joy.

Yes, I felt relief—relief that Johan and Lance might be less upset with me now—and I felt some pride in the efforts I'd made that day, in the execution of the ride, but there was another almost overwhelming emotion that hit me out of nowhere.

This is a joke, I thought, as I waved and smiled while clutching the winner's bouquet.

I'd spent fifteen years of my life, fifteen years of sweat and sacrifice, singularly focused on getting to that moment, and now all I could think was that it was a joke.

I now knew, with absolute certainty, that even if you had the talent and were willing to work hard, you still had to take enough drugs to make it all work. It was like seeing the strings in a puppet show for the first time. The magic was gone.

I'd beaten all my heroes that day, but they were no different than I was. I'd won, but I'd devolved into a hardened, cynical, and cold cheat to do it. Did I feel guilty? Did I think I'd beaten a clean rider? I hate to say this, but no, not really. Not in 1999.

The results from that era, from top to bottom, are a list of people who've been caught for doping, admitted doping, or have outstanding cases against them. We all knew what we were up to at the time. We had all succumbed to the toxic environment that cycling was back then. Anyone who managed to hang on to their principles and honor, and held out against the prevailing practices during that era deserves to be hailed as honorable and exceptional—they were racing at a disadvantage that the sport, at the time, did not acknowledge and the public was in no position to know who the true heroes were.

No, guilt wasn't the point in my feeling foolish about this victory. The part I couldn't get over was that it was just too mechanical, too predictable, too scripted. My heroes weren't heroes, I wasn't a "hero"—not in any real sense. None of us were.

We were all just flawed humans trying to make the best of a short life. It was a dirty game, and now I knew the secrets to winning it. The joy drained out of me as I stood on the podium receiving my yellow jersey.

This is a puppet show.

This is all a big joke.

Is this how all athletes feel when they win after doping . . . ?

For the next few days of the race, my head was spinning. I wore the yellow jersey proudly, but was nervous and scattered in my thinking.

On one hand, I badly wanted to win the Dauphiné, to show the world I was for real, to show all those in the peloton who had made cruel and nasty jokes about me that I was a winner. On the other, I couldn't help but roll my eyes at how I'd taken the jersey, and at why my teammates and I were so strong.

Kazakh rider Alexandre Vinokourov and Joseba Beloki of Spain proved to be my closest rivals as the week went on. Each day, the U.S. Postal team would patrol the front of the race like an armada, defending the lead and intimidating our rivals. The steady pace of riding up front with the team suited me, as I didn't have to fight for position and accelerate over and over again, as you had to further back in the peloton. As our road captain, Lance had taken control of the race tactics.

He would bark orders at us over the radio to ensure we all followed the plan. He was an astute tactician and strong leader for the team, but in his quest to motivate us he would constantly refer to the other riders in the race as "cocksuckers," "motherfuckers," "worthless shitbags," and so on.

The constant denigration of riders whom I quite respected and also liked just got to be too much at times. I'd just pull my earpiece out and think about something else instead.

Del Moral, too, had really upped his game for the Dauphiné, trying everything he knew to help me recover each day. The number of injections I was getting were mind-boggling by this point, and, to this day, I can't even say I know what half of them were, or what they were for.

He would come into my hotel room each night and push multiple syringes of all kinds of colorful liquid into my veins. Blue, green, red, clear—all with the intent of bringing me back to full strength for the next day's racing. I just lay there and watched.

He calmly smoked a bedside cigarette while giving me injections, reassuring me to relax. The days when I would nervously and cautiously consider everything I put in my body were long gone. No, this was war: we were here to win. Side effects weren't really that relevant to a soldier.

The second to last day saw the crucial mountain stage that we thought would determine the final outcome of the race. That morning, Lance and Johan sat down with the team and outlined the plan for the day. Lance started by saying that we shouldn't defend the lead, but instead attack, as my race lead was too small. He argued that Vinokourov could take the race lead with a small punchy attack at the finish.

Instead, Lance said we needed to blow the race apart and force Vinokourov to chase us. Attack as opposed to defend. I sat, quietly, knowing this would never work for me. While I could climb at a very high speed, it needed to be steady. Repeated jumps and accelerations killed me and my legs. It was my weakness and it was Vinokourov's strength.

I don't know if it was Lance and Johan's way of taking a subtle and cruel revenge for my falling out of ranks earlier in the week, or if it was just a lack of understanding that all riders aren't like Lance. Either way, I knew it would be a strategy that would hurt me and help my rivals.

Once the race began, the peloton was shocked that instead of riding a steady and fast tempo to defend the race lead, we started sending guys with each and every breakaway. Lance, Kevin Livingston, and Tyler Hamilton were all doing their best to get into moves. The stop-start racing was wearing on me, just like I thought it would.

By the time we got to the final climb I was exhausted and had already used my best efforts much earlier in the day. The gas tank was empty: now all Vinokourov would have to do would be to finish me off. He attacked some five kilometers from the summit, and I couldn't follow. Kevin was up the road in the breakaway, so as I got dropped, Lance waited for me.

He was clearly frustrated by me, by the situation, and who knows what else. But I suffered like I never have to hold his wheel to the line. He looked at me as if I was pathetic, over and over, trying to up the pace. When I crossed the line, I knew I'd lost the race lead as well as the respect of my team.

On the podium, I smiled a little bit, maybe a more genuine smile than what I'd won on top of the Ventoux. I just never really felt right about the prospect of winning that year's Dauphiné. This was not because I would have "cheated" Vinokourov, Beloki, or Lance out of a victory, but because it felt hollow to win like this. It wasn't honorable, and I didn't want to think of a victory like that as lacking honor.

Strange, conflicted, and twisted, I know, as I'd just doped to the first degree, yet when the fruit of all that came to bear, I didn't really want it. It tasted sour. My success felt spoiled and I felt numb.

But then in that era, if you were looking for a clean slate it was hard to find. There was one, though, riding in that Dauphiné. Christophe Bassons was a massively talented French rider who was genuinely robbed of a pretty successful career by doping.

During the 1999 Dauphiné, everyone was starting to hate him because he continued to be outspoken, saying that doping was endemic. I felt for Bassons, even though I was one of the people he was referring to. All he was doing was telling the truth.

On the last day, Bassons attacked and won the stage. I remember thinking, "That's great that Bassons won, because he's such a good guy."

But the amount of shit he was taking from the rest of riders in the peloton in every race he rode in was sickening. The peloton abused Bassons and, even now, it still makes me angry.

At the time, I didn't do anything other than ride up alongside him during a quiet moment and mutter: "Erm, sorry about my teammates—they're kinda dicks." People will say that I could have supported him. I could have quit doping, or I could have spoken out in support of him. I agree, but to be blunt, at the time I wasn't courageous enough to do either one of those things.

I stopped taking EPO, briefly, after the Dauphiné. I wanted to go to the next race, the Route du Sud, without worrying about my hematocrit and not sleeping due to stressing about early-morning UCI testers sneaking into the hotel. It was such a relief, and maybe a lesson for me in staying relaxed.

I wasn't as strong as I was at the Dauphiné, yet I won the Route du Sud nonetheless. The last stage was almost a repeat of the last day in the Dauphiné, with Lance being forced to wait for me on the climb up to the Plateau de Beille. However, this time it was because we were riding away from the field, just the two of us.

Lance was clearly stronger, but since I'd gained time in a breakaway a few days before, he had to wait for me so that we might win the race overall. It was, again, clearly annoying to him, but he won the stage and I took the overall classification. And so, one week before the 1999 Tour de France, French sports daily L'Équipe proclaimed Lance and me as co-leaders of the U.S. Postal Service team for the biggest race in cycling. Ha! Little did they know!

Because of my recent race performances, I had a few other teams asking if I might be interested in coming on board. The situation with Lance and Johan was not great and the tension between us was palpable at most events. They didn't like my constant philosophizing about what was right and wrong, they didn't like my questioning of authority, and they definitely didn't like that my hematocrit was always too high. I was an annoying liability to them.

That was fine by me, as after the Dauphiné I finally started to think about what my values really were and if I was really okay with being turned into a human pincushion all the time. To preserve my own sanity I knew I had to leave U.S. Postal and Lance behind.

I knew, too, that many of the French teams were trying to clean up their act after the 1998 Festina scandal. In France if they were caught with EPO it meant jail time. The post-Festina change was evident in their racing style—the French just didn't go up hills quite as fast as they used to. One of those teams looking to make a fresh start was Crédit Agricole, run by Roger Legeay.

Roger had always liked Americans and Anglophones, and he had expressed quite a bit of interest in me. It seemed like a potentially good choice, and as I was starting to become a bit psychologically addicted to all the doping, maybe going to a team that was trying to clean up would help me try and clean up, too? The other team interested was Saeco Cannondale. They were not trying to clean up and needed an American rider to keep their Italian sponsor happy.

Lance knew I was most likely leaving the team, but he also wanted to keep me happy, as he might need my help in the upcoming Tour de France. So, for a while, he was uncharacteristically nice.

On a training ride a few days before the Tour, I openly asked Lance what he thought about my transfer options. The answer was cryptic—loaded, even—but it helped me make my decision a few weeks later. He just said that Saeco was a "fast" team, and Crédit Agricole was a "slow" team. He said that I needed to make up my mind if I wanted to ride "fast" or "slow."

PASSAGE DU GOIS

The 1999 Tour de France started with a bang for the U.S. Postal Service team, as Lance unexpectedly won the prologue, claiming the coveted yellow jersey. It was a happy moment for all the team, even though it was a moment that almost didn't happen.

Earlier that morning, the entire team had been tested for hematocrit by the UCI. Del Moral had been meticulous about testing us every day with his massive centrifuge, and so we all felt pretty secure in what our hematocrit was and our certainty of not popping the test.

Just to be sure, on the morning of the test, del Moral gave me a saline infusion, but this time with glycerol added to pull more water in and further dilute the blood. It made sense to me, but about an hour after the infusion ended, I almost passed out when I saw my urine had turned a dark shade of purple.

It was one of many moments in 1999 when it just felt like things had gone too far.

Moralistic musings aside, we all went in to the test that morning confident that we'd all be well below 50 percent, as we'd been tested multiple times by del Moral in the lead-up to the race. However, on that particular day the UCI testing equipment was registering quite a bit higher than our own. Instead of being well below 50 percent, we were all—the entire U.S. Postal Service team—right on the absolute limit of legality.

I tested at 51.9 percent, just below my limit of 52 percent. When I found out the results, I started shitting myself.

I had taken a good amount of EPO right before I boarded the plane, as I certainly wasn't going to carry any EPO around with me after what had happened in France a year earlier. I reasoned that riding a good Tour was not worth a French jail sentence.

So, instead of trying to sneak EPO around for three weeks, I'd tried to "overstock" on it just before leaving for the race, meaning that although I was 51.9 percent at the start, it was probably going to keep going up for another few days. I realized I wasn't going to be sleeping much in the coming days.

Once again panic gripped me. I thought about what life would be like if I was kicked out of the Tour for a hematocrit over 50 percent. I thought about my parents, about my friends, about how I would have to rebuild my life as someone sullied, tainted by cheating.

How had I got to this point? Why had I wanted all of this? What had become of the kid who loved racing bikes? All of that came flooding in, as I thought about the potentially nightmarish consequences of being caught.

It wasn't a feeling of guilt, but one of revulsion. I was disgusted with myself, I was disgusted with the sport, and I was disgusted with how I'd let myself descend to this level.

The peloton discussed the high hematocrits before the start. The rumor was that the UCI had intentionally adjusted the machines to read high, so as to scare the shit out of the peloton, after what had happened in 1998.

While quite a few of us were absolutely scared stiff by the situation, Lance took a different view.

"Well, at least we all know we're ready to race." He shrugged.

I couldn't believe he had said that, as if he didn't care whatsoever if he got caught. No conscience. No fear. The contrast between where his head was and where mine was couldn't have been greater.

The Tour began, but I wasn't on the race for long.

On stage two, I crashed quite hard in the infamous Passage du Gois coastal causeway stack-up that has since become legendary. It was a spectacular crash, with some fifty or sixty riders hitting the slick seaweed-covered road at 37 miles per hour and immediately losing control, as if we'd all hit a giant banana peel. I looked bloodied and beaten after getting up off the road, but after pulling seaweed and clam shells out of my teeth and spitting out blood, I climbed back on my bike.

Yet my commitment had gone and I remounted the bike without conviction. My mind was anywhere but in the race. I'd hit my head hard, but then maybe that's exactly what I needed. I stopped soon after. To the watching world, I stopped due to the injuries. But that isn't why I crawled off the bike that day.

I quit that Tour de France because I couldn't handle the combination of a guilty conscience and crippling fear that flooded my mind after that opening UCI test. I'd got a small taste of what it might be like if I ever actually got caught doping. It scared me.

I wanted nothing more to do with the race, I wanted nothing more to do with the team, and I wanted nothing more to do with Lance. So I left the Tour de France, with the comparatively easy excuse of having been injured in a horrible crash.

The world thought I was brave for even trying to finish. I knew I was a coward.

PART 5
2001–2006

CHAPTER 13

ADDICTED

Escaping addiction is always tough. If it wasn't, it wouldn't really be an addiction, but more of a strong preference. I knew, after the last few months, that if I stayed with U.S. Postal Service, I would be addicted. Maybe not addicted to EPO exactly, but addicted to winning, addicted to being the best, addicted to money, and addicted to the success. But it may as well have been a direct addiction to EPO, as EPO was the central route to all of those things.

During my time alone after I quit the Tour de France, I decided to try and escape that addiction. I didn't want to quit professional cycling entirely, though. I needed to find a way to continue, but without my ten-injections daily routine. Joining the Crédit Agricole team was maybe a way out of that cycle.

French cycling had been forced into a genuine reassessment after the humiliations of 1998. Many of the teams in France were trying to end doping internally, and the French cycling federation had begun blood testing in what would be a precursor to the biological passport. Beyond that, those working in French cycling were scared shitless of the police.

Doping was now an offense punishable by prison; not so many guys were willing to risk that. I thought maybe the races in France would be a bit cleaner, reasoning that maybe everyone would be scared to dope. I could be competitive and clean; maybe Crédit Agricole would be truly a clean team.

"This could be like rehab," I told myself, and I needed rehab more than I needed any more hollow and empty race wins.

Clásica de San Sebastian in northern Spain was my comeback race after quitting the Tour, and I had a few hours to think on the drive from San Sebastian to Bordeaux. At San Sebastian I'd finalized a deal with Roger Legeay, manager of Crédit Agricole, to come to his team the following year. Just about everything was complete and in place, but he asked me to do one more thing before he would sign the contract.

"Jonathan, I want you to go to Bordeaux to be tested by our doctor," Roger insisted.

He was very clear with me. French teams could no longer play the game with doping; there was too much risk from law enforcement and, reputationally, French cycling could not take another blow. They had to stop the games.

Roger was trying to find riders who might be able to function well without resorting to doping, which, in 1999, wasn't the easiest of tasks. He knew that I had doped previously, but the point of the tests in Bordeaux was to find out if my hematology would be consistent enough to perform without doping.

Too many guys were falling off the map without using EPO, and teams were getting burned because of it. For many, years of keeping hematocrit much higher than normal had led to some sort of degradation of oxygen delivery once the extra red cells were gone.

Worse, for some at least, it seemed the body just wouldn't generate many red cells anymore and produced instead a severe anemia once EPO use was stopped. It wasn't that these guys were just returning to where they were before they used EPO, they were in fact sliding into a worse condition. The Bordeaux test was all about making sure I wasn't one of those guys, and ensuring that I wasn't a waste of money.

Roger was pragmatic. He knew I wouldn't be as good without doping, but he wanted to know how much worse I was going to be before he signed the deal. It was innovative thinking on his part, far ahead of its time, and excruciatingly difficult to execute.

On the drive through the flatlands along the Atlantic coast, I was nervous and my mind was racing. What if they found out I was going to suck without EPO? Would that be the end of things for me in cycling? I'd certainly burned my bridges well and truly with USPS.

I had chosen to go to Crédit Agricole for the same reason an addict chooses to go to rehab. I needed a clean break from doping. If I remained on a team with an environment in which doping was made easy, I would continue to dope. The money, the accolades, and the feeling of winning were too enticing, too seductive, to pass by.

Plus, if you're on a team that dopes, the social pressure to "be one of the boys" is immense. I certainly wasn't strong enough to say no—history had shown that. So I needed to remove myself from the situation entirely. I needed to go somewhere where I couldn't order a drink. Crédit Agricole was a bar with no booze.

But what if I was just a shit bike racer without doping, without the "hot sauce"? It would be one thing to be rejected by their team doctor and told the contract was a no-go, but it would be another matter entirely to discover I just wasn't that good, that I couldn't cut it without doping.

Would I be able to swallow that, the bitterest of pills? It was a long drive up to Bordeaux. I wasn't sure if I'd just ended my cycling career or if I'd just begun an entirely new one.

The doctor in Bordeaux discussed, in earnest, EPO use and doping in general. He reiterated Roger's words and made it clear to me that in French cycling—or at least on Crédit Agricole—those days were over. They all knew the team wouldn't be as good as it once was, but that was just part of the consequences of the Festina scandal.

He told me he had friends who worked in French anti-doping and that an EPO test was almost ready, so hopefully this whole sport-wide addiction to EPO wouldn't be a problem for very much longer. I was happy to hear that and hopeful that he was right.

I enjoyed my time in Bordeaux, riding through the vineyards and buying wine to bring home. But that didn't quell my uneasiness.

I wanted to know if I passed the test of being a formerly doped rider who might be able to race well clean. It was all I thought about. I went home after the second blood test and awaited the results from Roger and to hear if I'd be given a contract—or not.

Finally, Roger called. It was good news.

He was ready to sign the contract and said that my tests indicated I would be a great rider for their team. I was so happy. Not only was I escaping from my addiction, I was being told I might not be a half-bad bike racer, even without the drugs.

My time with USPS was coming to an end. I couldn't have been happier going back to the USA for the winter. It seemed like the perfect move at the perfect time, with a manager who understood the lay of the land, and who felt like he could still run a team and keep a sponsor happy without winning so many races and without doping.

I chuckled privately when many in the cycling media, especially in the USA, questioned my sanity as I moved from the world-beating, ass-kicking U.S. Postal Service to a funny, green-clad French team. If only they'd known . . .

I had been seeing Alisa, the girl who'd driven me around southern California for sushi in her red Toyota. She had been transferred to Paris as a flight attendant, and had been able to come down and visit me on a regular basis at my place in Girona, which was rapidly becoming a second home for many of the expat Americans in the peloton.

We had also hung out a fair bit in France. It was a very cosmopolitan and international romance between two people who shared a very suburban, American, and prosaic background. As the season ended, she managed to come to Denver to visit me, and, when the weather was bad in Colorado, I would go out to San Diego where her parents lived, to train. It was a lot of time on planes for both of us, but we somehow managed to have a budding relationship.

Through the winter holidays I felt like the king of the world. I had a great girlfriend, a new team, a new house, and happy parents. And, from now on, I would race clean. I was the toast of Paris.

The first training camp with Crédit Agricole was in mid-December in an odd little place in the middle of France called Center Parcs. Center Parcs was a French holiday retreat with swimming pools, water slides for the kids, and lots of booze for the adults.

The camp was a chance to meet new teammates and train a bit before the upcoming season. Jens Voigt, Chris Boardman, and Bobby Julich were among them, forming a little English-speaking clique within a French team. We stayed in cramped, cold cabins, rode bikes on icy roads, and then had drinks next to the indoor water slides.

It had a much more old-school and far less mafioso feel to it than USPS. Generally speaking, the riders and staff were happier people, and they absolutely loved Roger Legeay. He was a leader by example rather than by strength. He did things the way he felt was right and challenged those around him to do the same.

While he wanted to win races as much as anyone, he wasn't obsessed by it and realized that at that moment in cycling there were more important issues to think about. It's not that Roger was a lifetime anti-doper: no, he had tested positive himself, and had been in charge of teams that doped. But after 1998 he took a hard look at himself and his team, and made a big change, for the better. He is a man I will always respect.

I went home from the camp feeling very optimistic about my new team and my new lease on life. Alisa, fresh off a trip herself, met me when I arrived home. We were going to spend Thanksgiving and Christmas together that year. I was incredibly excited, both to see her and to be with her for the holidays. She was excited I was on a French team, as we'd be able to spend plenty of time in Paris together. It was a wonderful and glamorous fall and winter. I had journalists coming over from Europe to interview me, we were going to host a big Christmas party together, and we were madly in love.

Little did we realize that we'd also added a member to the family while we were enjoying our time together during the holidays.

One cold but sunny December morning, I went out on a training ride up toward the mountains, to meet cycling photographer Graham

Watson for a shoot. We got the photos knocked out and, despite quite a bit of snow on the roads in the high country, the training miles put in for the day. I came back home looking forward to a nice warm bath and some hearty winter food. I clumsily barged in the front door and greeted Alisa. She seemed a bit off, a bit quiet.

"What's going on?" I said, as I peeled off my layers of kit.

"I'm pregnant," she blurted out.

I was surprised—not shocked, as we had been doing those certain things that can lead to pregnancy—but I was still surprised. Alisa is, and was, a deeply religious person. Even though I can be a bit agnostic, I deeply respected Alisa's faith and her moral compass.

So, before she could get much more nervous or choked up, I said: "Well . . . I was thinking we should get married anyway, so maybe this kinda helps seal the deal?"

That was not perhaps worthy of an A+ for being romantic, but I was giving her the unedited version of what was going through my head.

"Really? Oh, wow, so that's good," she said, as she smiled and hugged me. "That went much better than I thought it was going to go!"

Going into the 2000 season, I was the most optimistic I've been in my entire life. I was on a new team trying to do things a new way; they had faith that I could race clean and race well; I had a baby on the way and I was going to get married.

Training each day seemed purposeful and focused. I had real responsibility now, and I needed to make good on that. I had a mortgage, a wife, and a family. It felt like the American dream, and, finally, I felt like an adult.

Gone were the days of living in spare bedrooms and buying one-way tickets. I was a real "professional" now, meaning I was working toward creating financial stability for my life by racing a bike. It felt good at that moment, like I was making progress in the world.

I was finally outstripping all the assholes in high school that had made fun of me. They were stuck in boring jobs; I was making big money as a professional athlete. Little did I realize all of this responsibility would backfire into pressure and that that would happen quickly.

The season started out with a bang for me. Immediately in February, I was fighting it out with French star Laurent Jalabert for victory in the Tour of the Mediterranean.

I ended up placing third overall, yet could not believe that I was actually battling with a guy like Jalabert. Maybe this whole racing in France thing, where everyone was afraid to dope due to the police, was going to work out? It seemed so, and as the spring progressed, my results kept coming in, better and better.

Paris–Nice, Critérium International, Midi Libre—they were all prestigious races in which I was in the hunt for the win. I wasn't quite beating the best of best, but I was right there in the mix each and every time. And I wasn't taking any drugs. It was absolutely wonderful, even if I didn't quite believe it was happening.

This was what I had hoped for my entire life: becoming a top bike racer and not having to compromise my ethics. It seemed that, through all the scrutiny of cycling and all the scandals, the French authorities were making my dream come true. The fear of law enforcement had cleaned up the peloton more in one year than anti-doping tests had in three decades.

While it felt a bit odd to be part of a sport where police raids were becoming a norm, the effect it was having on the racing was boosting my morale. I could race at the front with no fear of an over 50 percent hematocrit test. I could race at the front without turning my veins into corkboards. I could race at the front and be proud of what I was doing behind closed doors.

It made me realize how far my self-respect had fallen, against the steady drumbeat of cycling's doping culture. I had grown numb to doing things so shocking and degrading that they would make my mother cry on a daily basis. I'd grown numb to feeling any remorse or guilt about breaking every rule or moral code I'd grown up with. The vein in my right arm had grown numb to so many injections that I could no longer feel the needle puncture my skin.

But now I could feel again. I could feel pride, I could feel happiness, I could feel the joy of riding a bike. It propelled me to train harder and harder. I believed in myself again. I believed in the sport again. And I believed in my future again.

I returned to the USA after a successful spring campaign to get married to Alisa in her hometown of San Diego. She was a stunningly beautiful bride, if already five months pregnant. My father-in-law took me fishing on the morning of our wedding.

He was a religious man with deep convictions about what was right and wrong. For the first time in a long time I felt like I could finally make a man like this proud. I was going to support and love his daughter and grandson-to-be, and I was going to do it the right way.

It was going to be a short-lived utopia. It had been a little while since Festina, and things seemed like they were calming down in France, but as any good bike racer knows, the moment to attack is when things seem peaceful.

When I returned to Europe, I immediately began hearing worrying rumors. Perhaps many of my rivals had raced the spring program clean, but with the Tour de France looming, there was much talk of new ideas and new ways around French law enforcement.

I still lived in Girona, even though I was racing for Crédit Agricole. I was still privy to much of the inside knowledge of my old team, USPS, and I still had many contacts in the Spanish cycling world. Looking back, I wish that wasn't the case, but unfortunately it was, so I knew that for the 2000 Tour, things would not be clean for much longer.

As the Tour got closer, so the pressure began to build. I couldn't shut it out.

I knew that team management at Crédit Agricole had got used to me racing at the front, and that they expected I would be able to do the same thing at the Tour. My teammates had come to rely on me flying the Crédit Agricole flag in mountainous stage races. They supported me unselfishly in every race. I didn't want to let them down.

When I was home in the USA, it seemed like all my old friends and family knew how well I'd been racing that spring, and knew, too, that I might be an outsider for a top placing at the Tour.

These were the people who'd helped me become a bike racer. From Frankie at A Bike Place to Bart, my relentless training buddy, they all were my biggest fans now. My parents were pleased that I seemed happy and that I was racing well, making good money and ready to support a family. I didn't want to let them down, either.

Then there were the sponsors.

Sponsors smile when you perform well in races. They pat you on the back. They look happy when the team is riding at the front, and you're the one making them happy. When sponsors are happy, they let team management know. That ensures the team management is very happy, making all the staff and directors and riders happy, too.

I didn't want to let any of these people down. I knew the peloton would be back to full speed at the Tour, and if I wanted to keep not letting everyone down and keep everyone happy, then I needed to be at full speed, too.

This wasn't about me anymore, I told myself. I had responsibilities to many other people. I was responsible for a family and had bills to pay now. I needed to get the job done. Be professional.

I decided to take EPO again.

"Just one last time—right?" I told myself.

Just a small amount, just a small dose, I reasoned.

I had an awkward discussion with my beautiful newlywed, seven-month-pregnant wife as to why I was waking up every morning to take a small blood sample and spin it in the centrifuge to check my hematocrit.

I had told her this was part of the sport, that there was no other way to pay the mortgage in this sport, and she understood—I think. She'd spoken to the other wives and girlfriends around town about the topic, too. They all understood. They all worried, but none of them showed it.

So she would lie in bed, early in the morning, quietly dozing, while I switched on the centrifuge after pulling out a small amount of blood. The steady whirring of the machine would wake her up. Every time, I apologized.

At Crédit Agricole there was no doping system, with doctors or medical team supervising what you were up to. I figured everything out—centrifuges, dosages, all of that—on my own. It was my responsibility and no one else's.

It was my dirty little secret.

No one at Crédit Agricole could know, least of all Roger. Roger was genuinely anti-doping, but he was also a bit naive and idealistic when it came to what other teams would risk, even in the face of the police. I hated breaking the trust Roger had placed in me, but I had to do it. He might not have known it, but he needed me to do it. He needed to keep those sponsors smiling.

I thought I would do as I had prior to last year's Tour de France, taking EPO all the way up to immediately before leaving for France, and then not taking any during the race. I would avoid pushing it as hard as I did the year before. There was no doctor to go crying to at Crédit Agricole when you pushed it too high.

I would just do a little bit, like back in the days of Santa Clara, and I figured the effect would last just about three weeks, before I hit the dreaded "backside slide" of hematocrit falling after using EPO. It wouldn't be the full meal deal, like the guys at USPS would be doing, but it'd be enough to allow me to cling on to the back end of the lead group in the mountains, and not embarrass the team or myself.

Then, a few weeks before the 2000 Tour, the UCI announced that they were close to developing a test for EPO, and that they would be freezing samples taken at the 2000 Tour for analysis once the test was approved. No one was quite certain how serious they were, or if this was just a scare tactic. Rumors spread through the peloton. Some didn't believe they would actually freeze these samples and continued, business as usual. Others were mortified and stopped using EPO immediately.

The rumor was that the test would be able to detect EPO for about ten days after its use. This put a massive dent in my plans for using EPO right up to when I'd leave for France. Now I would have to stop ten days before entering France, meaning fourteen days before the race.

I'd get a week, maybe ten days of performance enhancement from EPO, and then my hematocrit would start sliding down for the last part of the race. I knew from experience that falling hematocrit meant the last ten days of the Tour wouldn't be too great. Of course, I did my best to convince myself otherwise.

Interestingly, while most of the peloton was scared stiff of this new EPO test, my old teammates from USPS didn't seem very worried at all. The least worried was Lance himself. On one friendly training ride with my fellow Girona resident that spring, I asked him about the test and what his thoughts were.

"I don't think the test works," he said bluntly.

When I inquired further, he started explaining more about the technicalities of the test.

"It's all about shades of gray with that test," he said. "You just have to know how to not be too gray."

Of course, he didn't give me more detail than that. I wasn't going to figure out what he meant on my own, but I took his words to mean he knew a way around the test that no one else did. That would be very Lance. He knew how to stay ahead of the riff-raff.

Our conversation shifted and then settled on Bobby Julich. Bobby had been my teammate for two years, and, in the eyes of many, had really underperformed.

He had stopped doping, entirely, and many in the peloton knew that, as he was a long way from the form that got him onto the podium of the 1998 Tour.

I shrugged when Lance brought up Bobby's performance.

"He's doing the best he can . . ." I said.

Lance didn't think so.

"No, he's not," he growled. "He's not doing his job. He's not doing what it takes to do his job. He's letting the team down and letting the sponsors down. What Bobby is doing is *wrong*," he said, damningly.

To Lance, Bobby stopping doping was wrong. It meant that he'd now become incapable of doing his job, which was a betrayal of his obligations and was the morally wrong thing to do. The conversation showed how twisted we'd all become in the way we saw things.

The guy from 1995, the old Lance, the one who was railing against doping and hoping all the cheats were caught, was long since gone. He'd been written off, left in a ditch by the roadside to die. The new Lance was fully committed to winning at all costs. It didn't matter to him anymore, not like it had in 1995, what everyone else was or wasn't doing. All that mattered was that this Lance was going to do it better than everyone else.

I stopped taking EPO ten days before I left for France, and thirteen days before the race actually started. I was confident I wouldn't get caught, but not so confident that the effects would last very long. But I convinced myself that as I hadn't really taken very much, it might not matter anyway.

I was fairly strong for the opening part of the Tour, with our team finishing fourth in the team time trial, and I was generally able to stay out of trouble for the opening ten days. When we finally reached the real mountains, on the stage to Hautacam in the Pyrenees, I was in an ideal spot to challenge for a top-ten placing in the overall classification. Unfortunately, however, it was also ten days into the race, and I could feel my form fading.

I can't remember all the details of that day, but I remember suffering intensely to make the lead selection of riders. It was raining, hard, all day long, and in order to make the typical thirty-rider initial selection that happens on most high mountain stages, I had to push myself much further than I normally would have.

It was touch and go in keeping contact with the leaders, and it felt like I was constantly in oxygen debt. I was clinging on the back for my life, fighting against the inevitability of just not having as many red blood cells as a few weeks ago.

"Don't disappoint Roger," I told myself. "Don't disappoint your fans and friends back home. Don't disappoint your mother. You can make up for it with suffering."

You can make up for it with suffering. It became my mantra.

I wasn't the only one suffering that day. Many of the race favorites were also surprisingly losing contact early. The entire ONCE team, the same unit that had crushed the team time trial early in the race and held the yellow jersey, were now creeping up the mountains, far from the front. I wondered if they were experiencing the same "backside slide" that I was.

Coming over the top of the Col d'Aubisque, the string finally snapped, and I lost contact. I would now need to catch back up on the descent. I took risks, massive risks, in the rain to regain my spot. I was never a great descender, and in the rain with my corrective glasses fogging up, I was even worse. But nonetheless I let it fly down that hill, using very little brake, and passing people very quickly to get back to the front.

I had to get back to the front. I needed to get back to the front.

Don't disappoint the team. Don't disappoint the sponsors. Don't disappoint Frankie at the bike shop.

It was all running through my head as I screamed down that huge mountain, much too quickly.

And then it all went black.

I don't know what happened, but I'd guess my front wheel went out from under me on a wet switchback bend. I hit the deck and hit my head, knocking myself unconscious.

I got up, quickly enough, and remounted my bike, but I had no idea where I was, and I had no idea what race I was in. I was shivering from the cold and the shock. Stunned and dizzy, I tried to follow an encouraging teammate on down the hill. But I couldn't.

When I started vomiting due to the dizziness, I knew my Tour was over and I was forced to quit. Unlike the previous year where I was trying to escape the addiction, this year I was just trying to keep everyone happy. And once again, I'd failed.

It was a strange season, full of early success in big races, totally clean, which gave me an incredible sense of hope. Then all that optimism unraveled in a short period as I watched the game of doping and deceit start up once again. I went home after that Tour, not a beaten man, but definitely chastened, and not really sure what the future held for me in cycling.

I was lucky, however, in that when I came home after being defeated, I was overcome by the joy of my son, Charlie, being born. He was healthy and full of spirit from the word go. Alisa was also healthy and happy after his birth. They say that becoming a father changes you and, while I didn't really feel that immediately, the change was very profound.

The responsibility I felt toward Charlie slowly eroded the reckless attitude I'd had toward life until that point. I now needed to consider my choices more carefully, more wisely. Think a bit more, act a bit less.

Perhaps that is why the guilt over doping started kicking in once Charlie was born. I was starting to feel more and more ashamed and was less willing to take risks in general once I became a father. I was pulling on the brakes sooner than I had before, backing off more on descents.

Becoming a father made me more reflective. I'd blocked out a lot of what my parents had taught me and I started to ask myself what kind of father I would be to Charlie if I could persuade myself that cheating was acceptable. It wasn't how I'd been raised, so why did I think it was acceptable to raise my own kid that way?

Since I had ended my season early in 2000 to be home for the birth of Charlie, I started my training earlier than normal for the 2001 season. I needed another contract to make sure I could pay the bills and support my newborn and wife for the coming years. Training was now a job. Riding bikes was something I needed to do to feed my family. I dutifully went out every day.

Somehow in the mix of morality and disappointment, cycling had turned into something I had to do, instead of something I wanted to do. I was a million miles away from the wide-eyed kid who'd motor-paced behind the orange Volvo.

Instead I was jaded and hardened. I rode my bike to pay bills—period. I went out and rode but now I dreamed about what I would do when I was done with training, just like I used to dream about winning races. My love for cycling itself was dying. Or at least, had been buried very deeply.

Despite all the extra training, 2001 started very poorly for me. I was struggling in every race I entered, getting sick and worn down each time. It just wasn't working like it had the year before. I was racing clean, and thought I could make a repeat of my early-season exploits of the 2000 season, but I wasn't even close.

Something just wasn't right. I was getting concerned that I might not be assured of another contract by Roger if things didn't improve. That would be catastrophic to my family's finances. I started to worry endlessly. I would sit up at night and calculate how many months I could pay the mortgage before going bankrupt if I lost my contract.

My buddies back at home all thought I was living the life, riding on a pro team, making good money, beautiful wife and child. It all looked incredible from the outside, but inside my mood was growing darker and darker with worry.

The stress just made my racing worse. I just wasn't getting anywhere, no matter what I tried. My roommate on the road, Christian Vande Velde, watched me slowly fall into a deeper and deeper depression. Christian had been a true friend over the years, and despite being on different teams, we were still very close.

He'd noticed me training less, not really being motivated, not pushing myself, and being unhappy with my situation. I wasn't racing well, and the depression over that was killing my training and my diet along with it.

He'd watched me slip into depression and I think he felt a bit of guilt and pity when he finally asked if he could help out a bit with my predicament and my downward spiral.

Christian explained what Lance had meant when he'd told me the EPO tests didn't work. There was another, more discreet way to use EPO, and other riders were now figuring it out. Lance had been first to catch on, but now everyone else was catching up.

Instead of injecting the EPO subcutaneously and in standard doses, you had to inject it intravenously and in a very precise and low dose, or micro-dose. If you injected 10 IU per kilogram that would ensure it was undetectable after twelve hours.

Finally, I had an explanation as to why everything had been going so shit for me. Now I knew how I'd be able to perform again, to pay my mortgage, to avoid going bankrupt. The dark funk lifted.

Once I understood what was going on, the addict in me surged up again and took over. I knew that if I micro-dosed that I wouldn't be starting every race at a disadvantage. For the start of my build-up to the Tour de France, I started using EPO once again.

There was one small detail that worried me about this new method of taking EPO. When you give yourself an intravenous injection, if you aren't a professional, you can sometimes miss the vein. With a large quantity of fluid, such as a vitamin B injection, you can tell that you've missed the vein, by a bubble building up and some pain.

You then just stop the injection and resituate the needle back in the vein. The problem with this "undetectable" EPO method was that if you missed the vein, got some EPO under the skin or in a muscle, even for just a second, the clearance time—"glow time," as it was known—would extend from twelve hours up to as much as ninety-six hours.

What made this an even bigger problem was the fact that at 10 IU per kilogram of use, the amount of EPO you were injecting was so tiny you would never feel the fluid under the skin. You would have no idea that you'd just made your clearance time ninety-six hours instead of twelve.

That's one of the reasons why I don't subscribe to the "everyone is still micro-dosing" theory that some cling to. There were quite a few guys in the early 2000s that knew all about how to avoid an EPO positive, but still tested positive for EPO. I think missing the vein was the reason why.

As I prepared for the Dauphiné Libéré, I worried incessantly about missing the vein. I was extra careful in making sure I was inside the vein, carefully drawing blood out before pushing the EPO in, but no matter how careful I was, I knew there was a risk of getting caught.

I tried to put it out of my head, but my anxiety was almost over-whelming. So, to be extra careful, I stopped taking EPO a few days before the Dauphiné began, just to allow for any margin of error.

My new motivation and form was incredible for the Dauphiné. I rode at the front the first few days, then made the lead selection over an odd stage that went up the north side of Mont Ventoux, and then descended to a finish in Carpentras.

The day after that was a long, hot, and fairly flat time trial in Valréas. I expected to do well in the time trial, maybe place in the top ten or so, which would set me up nicely to contend for the over-all victory later in the week. But instead of doing well, I was on a ripper of a day.

Quite early in the time trial, I flew past Iban Mayo like he was standing still, and at the halfway point I could hear Roger yelling from the car that I had the second-fastest time. I found myself, once again, in that place that just allowed me to reach into the depths of my soul for more energy.

Once again, the metronomic pounding of the pain and effort in a lonely time trial suited me. I relished the silence and solitude. I bar-reled along the finishing straight with my head down, racing at 37 miles per hour, and almost passing out at the finish line. I was back in the game.

I had set the best time, but British time trialist David Millar was still out on the course and was ahead of me at the first checkpoint. I figured Millar would beat me, as the second half of the course was flat and a bit downhill, so I went back to my hotel room and started to change and shower.

A few minutes later, one of my directors came running up the stairs, yelling.

"You won! You won!" he shouted.

I couldn't believe it. For a split second I was elated, but what he said next destroyed any sense of euphoria.

"Okay, we must go to anti-doping control," he told me, and at that moment I collapsed inside my head.

What if I missed the vein?

I'm going to test positive. I'm going to test positive. I'm going to test positive . . .

Fuck.

I lay awake all that night, thinking about what my friends would think if I tested positive. I was panic-stricken. What would my mom think, what would the world think? I unraveled entirely, imagining scenarios where I became a pariah of cycling, a black sheep, ostracized and alienated, an outcast.

How had I got here? Why was I doing this to myself again? How could I ever escape? Mentally, I melted down that night. I vowed never to dope again. I couldn't go on like this.

The next day I raced horribly, drained from worry and a completely sleepless night. My teammates were totally confused.

How could this skinny little twerp win a pan-flat time trial and then totally die the next? It made no sense to them. I had to hide the real reason, shrugging it off as a random bad day.

I clearly couldn't handle the pressure. My conscience and maybe my fear of consequences wouldn't allow me to do it. So, as the Dauphiné had proven, a good night's sleep would have more performance-enhancing benefits than using EPO. I could do one or the other, but clearly not both.

I started the Tour that year without having doped for a month. I knew that decision would get me killed in the later stages of the race. Maybe Lance would tell me I wasn't doing my job, just like Bobby.

No matter, I figured I would just try and enjoy being a mediocre bike racer. I was going to do my best for the team and not worry about the outcome. I wasn't going to dope anymore, and I needed to live with the consequences of that decision. I couldn't handle the uncertainty of everything hanging in the balance.

The Tour that year was sort of wonderful. Well, the first part anyway. In something of a miracle, we won the team time trial ahead of the USPS and ONCE teams. It was a miracle, in that I believe, to this day, our Crédit Agricole team was about as clean as it got in 2001.

I can't say I know exactly what each and every rider on that team was doing in private, but I do have my opinion. I think that while some of the riders on that team had doped earlier in their careers at various points, by 2001, they were no longer doing so.

In truth, I was probably the sketchiest character on the team, with my connections to USPS and knowledge of how to dodge the tests. The rest of the guys seemed genuinely to believe in the new EPO test, and felt like it would be plain stupid to try and dope again like they did pre-Festina.

I'll say it with as much certainty as I can: I think we won that Tour de France team time trial clean-ish on that day. I don't really know how that's possible—maybe there was a tailwind at the right moment or something—but somehow, against all odds, we won. It was and will always be my most cherished victory in cycling.

I was the recovering addict who won something big—and won clean.

THE STING

Unfortunately, my 2001 Tour de France ended on a very sour note.

Just a few days from the finish, I was stung by a wasp, right above my eye. At first the sting didn't seem to be too much of a problem, causing just some swelling above my eye. Quickly, however, the situation worsened. My eye had totally swollen shut.

Worried that I wouldn't be able to continue, we went to the emergency room to have a doctor, who wasn't our team doctor, look at it.

"Well, it's easy enough to solve this," he told the team's medics. "We just need to give him a shot of cortisone."

The Crédit Agricole doctor stopped him before he was able to give me the injection.

"I'm sorry, Jonathan," he turned to me and said. "We must find a different solution."

I was baffled. "Why? I don't understand?" I said.

Cortisone was used for everything in cycling. Knee injuries, wrist issues, tendinitis of all sorts. I was sure that restoring my impaired vision would surely be a legitimate use of the drug.

Considering the amount of illegitimate use of cortisone that went on, with riders lying about having a "knee injury" and getting team doctors to fill out the paperwork to make it legal, I really didn't think taking cortisone for a huge allergic reaction was that big of a deal. I hadn't applied for cortisone use in years but I didn't really find it that performance-enhancing, not compared to EPO, anyway.

The team doctor explained to me that while cortisone did indeed have a legal use for knee injuries and tendinitis, it was not permitted for allergic reactions. It was most likely an oversight, but allergic reactions were just not a listed use of cortisone in the rule book.

Instead, he tried giving me massive doses of intravenous Benadryl to try and get the reaction to stop. It didn't work, although it did succeed in making me so incredibly tired that I could barely move. I begged the doctor.

"Please give me the damned cortisone shot," I asked. "We just would say it was a sore knee, nobody would know the damned difference."

Still, I was being told I couldn't take it. Meanwhile my eye closed down even further. By the next morning I looked like a mess. The pictures prove it.

Most of the peloton was taking the shit to go fast anyway, while I just wanted to be able to see where I was going. Who the fuck cared? Still he refused and I launched into an angry tirade.

Then Roger came into the room.

"It's not his choice, Jonathan," he said, "it's my choice . . ."

I was furious. I called Roger a fucking idiot and a naive fool. Did he not know what the other teams were doing in this race? Did he know what ONCE and USPS were doing? I explained to him in no uncertain terms.

"Roger, you fucking ignorant moron, these guys are chugging down blood bags and EPO like Kool-Aid, and I can't take a little cortisone so I can see where the fuck I am going??! This is bullshit . . ."

Roger stood his ground, and calmly explained to me that while he understood what I was feeling and knew about the other teams, he believed that by saying my need for cortisone was for something other than an allergic reaction, we would be lying.

He said that lying was the problem this sport needed to correct. If cycling was going to survive, we needed to be truthful and honorable, and so we were not going to use cortisone.

At that moment, I hated him. He was taking my Tour de France away from me.

Even though I knew I had no chance of finishing the race, I showed up to the stage start that day, just to draw attention to how stupid the rules were. It worked. Journalists went crazy about the story. My swollen face was on the front page of newspapers around the world. I'd made a mockery of the anti-doping rules, and I felt good about it.

I swallowed my opinion of Roger—barely—in the interviews I did. Then I rolled up to the start line in an attempt to finish my first Tour de France. And there was my old compatriot, Lance.

"What the fuck happened to you?" he snapped. I told him the story.

He started laughing. He wasn't the only one.

"You need to get the hell away from that goody-two-shoes team, man," he said. "On this team, we would take care of the problem. It's that simple."

And at that moment, it all became clear. On Lance's team, they would take whatever they had to. Here I was, angry with a man, Roger, who was trying to make a stand and do what's right. And all the others could do was laugh at him.

I started the stage and rode about thirty kilometers, but the combination of dosing up on Benadryl and only being able to see out of one eye meant I couldn't go on. I climbed off and they put me in an ambulance. The doctor gave me a shot of cortisone and by the time we got back to the hotel, my eye was fine.

I understood that the problem had never been Roger; the problem was me and the lies I had told myself for the past five years, convincing myself that lying and cheating were the right things to do.

Cycling had convinced itself that lying and cheating were honorable. It was a sport that had lied to everyone, including itself. There was a deeply ingrained hypocrisy that prevented a rider from taking cortisone legitimately, but yet turned a blind eye to the hundreds of fake reasons for its use in every race.

Lance, the Tour's yellow jersey, had laughed at my situation. The whole sport laughed at me. And while I wanted to blame it all on Roger, he was the one who was right. I was angry with someone for just asking me to be truthful and honorable.

And somehow my anger with Roger was being justified as righteous by those around me who'd themselves been untruthful and dishonorable. How fucking crazy is that?

That was the moment my racing career effectively ended. I was done with professional cycling. Definitively and forever. I had to be, because none of it made any sense any longer to me. My passion died that day. More than hating Lance or Roger, I hated the sport. More than that, I hated myself and I wanted out.

I raced again in 2002, but without any of the same spirit I once had. Like any good addict, I slipped into doping again in 2002, but this time it had become pathetic and pitiful. I was only doping so I could train less, ride my bike less, and survive the races.

I just didn't care anymore. I was fading away. I only kept racing for the paycheck, nothing more.

And so, halfway through the 2002 season, I sat down with Roger and explained that I had reached the end of the line and was stopping. He was a bit shocked, as I don't think he fully realized the impact the cortisone farce had had on me. I still had two years left on my contract extension, and riders rarely quit while they still had time left on a contract, especially if it entailed leaving money on the table.

But he seemed to respect my decision and to understand why. It was the start of a great friendship that would last until this day. I didn't want to drag around the races with no passion, and I didn't want any more blood money. It was time to really, properly end the addiction. And the only way to do that was to stop.

It's important to say that I consider Roger's firm stand with me about that cortisone injection to be the most honorable action I've seen in sports, life, or business in my years on this earth.

Roger may be a flawed person, just like the rest of us. He may have a dark history. But in my years on Crédit Agricole, he was the model of what a modern manager in cycling should be like.

There were times when our team was desperate, when we were ranked outside the top twenty in the world. There were times when we were made fun of for going much slower than the pre–Festina affair days. Roger absorbed all of that without flinching. He never placed pressure on the riders, or conveyed the pressure he must have felt from the sponsors.

While I'm sure Crédit Agricole wasn't flawless in its anti-doping stance (my own actions are evidence of that) it was a team making a huge step in the right direction. I was a friendly-fire victim of that stance, and at the time I naively didn't think such ideological crap was worth it.

But as I look back, I look back with huge admiration for Roger. He taught me, the hard way, that sometimes there is a right thing to do. And sometimes it isn't very much fun doing it. I am eternally grateful for that lesson.

CHAPTER 14

INTO THE DARK

When a professional athlete retires and transitions from sports into the real world of jobs and family, bills and business, drudgery and deadlines, it's not easy. It seems odd to think that these people who are so gifted, who are such high achievers, who have lived their dreams, can so easily fall victim to deep depression.

If you'd asked me as a twenty-year-old if I found that hard to understand, I would have said yes, absolutely. But as a thirty-year-old, after stopping my professional cycling career and dealing with the harsh realities of "normal" life, I would have emphatically answered no, not at all.

The transition away from living the dream you've had since being a child, of being someone in the public eye whom a lot of people admire, of being in a glamorous location almost every day you wake up, with a very public, goal-oriented purpose to your life, is both harsh and cold. It is a move into the unknown.

That might not be true for someone who's won the Tour de France or is somehow otherwise very famous, but that wasn't me. I was a guy whose biggest claim to fame for the general American public was a photo of my wasp-stung face that made me look like the Elephant Man.

I was thirty, with no degree, no job skills, no experience doing anything beyond riding a bike. My reputation for going uphill fast in a bike race wasn't going to be of much value in the business world. I had debt, a wife and a child to take care of, and absolutely no knowledge of how to do that. Beyond that, the intensity of racing—the speed, the focus, the adrenaline—was all gone.

It left a huge void. Emotionally, I felt like a simmering volcano, as the outlet I once had put so much energy into was now gone. Once I was living back at home in the U.S., Alisa tiptoed around me wondering what had happened to the calm—read: sedated by excessive exercise—man she had once known.

I think Alisa was shocked when I called her and said I was coming home, for good. She knew I wasn't happy, and hadn't been for a while, but I think she thought I'd bounce back. After all, who would just quit professional cycling, a dream job, when you still had hundreds of thousands of dollars due to you in an already signed and guaranteed contract?

I felt like a man in rowboat out in the middle of the ocean. With one oar. Which direction was I supposed to start rowing in? Whichever direction I chose, I knew I had to get busy.

In 2003, I raced part time. I'd found a Continental-ranked team, Prime Alliance, with a ton of talent. That paid some of the bills. I'd also put myself through real estate school after coming home from Europe, so I'd set up a little real estate business on the side. It was a bit of a juggling act with a little kid and family in the mix, but it was a hell of a lot more fun than racing in Europe.

The guys on our little ramshackle team were mostly bright-eyed kids who still loved bike racing. I'm grateful, because they made me see bike racing as fun again. My peak years in the sport had already passed, but doing little races in the U.S. made me open my eyes to why I raced bikes in the first place.

We were staying in host housing again, eating burritos after the races instead of bland pasta, and traveling around the USA, not Europe. I loved it, and I loved those guys. It wasn't all great, of course, as they wanted to know what the real story on doping was over in Europe.

It was tough to talk about it, but I felt they needed to know the truth, so I'd explain to them exactly how it worked and how it was done. They needed to know what they were getting themselves into if they made it to the next level of the sport. But it felt odd. I wanted them to be successful, but I didn't want them to get in too deep.

My renewed enjoyment of cycling also led me to start up a little junior team. As Lance continued his winning streak in the Tour, U.S. cycling was very visible in the mainstream media, but the effects had little trickle down to the junior ranks. There were no more junior teams around like there were when I was kid. I figured I needed to do my part to fix that.

I rounded up six talented kids from Colorado, with Timmy Duggan, Alex Howes, and Peter Stetina among them, and I tried to figure out a way to support them. I asked all my friends about sponsorship, and a few of them wrote a check to get us started, but it wasn't until a funny meeting with Dan Brogan, the publisher of a Denver lifestyle magazine named *5280*, that the project got some traction.

Dan proposed a unique deal. He'd give my upstart real estate business a full-page ad in his magazine every month, and whenever I sold a property as a result of that ad, I'd split the commission between the team and me. I didn't think it would work very well, but nonetheless I agreed. Man, I was dead wrong.

The real estate business took off and, thanks to that, the kids got their expenses paid for the whole year. Team 5280 was the grandfather of what would become Slipstream Sports, and you can trace a line from that meeting with Dan right through to the current Education First World Tour team.

In addition to racing my bike a bit, starting a little team, and selling a bit of real estate, I was attempting to dip my toes in the waters of entrepreneurship. A friend of mine introduced me to a fellow named Steve Goldstein, the head of communication for Dow Jones and the *Wall Street Journal*.

Steve was convinced I was the coach that could help him to lose some weight and eventually maybe do a small race on a bike. I realized that I could probably learn just as much from him as he would learn from me. His life was so different than mine. He worked in a tall Manhattan office building and wore nice suits every day. It looked like a dream to me compared to riding a damned bike in the rain for six hours.

He was fascinated by professional cycling, and wanted to learn all about it. Meanwhile, I was fascinated to learn how the hell I could make a living in the real world. So I suggested a trade. I would coach him on how to ride and race a bike, and he'd coach me on how to operate in the world of business. He agreed and, with that, I had stumbled onto the greatest business mentor I could ever ask for.

Steve was a master of communication, who'd served under the second Bush administration as a press officer and then honed his skills further in the corporate world. He also understood the inner workings of how corporate politics worked and how to move the dial inside a major company. He understood how the world heard your spoken words, and how interpretation could be different from what you said. I don't really know why he agreed to take me under his wing, but he did, and it would change my life, forever.

After a few months of working together, Steve left Dow Jones for a new position as executive vice president of a company called TIAA-CREF. He invited me in to speak to his executive team about the life of an athlete, and to expand on what business could learn from professional sport.

Steve set me loose on my first project, a "community relations audit" of all the charitable giving and charitable board presence TIAA-CREF had in the three headquarter towns of Denver, Charlotte, and New York City. It was a fascinating project to be thrown into with zero experience. I loved it, but in truth, life was getting a little nutty with the real estate gig, the part-time bike racing gig, the little 5280 team, and now this.

I was regularly working eighteen hours a day. It didn't bother me in the least, however, as it was still much better than taking a ton of drugs to race six hours in cold rain. I was happy to work the long hours. Plus, I got to wear a suit.

But Prime Alliance was struggling to keep its sponsorship or to find new sponsors. I decided this might be the time for me to use my newly acquired business skills to try and help them out.

I sounded out Steve and he wondered if maybe TIAA-CREF itself would be a good fit for taking over the sponsorship of Prime Alliance. He and I came to a deal that they would test the idea by sponsoring one race in downtown Manhattan. We did the race with TIAA-CREF emblazoned on our jerseys. Some of his colleagues liked it, others not so much. Yes, it was interesting to them, but not enough to sign off on a million-dollar sponsorship.

TIAA-CREF services and manages the retirement accounts of thousands of teachers across the nation. Paying professional cyclists wasn't going to go over well with their client base. Still, the company was in the midst of a massive rebranding campaign. They had almost a trillion dollars of assets under management, yet no one knew who they were. I reasoned that maybe doing a few little sponsorships wouldn't hurt.

I suggested sponsoring a really small team, where all the kids were in college, rather than professional. We would call it a "development team," which, back in 2003, was a relatively new idea. It would cost $100,000, and we'd leverage collegiate cycling races and collegiate national championships, and create an employee health-focused effort using the cycling team as the centerpiece. Steve was reluctant, but probably purely out of annoyance with my ridiculous persistence, he finally relented.

Although I was now back in the cycling business, I still had to keep my real estate job to support myself. Prime Alliance, unfortunately, went belly-up. But I had a "development team" to run and real estate to sell. It hadn't been a pretty year of transition. I had flung as much shit up against the wall as possible and just waited to see what would stick.

The whole time I was an overworked, insecure mess who was

spending less time with his family than when I was racing in Europe. I just figured the only way to make it through the athlete-to-reality transition was by sheer force of effort and work hours. But I doubted myself every day and I often fell into some pretty dark holes.

But I was damned lucky to have great mentors. They helped me to find my way through to the other side. Many of my friends from my racing days have not been so lucky. Depression, unemployment, addictive behavior, divorce, and some suicides all impacted many of those who rode in the peloton of my era.

The list of names of those affected grows all the time: Marco Pantani, Frank Vandenbroucke, José María Jiménez, and, most recently, Jan Ullrich. There are other ex-professionals, not so famous, who are struggling. For all of us, a career in cycling was our holy grail. And, while it may not have been exactly what we thought it was going to be when we were fifteen, we got to live that dream.

You're living that dream for two decades of your life, and then one day, it's gone. Your career is over and you're finished. It's a shattering experience. Anyone who watched Andy Murray in bits as he realized that his career was soon ending can't doubt how devastating a feeling it is.

In Dan Coyle's book, *Lance Armstrong's War*, he cites the statistics that demonstrate cycling is among the most dangerous professions in the world. It looks pretty and peaceful on TV, bowling through the vineyards and past the sunflowers, yet it is anything but. We were an intense clan, who never really thought about the consequences of how extreme and unethical our sport had become in that era. When people ask me if I was ever worried about the side effects of EPO, the answer is "No, not really."

When you experience, from the inside, a high-speed Tour de France crash, guys screaming in pain, doctors rushing to revive them, blood spilled on the road, riders toppling over the side of a cliff into deep ravines—and yes, sometimes even dying—you don't worry so much about the possible health risks of EPO. The risk of doping is relative to the risk of racing.

Flying off the road in the high Alps at seventy kilometers an hour is a much bigger risk to your health than taking EPO. We trained our minds to erase those thoughts of risk, to erase the thoughts of what could happen. Doping was just part of that erasure, a part of our body armor. And it was the only way to survive in the peloton at that time.

CHAPTER 15

DOUG AND THE DEAL

We were up in Boulder one day, having a little 5280 training camp, and while I was driving behind the riders, my phone rang. Normally I wouldn't answer, but if there's one thing I learned in looking for sponsorship, always answer a number that starts with 917, the prefix for New York City. It's fair to say that it was a phone call that changed my life.

The call was from a guy named Doug Ellis. At the time, 5280 held a little annual fund-raising dinner in a restaurant in downtown Denver. The governor would come along, and we'd raise maybe thirty or forty thousand dollars for the junior team. Doug called me—on the day of the dinner—to ask if he could attend.

Initially, I wasn't that receptive.

"Well, sorry—it's sold out," I said, but when he told me he was coming all the way from New York, I felt obliged to try and find him a seat. Something else—a hunch, I guess, given he got from NY to Denver in four and a half hours from putting the phone down—told me that he was a pretty serious investor.

"If you can be in Denver by seven tonight, you can sit next to me," I told him. That evening was when the idea for Slipstream Sports took shape.

We got to know each other as we sat together. During dinner, Doug said: "Hey, I would like to make this into a Tour de France team. Can you fly to New York with a business proposal on how to do that?"

I thought about it for a little while over the next few days.

"Don't shoot too high! You'll scare him off!" my friends advised. But quoting a million dollars was a lie. You can have a great under-twenty-three team for a million dollars, but this guy said he wanted to go to the Tour. I had some voices whispering in my ear saying, *"Don't tell him the truth, don't tell him it's gonna cost twenty million dollars..."*

My friends and parents were a bit worried for me.

"You're flying to New York because you think some guy might give you twenty million...? Right. You're going to get abducted and sold or something. Be careful."

But I went out there, went up to Doug's office, waiting to be drugged and stuffed into a cage, and sat down with him to discuss how to build a Tour de France cycling team from scratch. This is not an easy thing to do.

I outlined how there were no assurances, and that as you build through the middle stage, as a pro Continental team, there would be little commercial opportunity from sponsors, and that he would be on the hook for the whole bill.

I didn't even realize that there are people who could spend $20 million, other than movie stars or Bill Gates or whatever. But I pulled out the page of my proposal showing the financial outlay needed to get the team to the point where we could race the Tour de France, and then maybe—just maybe—after that, we could get a sponsor that would cover the costs. The end of my little timeline quoted a figure of $20 million. He didn't flinch.

The next conversation was even more bizarre. I'd just warily convinced this guy to invest $20 million. Next, I did my best to convince him to walk away.

"I don't even know if I'm comfortable doing this," I told Doug, "because the way cycling is right now, I feel like I'd just be dragging these young Colorado kids—kids like Alex Howes and Taylor Phinney—into an environment where they're going to be forced to make choices regarding doping that they shouldn't have to make."

Doug listened. Then he looked at me, without judgment, and said: "Well, how can we change that?"

Over the next month, we met in New York and blueprinted how we'd go from this little Colorado-based junior team to a Tour de France team, how much money it would cost, when we'd be able to mitigate some of the cost with sponsorship and what phases the team would go through as it made the journey through the ranks.

We created the Slipstream cycling team based on the belief that people want to make an ethical choice. If you go into the supermarket, there's a big stack of beautiful, yellow bananas, and then there's the smaller bananas—maybe a little brown—and they're the organic ones, costing twice as much as the big yellow chemicals-induced bananas. But people still choose them.

We believed that, after enduring years of scandals, people would make a market-based preference in sports, too. They would choose a team they felt confident was clean and we would get more support and more sponsorship dollars if we differentiated ourselves in that way.

We made a bet that the world, cycling fans, sponsors, would prefer the little brown organic banana over the big beautiful yellow (but chemically enhanced) one.

We were going to become "team little brown banana."

Typically, a cycling team was run on the equation of "More race wins = greater publicity for sponsor = more value for sponsor." Nobody had thought beyond that paradigm.

So cycling had become like an arms race, with each team trying to win more than the others, and looking for ever more effective tools—including doping—to do that. Nobody was thinking: "How can we create value for our fans *beyond* winning more races?" The original seed for that was sown by Doug.

Interestingly, our "little brown banana" business model would change the sport. Our run toward the Tour de France generated much more publicity for our ethical stance than teams winning twenty times the number of races we did. We were the toast of the media and, because of this, we started pulling in some major sponsorship dollars. People did prefer the little brown organic banana.

Other teams took notice. Money always makes people take notice. Maybe clean cycling was a better business model? Maybe just winning more isn't the be-all and end-all? I'd love to say there are many idealists in the world of cycling that want a better world. But there aren't. The management in pro cycling is about getting cash in the door. You want to change the sport? Show them the money.

We were doing just that. We were beginning a massive cultural shift in the sport by showing the cycling world that the money wasn't going to follow the doping arms race anymore. The funny side effect of it all is that by 2011 to 2012 the sport had cleaned up to the degree that we actually did start winning a lot of races. That process of change in the sport was overwhelmingly joyful to watch.

By 2006, Doug and I had been working together for a year and he was learning quickly about how the cycling business worked. He loved the sport and was investing more and more into growing the team, but the one thing that always concerned him was that there really no way to build equity value for the owner.

Teams were just "cash in, cash out" entities, unlike, say, an NFL franchise that may not actually be cash-flow positive but is still very valuable to owners, because the franchise is worth so much at the point of sale.

In cycling, there was nothing to sell. This was due to two major problems. One, the owners of cycling teams don't have permanent rights to race in the biggest/best races. What gives an NFL team value is that they have the right to compete in the NFL, no matter what. A new team can't just come in and boot them out. It sounds silly even saying it, but that's the reality of cycling.

The assurances of racing the Tour de France for any team, say ten years down the line, is minimal, and therefore, the equity value of ownership is minimal as well. The second problem is that the identity and brand of the team is always tied up in the name of the sponsor.

Cycling teams didn't have a brand of their own. There's no orange and blue of the Denver Broncos or Yankee pinstripes. Instead, cycling was just all about coloring, naming, and branding your team to fit the needs of the highest bidder for sponsorship. The team would have the sponsor's names, colors, and brand all over it and would retain no identity of its own, which made year-to-year brand longevity a problem.

The UCI Pro Tour was an attempt to solve the first problem, but it had been seriously derailed by ASO, the group that organizes the Tour de France and many of the other most famous races, so the hope of someday having a franchise that had value was a bit lost. But the second problem maybe had a solution.

The other founder of the Slipstream start-up—and our original CFO/accountant/office manager/team photographer—was Beth Seliga. Beth was the heart of the team and the reason it ran so well in the early days. When you only have six employees, everyone has to be pretty good at everything. I wasn't good at much, so Beth made up for it.

She was a machine, doing the books until dinnertime, and then producing a video for our website at two in the morning. She was the third leg of the Slipstream stool that allowed it to stand.

I often get asked why the team has had argyle on every iteration of its kit dating back to 2007. Well, it isn't some story about how my great-great-great-grandfather was actually Charles Rennie Mackintosh and I felt we needed to respect the family's Scottish tradition or something. It was a purely business decision.

One afternoon in September 2006, Beth and I were bantering on about what our new uniform design should be. We knew that Doug liked a certain shade of orange that matched the sofa in his office and we had Chipotle signed up as a sponsor, so we needed to include something fun that would show their spirit off. But the uniform still needed some sort of overall motif.

Beth was also very good with graphic design software—of course—so we spent the afternoon playing with all kinds of designs. It was the norm in the early days to work well past dinner, and then eventually just start drinking in the office, before the Chinese food would arrive.

That night, after a few bottles of red, Beth jumped up and said: "I've got it!"

"We need to make our team brand something in the uniform that isn't a color that a sponsor could change, that isn't a name that definitely will change with sponsors," she said. "It's got to be like a little hidden sign in the uniform. Like something that quietly lets you know: 'Ooh, it's those guys.'"

It sounded like a secret Mason's insignia or something, but I got her idea. It just needed some refinement.

We kept throwing ideas around until we came up with a plaid pattern. We could have plaid kit. We tried it on the design software. It really stood out, although it overshadowed the sponsors and really wasn't very racy. I mean, I loved plaid, but it seemed like it needed wool rather than Lycra.

We tried every pattern we could think of: polka dots—that's already been done in cycling—and also herringbone, which was nice, but then we weren't a pheasant hunting team.

Finally, and admittedly after some more wine, we tried argyle on the screen.

"Holy shit, it works!" exclaimed Beth.

It did. You could make argyle bold, you could make it subtle. You could make it modern, or you could make it vintage. It would fit almost anywhere on the uniform: socks, jersey, collar, shorts. We checked patent laws to see if there would be a problem. We seemed clear.

Doug was going to be so happy.

"Let's call him," I said.

"Wait, it's three a.m. in New York . . ." Beth cautioned.

"Ah, fuck it, let's call him anyway! We've got argyle!"

I have learned a lot from Doug. He taught me patience, he taught me how to create a system and delegate, how to manage thoughtfully. He taught me *how* to think, but not *what* to think.

I showed him how tough and cutthroat bike racing can be, and how nimble and fast on your feet you have to be to survive it and to adjust. He learned how unpredictable it was and what it took to be a competitor, and how sometimes you have to be mentally mean to win. He acquired a new steel that wasn't there before.

At the same time, I was thinking that for the sport to move forward, we couldn't just keep trying to obliterate or deny the past. I knew we had to acknowledge it, learn from it, and move forward.

At this point, the sport was busy trying to make scapegoats out of a few riders who had been caught doping. They were all being burned at the stake by those who governed the sport. The other teams chimed in with the hypocrisy, saying they would never do such things as these naughty fellows. This just smelled like fresh bullshit to me. To me, I thought we had to own the past, and get beyond it.

The thought had been churning in my head for a little while, and while attending the Tour de France presentation, I ran into David Millar. He had been arrested for having doping products in his house and then gone on to admit his culpability. He was now attempting to come back into the sport as a reformed man.

I knew from my days at Crédit Agricole that David was massively talented. The word was that he'd won the opening time trial to the 2000 Tour totally clean. It was a rumor that made him a legend in those dark days. "You mean he actually won clean . . . ? Whoa!"

Maybe having an admitted (but apologetic and repentant) doper leading your team was the way forward? It certainly was better than playing pretend, like most other teams were doing.

That's why the first rider we signed was David Millar, with the focused intention of not being hypocritical. I knew that with David as the center of the team, we would be making it clear that we were offering a second chance to a guy who'd admitted to doping, served a ban, and was now riding clean.

Close to the end of my career, when David was at Cofidis, I got a call asking me if I'd like to join the team, on Millar's recommendation. I thought I'd been pretty much forgotten, so it was heartwarming—I'd disappeared off the scene, effectively, but somehow David had thought I would be a good addition to the team.

When I saw him again, at a time when he'd been ostracized by the sport, I thanked him for thinking of me and then told him about what Doug and I were planning. We talked a little more and I said, "Listen—I think you'd be the perfect spokesperson for this team."

He'd served his two-year ban but seemed a little taken aback.

"You want *me*? Nobody wants me!"

It was critical to establish David as the linchpin, because it set the tone for the whole team. It set a precedent and won a lot of people over immediately, including some in the media, because people were sick of denial. They liked that Slipstream talked openly about transparency and redemption. Everyone was being hypocritical about doping at that point. It was hard to find anyone who wasn't.

It was a hard culture to break, but we had to try. I remember once having a conversation over dinner with Thomas Dekker, before he joined the team. He didn't understand why people were being penalized for being truthful.

"If you lie about it, you get to carry on racing," he said, "but if you tell the truth you get kicked out of the sport."

Others had said they wanted to make a comeback after bans, like Dekker and Floyd Landis. But to me, David showed more genuine remorse and had more real desire to come back than some of the others. That's why I felt he was different.

People have said to me, "Why did you take David and not Floyd? Was it because Floyd was more outspoken?"

Well, no—that wasn't the reason.

It was because Floyd wasn't ever going to race well. He proved that when he made an attempt to come back with the UnitedHealthcare team. Floyd's head wasn't in the sport any more. He was tied up in exacting revenge, and not in racing well. Thomas was the same. Hiring him was a mistake on my part, because he wasn't ever going to race well again.

Thomas and Floyd had played around with the idea of coming back after their bans, but neither of them ever truly believed they could race well clean. They didn't believe in themselves, whereas David did. You could see that: it was clear that he could race well clean and that was the whole point.

So yes, there was actually a very hard-nosed business sense to who we signed. We wanted riders who could perform well without doping and who had the seriousness to prove that they could. I took a bet that Millar, Christian Vande Velde, and Dave Zabriskie, could all race well clean and I was right.

That judgment was based on a lot of things, like watching them closely when they raced. When you're there, in the middle of the peloton, you know when somebody is "on cycle," or not "on cycle" and you can see the difference it makes. With David and Christian it was smaller than I'd seen with others. Certain guys had the raw talent and the engine to race well clean and others hadn't. They all get lumped in as dopers, but there are degrees, differentials.

Millar was a massively talented underachiever. Had he been more focused on success in the sport, made adjustments to his lifestyle and gone for it on a flatter and more time-trial focused course, like the one that Bradley Wiggins won in 2012, David could have won the Tour de France. I still believe that and I told him as much in 2008.

"That's the nicest thing anybody has ever said to me," he said, but I think maybe he's forgotten that since then. He doesn't see me as so nice anymore.

For David to be a Grand Tour rider would have required a lifestyle change that I don't think he was capable of. Emotionally, he was too volatile. Three weeks of the sort of pressure the Tour brings would have crushed him, even if physically he was capable of it.

As a team, our anti-doping platform won over fans and sponsors. Pretty soon, other teams realized that an anti-doping stance was good for business and were doing it, too. I think even Johan Bruyneel had actually turned that corner by the time 2009 rolled around, which, oddly, is why I disagree with the USADA assessment that Lance was doping that 2009 season. I don't think he was.

Slipstream became good at knowing how to deliver the message.

We were always very clear and we didn't flinch from our position. It was never dressed up as "zero tolerance," but as "here's the line in the sand—from here on out we are not going to dope anymore." I felt from day one that that was much more real and that zero tolerance was effectively an empty promise. It still is.

Even so, when we first started racing in Europe in 2008, I think other teams saw us as an annoying little team that didn't deserve much attention. They didn't display much resentment; they just didn't really take notice of us. But then a lot of teams were still tangled up in the aftermath of the Operación Puerto blood doping scandal.

They were watching us though, wondering if maybe it was the way to go. Maybe, too, that's why, in spring of 2009, I was elected president of the teams' organization, AIGCP, or the Association Internationale des Groupes Cyclistes Professionnels. They were increasingly thinking that anti-doping was good for business and "this guy can speak for us."

ELECTION DAY

In many ways, I was still naive in 2009. I brought that naivete with me to the first AIGCP meeting that I'd attended since our team rode our debut Tour. I dressed up in my best dark suit and finest blue tie for the occasion.

I felt important as I entered the IOC headquarters in Lausanne, where the meeting was being held. Scheduled around the UCI's annual presentation to the teams and a presentation regarding the continued development of the biological passport, the meeting drew all the big team managers: Bjarne Riis, former Tour winner and then boss of the CSC team; Lance's long-term manager and multiple Grand Tour winner, Johan Bruyneel; and legendary Belgian Classics guru, Patrick Lefevere.

To me, still new to the management of cycling, it had the feeling of great pomp and circumstance. We shook hands, congratulated one another on our great successes, and sipped cocktails together. It was a reunion of men coming together to smell their own farts and marvel at the wonderful bouquet of self-importance. And I was about to become the king of them all.

*

As I finished writing this book, a few more blood doping cases surfaced in Austria. As a result, many questioned the biological passport's efficacy. Many more will question my integrity, because I will continue to defend the use of the passport.

The biological passport, by nature, is not an exact device to detect doping. It is, instead, a method by which you look at the body's own parameters and observe if there are changes. It is indirect testing. It looks for smoke, not fire.

Why do I defend it, if athletes are still blood doping, and the biological passport didn't catch them?

Simple. It was never designed to catch them. It was designed to prevent them from transfusing enough blood that it would actually make much of a difference. It isn't about catching people and burning them alive in public. It's about keeping the races fair as possible.

If the bio-passport's effect on the sport is that a blood doper transfuses 350 milliliters of blood instead of 1 liter, well, then, it's been effective in its job. I'll take a talented rider who is able to sleep at night over a stressed-out rider that just transfused 350 milliliters of blood anyday in a race.

To my mind, the biological passport works. Imperfectly.

But it wasn't easy to sell it to the anti-doping authorities. Montreal in winter is a cold place, and in January 2006, I spent a week there, largely indoors, trying to convince WADA—the World Anti-Doping Agency—to endorse the biological passport.

WADA was naturally very skeptical. An ex–professional cyclist with close ties to the evil U.S. Postal Service team was coming to meet with them and suggest some sort of partnership? I hardly got a warm welcome. I got the impression that some people felt it was repulsive that I was even there at all.

But each day I would manage to convince perhaps one more person at WADA that my intent was genuine. Slowly, after a week of trudging through the Arctic freeze every day to meet with various groups at WADA, it began to work, and the funding was approved.

The first year of testing was a disaster. Samples were mishandled, overheated, accidentally frozen; different labs would show different results;

different collection officers had different rules; different times of day created different results. It was an unmitigated mess.

But we learned and we learned quickly, because many of us used to be the thieves and the cheats. The lessons were very concrete, even if the results were not. But even as we improved the process, there were still large inconsistencies. It was imperfect. It was flawed.

We started to realize that this would never be a perfect process. There would always be some subjectivity, no matter how much we improved the procedures. Most important, we learned that this was okay.

The fundamental idea behind anti-doping is to create fair competition and to protect the health of athletes. This ideal gets lost in the push to catch people. To find the evildoers and burn them at the stake. That is what the world wants from anti-doping. Creating fairness seems a distant second. It shouldn't be.

We realized that while the biological passport method wasn't going to be very good at catching the evil ones, it could be a way to create an imperfect path to fairness.

The biological passport's greatest efficacy is in its ability to limit doping, but not to eliminate it. The parameters measured can and will shift around to a point, naturally. This is hard to differentiate from intentional doping. However, if the shift is large enough, then it does indicate doping. But that shift has to be large enough to trigger the algorithms used.

So, the skeptic can say, "then just don't dope enough to shift the parameters too much, and you will get away with it," and, yes, they would be right. You will get away with it.

But now this is where the pragmatism of imperfection comes in: Did that tiny bit of doping actually help? Did it change the race result? Was the race unfair?

The biological passport wasn't about catching people. It was always about dissuading them. It's about limiting them. It's about keeping things fair.

*

After the first day's UCI seminar in Lausanne, we spent the next day gathered at the AIGCP meeting. That was in the presence of the two entities that, de facto, run professional cycling: the UCI, who legally, technically, and nominally, run the show, and Tour de France promoters ASO, who actually hold the power.

To me, a neophyte, the AIGCP appeared to be a highly organized and coordinated group of high-level team managers that helped the UCI and ASO successfully manage the strategic direction of the sport. I was about to find out that the truth of the matter was pretty far from the dreamscape in my mind.

The AIGCP meeting started early that morning. First, we met to elect the new board of directors. They would then meet afterward to elect the new president from among them. But there was already a lot of bad feeling in the air, and before the hotly contested elections even began, the majority of the old board stood up and, in exasperation, resigned their positions.

This included outgoing president Lefevere, whose parting speech consisted of dropping the mic on the stage and storming off. I didn't quite get what this mass stepping-down was all about, but the look on everyone's face was a cross between deep contempt for one another and a hollow resignation about the whole situation.

During the meeting, a few voices would spring up here and there, and start ranting on about how no one ever came to their local race anymore, or how the biological passport fee was too expensive. Marc Madiot, boss of the French lottery–sponsored FDJ team, was the king of the mighty rant. Holy shit, that boy can go off.

By the end of one of his diabolical monologues, you felt like Napoleon had risen from his tomb and was marching toward Waterloo once again. Madiot would loudly and passionately express his hatred for anything that threatened the patrimonie de France or future Époisses production.

When Madiot was finally done, some two hours later, and everyone was completely confused as to why we were even in the room, it was time for the voting to begin. There were priorities, though. The voting needed to get done quickly, otherwise it would interfere with lunch. So, with that in mind, the nominations began for new board members.

For some odd reason, I was nominated as a board member by legendary Spanish team manager Eusebio Unzué. The nominations saw me running against former professional Andrei Tchmil. I defeated Tchmil, thirty-six to one, without actually having even said anything at all about my platform.

But, hey, it was time for lunch, so no need for that anyway. Tchmil left before lunch started.

After lunch, the board convened to elect the new president. Again, Unzué threw my name out there. I proudly accepted, having no idea what I was getting into. French team-management guru Jean-René Bernaudeau was running against me. I figured, he's French, so will probably win, but during a coffee break I got a call from Jeremy Botton, who at the time worked for ASO.

"Hey, bonjour JayVeeeee . . ." Botton said. "We want you to win . . . we think you must wiiiin. C'est bien!"

And with that, I realized that I had ASO's backing to become the new AIGCP president.

In order to avoid missing cocktail hour, I was quickly voted in unanimously as the new president. I was so proud. I was now the president of the league of teams in all of professional cycling. I was drunk with power. But I checked myself and remembered many of the Thomas Jefferson quotes about democracy my father had taught me. I would be a benevolent and kind dictator.

After drinks, Patrick Lefevere came up to me, shook my hand and congratulated me. Then, as outgoing president, he gave me one small, valuable piece of advice.

"You're fucked," he said. "I'm sorry . . ."

I learned very quickly why Patrick said this, and why the entire board of the AIGCP had resigned that morning. In 2007 and 2008 the AIGCP had effectively been broken into pieces. In the dispute over how many teams would be allowed to race in the World Tour, and still more important, ASO events, Lefevere's job was to protect the rights of all of the World Tour teams.

In a bold, yet very inflammatory move, the UCI decided to grant twenty World Tour team licenses. ASO hated this, as they wanted much greater discretion in who was entitled to compete in their races.

Their attitude was very simple: "It's our party, we can decide who to invite."

The UCI stood firm and told ASO that they'd be accepting twenty teams to all of their events.

"Non," ASO said, "we will not."

ASO had decided who to cull from the herd, and a team named Unibet was selected to be the sacrificial lamb. They would not be invited to ASO events, especially not the Tour de France. The UCI protested this exclusion, and then asked the AIGCP to help them battle the tyranny of ASO.

The final battleground for this came at Paris—Nice in 2008. ASO and the UCI were at odds over the number of World Tour teams invited to compete, and so ASO decided to make Paris—Nice a race that would be run without the UCI. ASO's move would turn the Tour de France into an invitation-only event and completely destroy any true value a team owned. The AIGCP needed to stand up.

So in order to protect the rights of teams whose participation was guaranteed by the UCI World Tour license, it fell on the AIGCP to decline ASO's invitation, on behalf of all the teams, to Paris—Nice.

But as would happen over and over in the history of the AIGCP, as soon as it was announced that the World Tour teams would collectively decline participation in Paris—Nice, the teams started to break ranks.

Sponsors called team management and asked: "Why the hell are you risking our invitation to the Tour de France by boycotting Paris—Nice? You do realize we only sponsor your team because of the Tour de France!"

Once that happened, the boycott started to crumble. One by one, the teams sloped off and signed individual deals with ASO to race in Paris—Nice, eroding the power of the AIGCP to almost nothing in the process.

The animosity between the teams grew. Those who broke ranks were seen as traitors. The group was broken to pieces. I had just become president of a group that hated one another, and had no intention of ever working together again. I think they figured it might be funny to throw this green American kid to the wolves as AIGCP president. Hence my election.

Over the next four years, I worked very hard to try and bring the integrity of the group back as a collective. I looked for small victories in the infighting with the UCI or ASO, as opposed to seeking big ones. The use of in-race radios, or the quality of hotels, seemed more reasonable battlegrounds than fighting about the rights of entry into the Tour.

I engaged with the riders' union, the CPA, to try and move things together in a positive way, while slowly raising the minimum wage of the riders. And little by little, it started to work. The AIGCP meetings, which, when I came in as president were only attended by maybe half the teams, became full. For the first time, the AIGCP had a voice in the media. In reality, we may not have actually been much to reckon with, but from the outside it certainly looked like we were.

The AIGCP had its mojo back.

Still, despite the AIGCP being cool again, the big issues had not receded or gone away. Cycling teams still had no real rights to participation in the world's largest events. Even more contentiously, the media rights revenues for these events were not distributed among the various stakeholders of the sport, and certainly not to the teams.

Cycling's biggest races always receive all of the revenue from television or digital media rights. The team and riders take none. This is viewed as normal in cycling, but it is a long way from the way other sports operate. Events and teams compete with each other in their interests, and for the same sponsorship dollars.

In other sports, teams, event venues, and athletes worked together to create the best possible experience for the fans and viewers, so that the product was the best it could possibly be. The best athletes were invested in growing revenues, as were the best events and the best teams. They came to market thinking of other sports and types of entertainment as their competition, but not each other.

Cycling was the equivalent of a Broadway show where the actors didn't get paid, and where only the theater collected money from the audience. So the actors hijacked the show by wearing shirts that had advertisers' names on them, and got paid that way. Everyone was pissed off at each other all the time, the stage costumes looked really dumb, and little by little other forms of entertainment became more popular.

In sports like the NFL, while the competition between teams might be fierce on the field, when it comes to the business side of the sport, everyone works together. The players, teams, and venues are all in the same business. A business called a league. And that business views its competition as other sports—or maybe Netflix or reruns of *Friends*.

In cycling, the teams, events, and riders aren't in the same business at all. So, instead of working together, race organizers, teams, and riders work to kill each other off in a parasitic and cannibalistic way.

Very few people even understand this to be a fundamental issue in cycling. They just view it as "the way it has always been," and then worry about burning issues like inappropriate sock length and bikes that weigh too little.

However, there are a few visionary souls out there in cycling. I was lucky enough to get a brief glimpse of what cycling could be like if teams and races worked together when a man named Michele Acquarone came to be the boss at RCS, the Italian promoters of the Giro d'Italia.

Michele is a man out of place in his own country. Instead of the sleek Italian leather shoes I love so much, Michele clunks around the streets of Milan in Air Jordan high-tops. He loves American sports, was never a bike racer, and has a university degree in business. All of these things make him a total outsider in European cycling.

While his fashion sense was hard for me to bear, I would listen intently to what the man had to say. And what he said was truly visionary.

Michele didn't view cycling teams as the evil, pesky bastards trying to ruin his race. He viewed them as the stars of the show, and the more stars he could have, the better the show. For him, as the boss of the second-largest race in the world, his competition was very simply defined as the Tour de France. If he wanted greater market share, he would need to beat the Tour. He would need to make the Giro more attractive and exciting than the Tour.

In cycling, the response to this type of thinking is a shrug and eye roll followed by: "C'est pas possible . . ."

"That's not possible . . ."

Michele didn't believe that. A few days after Ryder Hesjedal won the 2012 Giro d'Italia for our team, Michele and I talked.

"Jonathan," he said, "I want the Giro to become the most popular race in the world, and I need the teams' help to make it possible."

Over a long and lazy lunch in Milan, he explained his plan to me. It was quite simple. Michele proposed that in exchange for bringing their best and brightest stars, being available for the production of behind-the-scenes media content, and helping to actively promote the Giro, he would split the media rights revenues with the teams.

It was a huge risk and a huge investment on his part. RCS would definitely lose money the first few years, and then maybe, but only maybe, would it be recouped later, if the race became much, much more popular due to the teams prioritizing the Giro.

It was a long shot, but it was exactly the type of thinking cycling needed to move forward and, if it worked, would push ASO to eventually do the same. It would, through good old-fashioned competitive marketplace economics, force teams and race organizers to finally be in the same business, with the same interests. Everyone would be pulling in the same direction.

Michele and I agreed that we would present his proposal of media rights revenue sharing at the annual AIGCP meeting in October that year. I couldn't believe how nonchalant he was being about something of such extreme entrepreneurism. He was pissing against the wind of tradition with the force of a fire hose. It was inspiring to watch.

I worked to make sure the AIGCP would have the information it needed, and Michele developed a PowerPoint presentation to show to all the teams at our big annual powwow in October before the Tour de France presentation. It would be the most significant deal the AIGCP had ever been a part of. It would change the face of cycling, and truly modernize the sport's business model. I couldn't sleep, I was so excited the night before that meeting.

The next morning, ASO called Michele in to an emergency meeting to tell him he was a madman, and that his plan would hurt the business of all race promoters. But Michele didn't back down. Instead, he quietly prepared for his afternoon presentation to the teams.

Once the AIGCP meeting started, I rushed through the normally dull housekeeping agenda—"Here's the adjustment to the three-kilometer rule. Here's the new fee for the biological passport. Blah-blah-blah . . ."—just so that I could get to Michele's presentation.

When I introduced him to the group of team managers, there was a quiet air of suspicion in the room. Why was the new boss of the Giro at an AIGCP meeting? This must be a trick or a trap. Is he wearing a wire?

I briefly introduced the concept of what Michele would present, and then let him take center stage. He went through his ideas of how the teams could help build the Giro. "Bring your star riders," he said, "and base your calendar around the Giro . . ."

The softer points—to produce and distribute compelling video and digital content of the behind-the-scenes life of a cyclist training for or competing in the Giro—were equally as important. There was also an expectation that the top riders and their team's platforms would talk about and promote the Giro as the "best" race.

In return, the teams would get 50 percent of all media rights revenue from the Giro. While not ASO/Tour de France–level money, the figure was substantial. In fact, if you consider that most teams currently get around a $60,000 as a start fee from the organizers to ride the Giro or Tour now, it was massive. He was betting that within three years, the teams' efforts could grow the Giro's media revenues by more than 50 percent. It was a huge gamble.

The room politely applauded as Michele ended his presentation. He asked if there were any questions. Yet the room was silent and subdued. So he left, and I told him we would discuss the proposal in private and get back to him.

I couldn't believe the cold reaction of the teams. This was what we'd all been screaming and crying about in the press for years, and here it was, on a golden platter in front of us. Yet no one seemed excited.

I told the group I wanted to sign a brief memorandum of understanding with Michele soon, so that we could get to work on the details of a contract. The group disagreed and the usual infighting followed.

The French teams were immediately squeamish, knowing that being a signatory to such a thing would upset ASO. After all, you don't want to upset the boss. The rest of the teams uncomfortably cast around for reasons why it wasn't really such a good deal.

"Does this mean we have to have cameras in the riders' rooms? What if my best riders don't like Italian food?" On and on went the examination of the gift horse's teeth until any positive energy had been totally lost.

All the teams knew, just like the French, how angry this deal would make ASO. Nobody wanted to be seen as being a part of anything that contradicted ASO, all-powerful promoters of the Tour. So, they all hid under their desks, just like at Paris–Nice in 2008. Nothing had really changed.

I should have listened to Patrick Lefevere when he told me I was fucked. He's been around longer. He knows the game.

I resigned as AIGCP president. I just couldn't believe the lack of conviction and the fear that pervaded the group. I couldn't bear to go on battling fights about sock height limitations and maximum wheel rim depth. We had the big one in the palm of our hands and we threw it away.

A massive fraud had been uncovered at RCS and, as Michele's suspension from the company was announced simultaneously, people naturally assumed he was connected with it. I can't help but wonder if, like Icarus, he had flown just a bit too close to the sun. His idealism and vision was maybe a bit too much for cycling's closed world. And so, he was removed from it. Maybe all the fear in the AIGCP group was justified? They'd all been through this before. They already knew the end of the story. Now so did I.

PART 6
2009–2012

CHAPTER 16

THE BATTLE FOR BRAD

I n 2009, Lance Armstrong made his comeback to the Tour de France. This made for an incredibly uncomfortable Tour for me. With Bradley Wiggins on our team, we had a guy who could win the Tour riding for us. But we also had a guy who was going wherever the money was, and the money was with Dave Brailsford at Team Sky.

In public, there were lots of accolades for our team and the way that we were riding, but with Lance trying to settle old scores and Team Sky courting Bradley, behind the scenes it was pretty dark.

Nowadays, Brad might admit that he was naive and immature in the way that he dealt with it, but at the time he felt very righteous about his every move. The whole thing was hurtful.

Being scuttled by your ex-teammate and by your best rider at the same time is quite confusing. In between that year's Giro and the start of the Tour, Brad would wax lyrical about how much he loved the Garmin team, yet by the end of the Tour he was doing his very best to find a way out.

Although Team Sky didn't formally exist in 2009, they made it clear that they were going to buy their way straight into the World Tour by 2010. They were rich, they were bold, and their behavior around Brad during the Tour was blatant.

Dave Brailsford and his posse were just hanging around Brad all the time. They realized that the only way they could be seen as successful as a team in the UK was if they got Brad on board, so they were putting in an enormous amount of effort into recruiting him during the Tour, even while he was still racing for us.

We'd only had him on the team for a year, so the thought of losing him was tough. He was a big personality with the media during that Tour, but then a lot of his largesse was with the Brits, and not with the team. It was a little lost on us really, as we weren't attuned to the British media.

The situation was even more complicated because that spring, before Brad's breakthrough ride in the Tour, we had started talking to Alberto Contador about joining our team. He had started the year riding with Lance at Astana but they were having trouble paying their riders and were in danger of losing their license, which meant that he would have been free to join another team.

It was complicated for him because after he'd already signed with Astana, Lance joined the team to make his comeback, which meant that the team had two Grand Tour winners and two strong egos. Inevitably Alberto's relationship with the team went downhill.

Alberto hated being in the same team as Lance and by March that year, Alberto wanted badly to get off the team because things were just getting worse. I felt for him—he was going through the same demoralizing experience, the same mincing machine, that I'd been through with Lance and Johan. It was like a rolling frat party working with them. I'm sure that didn't make much sense to him because he's rather a genteel person.

We had a sponsor lined up, Herbalife. They were very interested in the Spanish-speaking market and felt that Alberto would have been perfect for them. Essentially, they would have paid his salary, which would have made it possible for him to come to the team. We even had jerseys printed up—the Garmin-Herbalife team—but eventually they ended up in the shredder.

I know that some people thought that there were potential

doping issues around Alberto, and, obviously, he did later test positive for clenbuterol. So why was I interested in him? Well, because I believed—and still do—Alberto to be the most talented GC rider of his generation. I believed he could win a Grand Tour clean, and that the stricter the anti-doping controls became, the more he would win due to his physiological superiority. I drew that conclusion from a few points of reference.

One was Iñigo San Millán, who had tested Alberto at a very young age. Iñigo said it was the most remarkable and eye-opening physiological test he'd ever conducted. Iñigo had conducted a lot of tests, on both clean and dirty riders.

Alberto gave us no cause to worry. He released all his blood values and his biological passport to us and our doctors. They reviewed them and said there was nothing remarkable to be seen in the blood tests, which, in light of how well Alberto was riding in 2008 and 2009, is really a statement. The 2007 season was pre–biological passport, so 2008 was as far back as we could review.

Anyway, clean rider versus clean rider, Contador wins. That's why I liked him.

That was the way you had to operate back then. An idealistic, head-in-the-sand approach wasn't realistic at the time, but a pragmatic approach acknowledging the hard facts worked well. Sad to say, but in 2009, "We only want riders that have never doped" would have been an absurd proposition.

My attitude was, I want a rider that has the talent to race well clean, and has the volition and discipline to do it. I stand by that, and if Contador had come to our team and finished third or fourth in the Tour, we would have still seen that as a success.

We discussed our expectations with him and he was fine with it. There was a reticence on his part to disclose much about his past, but he knew what the score was and that if there were any doping issues, we would effectively burn him alive.

If Alberto hadn't been paid by the end of June, he was going to leave Astana and come to us. The plan was that we'd change our kit and take him on from the start of the 2009 Tour. Brad knew about the idea before the Tour began and, at first, was totally behind it. But, of course, neither of us knew how close Brad was going to run Alberto in the Tour. By halfway through the Tour, when Brad found himself in contention, his attitude had changed. By then, he didn't want Alberto on the team, and I can't blame him.

We had one final, decisive meeting toward the end of the Tour with Alberto, supposedly in secret. We chose this big field in Annecy where all the team buses were parked for the final time trial. We set out from our bus and he set off from his, like Napoleon meeting Wellington at Waterloo.

Alberto and his brother Fran marched out across the grass to meet Doug and I in the middle of a field, in hindsight the most visible place possible. Anybody could have filmed the whole awkward meeting. Ultimately, the deal didn't happen because Astana continued paying him, so he had to honor the contract and the moment was lost.

Meanwhile, Lance was actively encouraging Brad to move to Sky. He was whispering in his ear, as was Brailsford, even as we were trying to get him into the top three. It was a very tricky situation, as some of the other riders on the team also thought they might be moving to Sky, David Millar included.

I understood that, because David's sister, Fran Millar, was one of the founders of Team Sky. He was our poster boy, but he couldn't go to his sister's new team because of his past misdemeanors and their zero-tolerance stance.

I knew that David found our team useful but I also knew that he had very little loyalty to us. We were good at building up his brand and profile, because we were good at dealing with the media and getting our message across, but I've never doubted that if David could have left for Sky, he would have. Blood is thicker than water.

David was also actively recruiting riders from within our team to go to Sky. But after the news was broken to him that "No, you can't come to Sky, you don't fit within our policies," he went from being pretty brash about how bad we were, in relation to Team Sky, to then saying, "Oh, but I love this team, I love you, I love Doug."

Even so, I never felt that he was interested in what was best for the team, but in what was best for David. However, I'm a forgiving guy, and David was a damned talented rider, so we didn't leave him out in the cold due to his turncoat ways.

The policies that prevented David from going to Team Sky soon became clear. When they launched the team in 2010, they shouted from the rooftops about zero tolerance. They built a successful team by padding it out with ex-dopers and then later fixed them when they were honest enough to admit what they'd done.

The reality was that Sky was never going to be able to find people competent in the jobs required in pro cycling that hadn't had brushes with doping, either actively or passively. Unfortunately, of the generation of potential staff they had to choose from, a lot of those people all had knowledge or experience of doping. That doesn't mean they were involved in doping at Sky, but straight away, the zero-tolerance policy fails, even as you're recruiting.

They wanted to come into the sport—boom!—at the top, riding in the World Tour, and because of that ambition they were forced into hiring people who had been connected to, or involved in, doping stories. To me, zero tolerance was purely a marketing ploy on their part, without any basis to it.

Simply put, the philosophical differences between Team Sky and our team were massive. The Wiggins negotiations in 2009 would turn this philosophical difference into a cold war and put us at serious odds with each other. We were opposed on many levels—how to conduct business, how to treat people fairly, how to run a negotiation—not simply in our stance on anti-doping.

Unlike Sky, Slipstream was very much a hands-on team in which everyone pitched in, so our head of sports science would stand on the side of a mountain handing out water bottles. Brailsford wasn't like that. He was into organizational charts and ensuring that every department reported in to the next department. To me, he was trying to operate something that was outsized for the sport of cycling.

That said, eventually you could see that some of their systemization and execution worked quite well. For example, altitude training works, and because of their resources, Sky would rent out rooms in the altitude hotel on Mount Teide in Tenerife for twelve months. That meant the riders could come and go and get the benefits of altitude more often than any other team. Many other teams would love to do that, too, if they had the resources. Innovation is one thing; executing on the basics is another.

The rest of it, the marginal gains—well, most of it was nothing new. We were using ice vests in 2008, we were warming up and warming down then, too. We were testing vortex generators on skinsuits in 2009. The real innovations didn't come until later on, with the $50 million iteration of Sky.

But in 2012, the year they first won the Tour, they weren't that innovative—they just had a fucking good rider, Bradley Wiggins, in the shape of his life. The very same Bradley Wiggins that we once had.

When a Russian gangster walks into a room in an all-white tracksuit, one feels something like fear. When Dave Brailsford walks into a Manhattan meeting room full of suited and booted attorneys in an all-white tracksuit, plastered with Team GB logos, one feels something else entirely. How we all got there, in that tense and confrontational New York City meeting, began and ended with Bradley Wiggins and his performance in the 2009 Tour de France.

Contrary to cycling folklore, Brad Wiggins wasn't discovered or coached by me to make the Herculean transition from winning four-kilometer races on the track to almost, in 2009, winning a three-week, three-thousand-kilometer race in France. I wish I could make that claim, but there's only one person who can actually say that, and that's Brad.

He had the vision that he could be more than a track rider, and he put in the work. The reason his career blossomed under my watch was only because I didn't stop him from trying. Instead, I encouraged him to take the risk.

Wiggins was a special person and special rider, prone to extremes in performance and behavior. His focus is razor sharp, but it is double-edged. When he loses that intense focus, he falls totally off the rails. He's self-destructive and destructive to all those around him, with very little thought for anyone beyond himself.

I signed Brad to our team at the end of 2008 with high hopes. I had a hunch that if he focused 100 percent on road racing he had a lot more to give than he'd shown previously. At the time, he was thought of by most as a limited specialist: competitive in short time trials and a reasonable lead-out rider. Nothing special, really.

However, I saw Brad differently than most others and I signed him to a modest contract to race for us in 2009 and 2010. It was a humorous negotiation.

"I hope you can appreciate I don't really want to play this bullshit game of negotiation," I wrote to him. "I'd love to have you on board, I will pay you the most I can scrounge up. But that isn't so much ... Sound good? That said, how much do you want to get paid?"

Brad wrote back: "I too hate bullshit, so here's what I think I'm worth, and here's why ..."

I loved his attitude. No useless pleasantries, no pointless decorum, just straight to the issue. Plus, there was this little glimmer in Brad you didn't see in other riders. A confidence and self-belief—backed up by an enormous chip on his shoulder—fueled the psychological makeup of someone who was going to win a lot of races.

He was an Olympic gold medalist, and though this didn't matter much to most team managers on the European road scene, who'd all seen many a great track rider fail on the road, I thought it all amounted to something extraordinary. It showed Brad could deal with extreme pressure. It also indicated he had extreme ambition. It showed who he was, emotionally—a champion.

However, it takes more than great desire to be a top rider on the road. It takes a huge engine of oxygen carrying, which can't be seen or determined on the track. This was the unknown element with Brad, but one that I had gained unique insight into a few years before.

In 2005, a full year after Wiggins had snagged his first Olympic gold, he decided to take a year off the track and focus entirely on road racing. While the first part of his season was unremarkable, by the late part of 2005 he'd lost quite a bit of weight and had finally built up the resistance needed for the road. Coincidentally, in the late part of the season, I took a fledgling young team to the Tour de l'Avenir, a baby version of the Tour de France, where Wiggins was also competing.

As expected, he was quite competitive in the time trial stages. However, when we hit the mountains, to the surprise of many, Wiggins impressed mightily. He rode away from the front group with his teammate, Saul Raisin, romping across the Cantal mountains with ease, and crushing the competition. While it wasn't enough to win overall, and it wasn't the biggest race out there, winning the queen stage of l'Avenir showed that he could handle longer climbs. It made a big impression on me, and highlighted his capabilities and his potential as an athlete.

Looking back, this was an obvious indicator of his future talent on the road, but somehow that day went unnoticed. And it would remain unnoticed, because when 2006 and 2007 rolled around, Wiggins had started back on the track and was mainly focused on time trials when he did foray into road racing.

Brad's climbing skills reverted back to subpar for the pro peloton, and no one remembered his mountainous victory in 2005. I remembered it well, though, and as I signed the deal with him, I had some secret hopes in the back of my mind that he might become more of a prospect on the road than most people thought. I asked that he focus 100 percent on the road and give up the track for 2009. He agreed.

The first encounter Bradley had with our team was at our 2009 season orientation camp in Boulder, Colorado. This camp was in the middle of the off-season. Wiggins fit right in with the raucous nature of our team, and was the victim of it as well.

I can still remember the phone call at five a.m. from the management of the St. Julian Hotel, asking if I could come help resolve an issue. After a night of drunken debauchery, Wiggins's roommate had decided that it would be fun to rip the fire extinguisher off the wall of the hotel stairwell and discharge it in their room while Brad was asleep.

Seeing Wiggins emerge from the room looking like a powdered gingerbread man still makes me chuckle. The room looked like the inside of a snow globe, with open suitcases covered in a layer of white powder. Both Wiggins and his roommate had just a few hours to make their flight at this point. They left for the airport, lugging bikes, suitcases, clothing and the rest, dusted in white.

Wiggins's 2009 season did not start well. He showed up fit and ready to win the opening time trial at Paris–Nice in March, but didn't. It was downhill emotionally from there, because when he finished second to Alberto Contador, he simply couldn't accept it.

Brad had a completely childish meltdown, ranting about the helicopters pushing a downdraft against him, that Contador was doping, that the French didn't like him. He would not and could not accept that Contador had beaten him in a short prologue. We initially thought it was just the normal disappointment of losing, but this was clearly something more.

Wiggins hastily packed his bags and left the race. He didn't ask permission; he just left the hotel, and left us all wondering if he'd disappeared forever. It was not a great way to impress his new team nor his new teammates.

Cycling is not a "throw your toys out of the stroller when it doesn't go your way" sport. It's a hard sport, demanding resilience and durability. That's because it rarely goes your way, and it's how you overcome that that proves your value in this sport. I was hardly impressed, and all the team expected me to take some punitive action regarding Wiggins. You do get used to dealing with temperamental people in cycling, but this was one of the oddest things I'd seen a rider do in quite some time.

It proved to be a little glimpse of who Wiggins really was. He desperately wanted to win—and he was a born winner, a champion thoroughbred. But he was also completely self-absorbed and lacked any skills as a leader of men, as someone who would inspire people. It was an odd paradox: a born champion, all alone on the battlefield.

Wiggins remained out of contact for some days after his strange departure. There was no response to calls or emails. Nothing. We had no idea what happened to him. We thought he may have just quit cycling entirely. An old soigneur who had worked with Brad since he was a small child told us: "That's the way his father was—he would just go missing for days."

He eventually showed up to race again, though he never expressed any genuine remorse for disappearing on us in March. I realized sadly that Wiggins had an outsized desire to be great, but that he had very little loyalty to anyone around him. It was so very much against what our team was all about, but we had to work around it as he was quickly becoming the best rider we had.

The next big objective for Brad and the team was the opening team time trial in the 2009 Giro d'Italia. We'd won the team time trial in the Giro the year before and were considered the favorite to repeat, with Wiggins providing a notable boost.

I'd stirred up trouble in the run-up to the race when I made some ill-advised remarks in the press, saying that anything less than winning would be a disappointment. My public display of optimism was working against the team spirit and the riders now had quite a bit of pressure on them.

The other force working against the team's hopes of success was Brad's brutal strength. The rest of the team were intimidated by him, daunted by his speed and power, worried they'd be unable to hold his wheel, when he came through the line of riders to take his turn at the front. He was incredibly strong, and the added weight of expectation didn't affect him in the least. He almost ripped the team to shreds every time he was leading.

For the poor bastard who had taken a turn before Brad, it was almost impossible to latch back onto the back end of the line. It didn't turn out well; we ran an overthought and anxious second.

Wiggins was the shining light of the performance even if his pulls at the front sent his teammates deep into the red.

When Wiggins was focusing on the track, his primary interest was his ability to produce power for the four minutes of a pursuit, and intensely, for the first twenty seconds of getting up to speed. This effort required a massive ability to produce torque, which meant more muscle was going to be an advantage, and since the track is flat, gravity plays no part and extra weight is not a penalty.

But on the road, extra muscle—and when climbing, extra bulk—is a huge penalty, and since the efforts on the road are so much longer, the torque needed is much lower. The key to producing power for twenty seconds is muscle mass—the more the better—but the key to producing power for twenty minutes has very little to do with muscle mass but instead relies on how well a rider's body can supply muscles with oxygen. You can be skinny as a starving rat and produce tons of power for twenty minutes, as long as you have a heart big enough to pump the blood to the muscles.

As I learned when I turned pro, although road races are often six hours long, the crucial moments that determine the race are much smaller segments of time. Twenty minutes represents the point at which the body must produce a large output of power by using oxygen efficiently. This distinction is the downfall of most high-level track riders who look to race on the road: they can produce power for four minutes but are never able to extend that high power much longer, as they don't have the oxygen-carrying capacity of a top-level road pro.

Wiggins, however, was proving to be different. I'd already seen that in him when I'd watched him climb to that stage win in the Cantal. It seemed he was producing the majority of his four-minute power on the track using oxygen rather than muscle, meaning it could be extended to much longer than four minutes. At least, that was the theory.

In both 2005 and 2009, when Wiggins had forgone the heavy-weight training and short, intense track workouts, he lost quite a bit of muscle. In 2009, when he focused on losing weight as opposed to gaining it, he "leaned out" considerably. Many people thought he'd no longer be able to produce the power he once did, and they were right.

Over ten seconds to two minutes, his power output was way down in 2009. But for the four-minute mark, it remained similar. What was more interesting is that he was producing 95 percent of the same power for twenty minutes as he once did for four. That was the simple fact that would make Wiggins a Tour de France winner one day.

And I knew it. Back then, though, I was one of the few.

Between the Giro and that July's Tour de France, Wiggins spent time back at his home in Manchester, and trained a significant amount indoors on his ergometer. His recovery from the Giro and the power numbers he was producing were incredible. He was demonstrating a consistent ability to produce more than 6 watts per kilogram, showing his power-to-weight ratio was among the best in the world. He had made a definitive step forward during the Giro, but to see that people had to know what to look for. Since he didn't race between the Giro and Tour, his form remained hidden.

It was during this time Wiggins wanted to discuss extending his contract. It was a casual, but significant, conversation during a stroll along the narrow, cobbled streets of old town Girona, some ten days prior to the Tour de France. Wiggins told me how great the team had been, how he would not want to race for any other team, and how our lighthearted and fun atmosphere helped him rise to his best level.

I was flattered. Of course, I wanted to extend his contract well beyond 2010, but we did not have visibility into our sponsorship and revenue situation beyond that year—that's often the case in cycling—so I had to delay the conversation from becoming more serious. Looking back, I think Brad interpreted the delay and my reluctance to commit as my not believing in him and his talent. So he went to the start of the 2009 Tour de France light, fit, motivated—and pissed off at his boss.

At the start of the Tour de France that year in Monaco, there was a whole crew of new people slithering around every team's hotel, wearing cheap, poorly fitted Sky-emblazoned polo shirts. They were recruiting from other teams right in front of them for their lavishly funded upstart, Team Sky. Of course, they denied their motives, saying they were simply observing how the Tour was run and picking up a few pointers from the established teams.

I recall one meeting with Dave Brailsford and Doug Ellis in Monaco. Dave sat us down and reassured us he was not at the Tour to lure our athletes away from our team to the upstart Sky. He put on the jovial, nice-guy act, telling us that we needed to be allies, not enemies, in this crazy and dope-ridden sport full of non–English speaking types.

Sky or no Sky, the 2009 Tour de France was to change how the cycling world viewed Bradley Wiggins. He would become a star in those three weeks, and the most highly sought-after rider in the world, once contract season had started.

Wiggins immediately showed he was there to race the Tour with the best, by finishing third behind Fabian Cancellara and his old nemesis, Alberto Contador, in the Monaco prologue. But this time, Brad didn't pack his bags and go home after losing to Contador.

Instead, he kept his cool, because he knew big money was at stake. With Armstrong making his comeback to the Tour, Brad's performance didn't make the headlines that day, but it should have. It was the start of his ride toward one day winning le Tour.

We knew within the team that this performance was different from Brad's typically impressive short time trial performances. It was a very hilly course that normally would have precluded a high finish for Brad. But instead of losing time on the uphill sections, Wiggins was on par with the best times. He only lost the top spot due to the more daredevil downhill skills of his rivals. While the placing was impressive, the downloaded power file revealed a rider ready to contend with the best of the best.

As the peloton raced through the first week, Wiggins continued to quietly demonstrate he was now one of the best in the world at all disciplines. Yet, amazingly, it still hadn't hit the radar of many people. Most in the cycling world thought he would fail when the race hit the mountains. That theory was disproven on stage nine to Verbier.

Inside the team, we had been watching how strong Brad really was, and realizing he would be fine on the twenty-minute climb up to Verbier. To many people's surprise, we decided to dedicate the team solely to working for him on stage nine, and not to Christian Vande Velde, who'd finished fourth in the Tour the year before. It was a risky move, and ill-advised by most, but we rolled the dice and put our full faith in Wiggins. It was the right call. Brad performed beyond anyone's expectations.

Most attention was focused on Contador's attempts at displacing Armstrong, both physically and psychologically, but within all that drama, Wiggins's performance was the most remarkable feat of the day. He gracefully matched the best in the world, carrying his improbably lanky frame up the steep slopes. He shocked the other teams in cycling, who had assumed this would be the day of his unraveling. Instead, he showed that day he had the talent to one day win the Tour.

It was a great day for Wiggins and for the team. Our sponsors were happy, our riders were happy, and I was happy. But that happiness would not last very long. It marked the day that Team Sky began shadowing our relationship, as it was the day they began, in earnest, trying to unravel Wiggins's future with our team.

I knew this was always a risk. Brad had tight connections to British Cycling and to Brailsford through his years as an Olympic competitor. Yet despite that, I wasn't all that worried, because Brad had consistently voiced his dislike of all things Brailsford.

But little by little during the Tour, that tune began to change. Dave B. was successful in creating a campaign of whispers by having people talk to Brad's wife, Cath, and to Brad's inner circle of friends.

Bizarrely, even Lance decided to try and convince Brad to go to Sky. It was a strange twist, as Brad had once been rather vocal about his dislike for Armstrong, and certainly knew of Lance's transgressions in cycling from his former U.S. Postal teammates, some of whom now worked for us.

Despite that, Brad befriended Armstrong during the endless July miles. Armstrong used his star power to befriend and then influence Brad. As Armstrong and Wiggins were fighting for the final spot on the podium of the 2009 Tour, this was an interesting move, but Armstrong's competitive nature is only supplanted by his vindictiveness. And, of course, this vindictiveness was often aimed right at me, particularly back in 2009.

Anything Lance could do to undermine me, he would. What better way than by convincing my star rider to go to another team? It surprised me that Brad, who was so often vocal about being anti-doping, would be so open to what Lance was selling. Yet the seduction of fame and money were strong for Brad. Lance already had both, and so Brad listened.

What shocked me was Brad's sudden about-turn toward Brailsford and Shane Sutton, Team Sky's head coach. He'd spent so much time poking fun at them, bemoaning their limited view of the world, and doing funny imitations of them on the bus, that I just didn't see it coming.

As the Tour progressed, you could see Brad was less and less interested in the well-being of the team and more and more interested in his own financial well-being. He became focused on the big payout that would be coming if he could figure out a way to exit his contract with us. And to do that, he knew he needed to upset me, upset his teammates, and upset the staff.

On the final day of the Tour, into Paris, we felt we had an honest shot of winning the stage with our sprinter, Tyler Farrar. We had always been a team all about helping one another, and even though Brad was lying fourth overall, our expectation was that he'd help in the earlier, safer parts of the lead out prior to the sprint.

No dice. At the team meeting that morning, Brad put his hand up and said: "I'm not doing the lead out today. Period." The child was once again throwing his toys out of the stroller.

Given the level of support and belief he'd been given by the team, it was incredibly selfish of him and against everything the team—a team he later admitted to loving—was all about. The guys helped him every step of the way during the 2009 Tour; given a chance to give back, he refused.

There was nothing we could do about his adolescent behavior; he wanted us to get upset and fire him. Then Sky could step in and just start paying him immediately. That was his game. That was Brailsford's game. And I knew it.

Brad and I had one final dinner, outside Girona in a fun and cozy little restaurant in Madremanya. As the hummingbirds flew around the lavender, we shared a great meal, a few bottles of wine, and many laughs about what an incredibly fun journey the last year had been. I presented Brad with the best offer we could possibly make, hoping that he'd remain loyal to us.

Yet, as the wine sunk in and the dessert menu appeared, I could see in Brad's eyes that he desperately wanted out. He dreamed of being just like Lance, with private jets, vacation homes, and few financial worries. Struggling with a band of misfits had lost its appeal. In his head, he was already gone.

Over the next few months, things deteriorated and the separation became inevitable. Brad acted as if he had decided the best way to get out of his contract would be to enlist various sports agents to contact me and try to negotiate the buyout of the contract, and to be as obnoxious to us at races as possible.

He was showing up late to team meetings, if he showed up at all, and then at the Eneco Tour, he decided to veer off the course with two hundred meters left in the individual time trial, just so the results would show "DNF" (did not finish). It was like dealing with a five-year-old that wasn't getting his turn on the swings.

I recall having dinner one night with one of our riders, Will

Frischkorn. He lived above Brad's apartment in Girona. You could look down and see right into Brad's living room. He pointed out that Brad and his family had not been there in months. The place looked like it had been abandoned.

The funniest of Wiggins's attempts to get out of his 2010 contract came when he threw me a highbrow sports agent named Jonathan Marks. Jonathan went about his business by trying to befriend me, and quickly noted that I had a taste for nice wine and gourmet food.

However much my love of grand cru Burgundy was indulged by Mr. Marks, I held a firm line on Wiggins's contract. He would be riding for us in 2010, and only lawyers or a crowbar had any chance of changing that. It was ludicrous to think I'd let a potential Tour winner go off to another team for a few nice dinners and a small payment. That said, Jonathan really was quite generous in always picking up the bill.

After some months of playing tiddlywinks and Brad throwing various new characters my way to solve the issue, Sky finally realized that third-party sports agents weren't going to move the dial. They began to put some real resources behind the effort to "free Wiggins."

This was fine by me, as the backstabbing, emotionally charged campaign of rumors Brailsford was using to try and create a personal rift between Wiggins and me was getting old. Tactics of persuasion, from my emotional reaction to the situation, to the fact that our sponsors weren't signed to decade-long contracts, were whispered in Brad's ear. It became tiring and childish. Finally, hard facts and lawyers got involved.

Fact number one: under EU law, you cannot compel an athlete to work for you, and certainly not at a lower wage than another team is willing to pay. This would work against us in any dispute. However, fact number two made things more interesting. Part of Wiggins's compensation was paid as an image rights contract to a company that he set up.

This contract was under the jurisdiction of the state of Colorado.

We owned Wiggins's image rights, 100 percent, through the 2010 season. So while he had the right to go and ride for another team in 2010, he'd have to be wearing a Garmin kit while doing so. That was when the attorney marathon began.

Brailsford, a few attorneys from Sky, our Slipstream Sports attorney, Matthew Pace, and I had all agreed to meet in Pace's office in midtown Manhattan. Brailsford and his crew were arriving from London in the morning, and we planned to sit down and figure out what was going to happen with the Wiggins saga.

Brailsford and the armada of Murdoch attorneys were late. When they finally did arrive, it was a sight to behold. Among all the dark pinstripe suits, crisp collars, and cuff links that a midtown Manhattan law firm can offer, there was Dave Brailsford, in a bright white Adidas Team GB–issue tracksuit. It made me laugh.

In contrast to Brailsford's Tony Soprano chic, his sidekick, an attorney named Richard Verow, looked like someone who was to be taken seriously. They had a flight to catch back to London in six hours, so they wanted to get on with answering the fundamental question of what it was going to take for me to let Wiggins out of his outstanding obligations.

To me, it was simple: Wiggins was a future Tour de France winner from a quickly expanding cycling market—Great Britain. This put his value to any current or new sponsor wishing to enter cycling at a sum near $100 million, as that's the advertising equivalent return on investment that he would generate for a sponsor if he were to win the Tour.

Brailsford and Verow saw it another way. They felt that Brad should be free to choose whatever team he wanted, despite having a signed contract with us. We couldn't have been further apart on the issue.

Hours passed and tempers flared, and at one point Brailsford exasperatedly declared: "It'd be easier to get Alberto Contador under contract!"

Dave still didn't realize, even then, what a gem he was after. Wiggins, in terms of pure marketing value, would be bigger than Contador by a mile. It was a tough deadlock to break, as we both knew the conflict that the UCI contract and the image rights contract presented, and the consequences if we could not reach an agreement.

But in promising him the moon, Brailsford had poisoned Wiggins's mind-set. There was very little chance Wiggins would happily ride for Garmin in 2010. And even if he did, he would know that his future employment was secured, so he could just show up to every race totally disengaged. Still, there was nothing in this world that would make losing a future Tour de France winner really worth it.

When you manage a team, it becomes part of your identity. And when you find a diamond in the rough like Wiggins long before anyone sees the potential, you relish that discovery as your own. It is the ultimate dream of any manager to win the Tour, but it takes a very special talent to make that possible, and Wiggins had that talent.

No matter what deal we arrived at, it was always going to be raw for me. Feeling strong-armed and manipulated into it is something I have never, in all honesty, forgiven Brailsford or Team Sky for.

CHAPTER 17

DO THE RIGHT THING

had left Europe and retired from racing with an incredibly bitter taste in my mouth. I was more than a little resentful of the guys who'd had the opportunity to walk away from doping when EPO stopped being so widely used. My frustration with cycling's spiral of doping and denial grew after I retired and moved back to the States.

Instead of grabbing the opportunity that came with the introduction of the new test for EPO, most of the riders competing as team leaders, particularly in the Tour, just found a way around it. Toward the end my career, I was doing it myself, running around sleazy little pharmacies, planning micro-dosing, and stockpiling for the Tour, but then at the last minute I just thought: "What are you doing? This is fucking crazy! I could kill myself . . ." It was incredibly sordid.

From the 2001 Tour onward, it was increasingly apparent that for the biggest races, some other methods were being used. Living in Girona, among all the U.S. Postal riders, I soon learned that they had moved on to a new method of using EPO, which was intravenous lower doses, administered more frequently. They were also using blood transfusions.

I knew, too, that my teammates on Crédit Agricole were really hurting. Their careers were suffering, their morale was tumbling. It hurt me to watch them get mocked by the media for not performing.

I sensed that Roger Legeay's idealism was starting to get beaten down; his morale was suffering, too. You could see the resolve of the team wilting.

When that happens, the riders start to question what they're doing. "*We can't function like this—what are we doing?—what's the point?*"

It was cycling at two speeds. There were the haves and the have-nots.

Watching my teammates in those Crédit Agricole years try and race without doping, try to convince themselves they could fight and win, honorably, only to see them get slaughtered, fueled my resentment. Yes, I was done with racing and I had walked away, but I carried that grudge with me like a two-hundred-pound duffel bag.

And when guys finally got caught for doping and then dared blame it on the system? That drove me nuts.

Going back to August 2004, my old USPS teammate Tyler Hamilton tested positive at the Athens Olympics, and immediately started disparaging anti-doping and USADA, the U.S. Anti-Doping Agency. I thought of my old teammates trying to race clean and then of Tyler and all the other U.S. Postal Service guys taking everything they could, and then, when they got caught, trying to tear down anti-doping.

It made me angry. It was just bullshit.

One morning when Alisa and I were taking a few days' vacation in Colorado Springs, at this hotel called the Broadmoor, I read another article in which Tyler was attacking USADA and anti-doping. And I just thought, *I've had enough . . .*

I called up USADA and scheduled a meeting with Terry Madden, then their CEO, and Travis Tygart, who was their counsel, for the next day. Alisa stayed by the pool with our son, having drinks and eating fish fingers, and I drove across town to USADA, where I sat down and, under conditions of confidentiality, told them everything.

That was the first time I'd met Travis and it was the first time I disclosed everything I knew. At the time everyone else in sport, not just in cycling, was trying to keep the anti-doping authorities in the dark as much as they possibly could. Nobody was helping anti-doping back then and it was the first meeting of that kind that they'd ever had with an athlete.

They were shocked by what I said, but they were also grateful. Travis is a very idealistic person with commensurate convictions. "You are doing the right thing, even if it doesn't feel like it at the moment," they said. "Eventually this will turn the sport in a better direction."

They were interested in taking down a system; they had no interest in taking down individual riders. Talking to me was the first step in taking apart that culture of doping.

For my part, it felt like a massive relief. I felt strongly that Travis was a good guy, that he was someone who wanted to do what was right. He gave me the same sort of feeling that I got from Roger Legeay, that he was a genuine and sincere human being. It's a feeling that I'd never felt for a single second with Johan and Lance.

I had more contact with Travis in 2006, in the period after Floyd Landis tested positive following his victory in the 2006 Tour. I had been in Annecy in the French Alps, with USA Cycling and with Doug, when the news came through about Floyd's big Tour-winning break to Morzine.

I was driving back from the Alps to Girona, listening to commentary of the race on the radio, thinking: "Holy shit! This kind of move hasn't worked in cycling for years . . ." But I wasn't that surprised. Floyd had balls and he was smart. He'd pulled off the truly extraordinary.

Floyd had looked beaten the night before. While I knew he may have been doping, you don't get a quick turnaround like that from testosterone, or from a blood bag. Yes, doping was obviously part of his performance, but tactically he also executed a high-risk plan on that stage. The fact that he was ever in contention to win the Tour that year—that was down to doping, but his ride to Morzine was no more down to doping than the day before, or the day before that.

After word started to filter out that Floyd had tested positive, I called him. We'd lived in Girona together and had some history. I'd known he didn't really fit in when he was on the U.S. Postal Service team, that he was butting heads with Lance, that he was lonely. I really liked him, his free spirit, and I always thought that he could have been a great bike rider if he'd just calm down, stop drinking fourteen cappuccinos a day and quit trying to be the rebel.

It was pretty late at night when I called him, but he answered on the first ring, crying so much that he couldn't even talk.

"What am I going to do?" he said between the sobs.

He couldn't go home because the media was there, and he couldn't go to his mom's house, either, because they were camped out there, too. He was in a terrible state, and desperate to escape the situation. There had been some big endorsements lined up for him but now all that was falling apart.

Within a few days, he was in New York and looking for somewhere to hide out. So Doug and I told him that he could stay in Doug's house in the West Village until the whole thing calmed down. There was a band of people who rallied around to support Floyd and at times it felt that we, and everyone else who was close to him, was effectively on suicide watch.

To this day, Floyd maintains that he wasn't taking testosterone—he accepts that he was doping but insists that the test was wrong and that it caught him for something he wasn't using.

Doug's attitude was that Floyd, whatever else he may have done, deserved due process, that everyone deserved their day in court, and that their case should be heard. That was why he helped Floyd afford a robust defense.

Most of the time, the slant in these cases favors the anti-doping body. The athlete has very few rights compared to a normal legal system, and there is a presumption of guilt. After the A sample is positive, there's a 100 percent presumption of guilt. My gut feeling is that there have been multiple cases when athletes have been wrongly sanctioned.

At the same time, we knew what Floyd had done, we knew he'd doped, and we knew that doping was serious, but we also believed him when he said he hadn't taken testosterone. Doug and I had long philosophical conversations about who was in the right, but at the same time, we needed perspective. Floyd wasn't a hardened cynic. He had a vulnerable, childlike quality, which was maybe why we felt protective toward him.

When he was still in Doug's house in New York, I spoke to Travis, and told him that Floyd and I were old friends. Travis told me he did not want to bring Floyd down—again he said he wanted to bring down a culture and I trusted him when he said that. He asked me to talk to Floyd and explain to him that, if he was honest, USADA could make things easier for him and help him get out of the hole he was in.

I talked to Floyd some more.

"You can make a deal with them," I told him. "If you just disclose everything it will be more favorable to you and you'll be seen as someone who's helping the sport."

There might have been a brief moment when he was actually considering it, but Floyd doesn't really trust anyone. There have been moments when he has trusted me, but he yo-yos between an incredibly intelligent, thinking, and considered person and a very angry, vengeful person. Unfortunately, that was where he bounced to. He decided to fight USADA.

When Floyd gave an interview to Paul Kimmage in 2010, he said he regretted that decision. "In the context of what happened since," he said, "I would do everything the same and I would just admit it [doping] afterward."

"Vaughters sent me some texts," Floyd told Kimmage, "saying 'just tell the truth.'"

Yet in the same interview he also suggested that his decision not to talk had been influenced by me. "I had some correspondence with Jonathan," Floyd said, "because he knew before some other people did—and his advice was, 'Just say what you know about you and don't say anything about anyone else.'"

But that's not exactly accurate. The reality was that I was trying to get him to talk to the proper authorities. I told him to speak to USADA directly and not through the media.

Travis's reaction to Floyd's decision to fight USADA was one of intense sadness. His response to Floyd taking on USADA wasn't competitive; he didn't want to "beat" Floyd. It was much more that an opportunity to take down a system, rather than an individual, had been lost.

In September that year, only a matter of weeks after the Operación Puerto doping scandal and Floyd testing positive, my ex-teammate Frankie Andreu came out and admitted to doping while at U.S. Postal Service in a *New York Times* story by Juliet Macur. That story couldn't have been published without it being corroborated, and it was— anonymously—by me. It quoted me saying: "To be accepted, you had to use doping products. There was very high pressure to be one of the cool kids."

I was scared shitless of the fallout when the story ran, but nothing really happened. Travis knew that the anonymous rider was me and the next time we talked he said: "Eventually there will be a day when I ask you to formalize this admission," which was when I realized that I might one day go public and sign an affidavit.

I'd actually wanted to admit to doping for some time, but it was a case of waiting for the right moment. Doug and I talked about it and he advised me to wait.

"At the moment, it's just you alone sticking your head above the parapet and taking a bullet. It's a tree falling in the woods," he told me. "Wait for the right moment, then it will be all the more powerful."

I didn't ever set out to become a main player in the Plot to Bring Down Lance—it was just circumstances, momentum, and a chain of events that made it happen.

When Slipstream started, there was the inevitable sledging directed toward us from Texas. Lance thought the whole thing was absurd. His attitude was: "What the fuck? The anti-doping team? All those fuckers doped like it was going out of style . . ."

Lance didn't want our redemption story out there, because it

acknowledged what had happened during the time he'd been dominant. I know that trying to crush our story and damage us was one
of the key motivators for his comeback in 2009. He dogged our
progress and tried to undermine me as we grew the team.

Lance is clever. He doesn't directly throw something at you, but
he'll just drop doubt in by suggesting to mutual contacts, spreading
the word along the lines of "Do you really think you should be involved with this person, with this team?" In the autumn of 2008, he
spoke to Doug Ellis and openly suggested that he should change the
management of the team by getting rid of me.

"Vaughters . . . ? Doug, I know you're a good guy, but you've got
the wrong guys on the bus," Lance wrote to him in an attempt to
redirect Doug's investment into his hands.

I think that briefly, Doug did think about it. Lance can be very
charming, and very persuasive. Now Doug says "Thank God, I
didn't listen to him," but at the time, certainly for me, because Doug
initially took what he said seriously, it was scary.

Lance enjoyed intimidating people, too. When the affidavits were
published as part of the USADA Reasoned Decision, there were
some chilling stories in there, particularly the one told by Levi Lei-
pheimer, another ex–USPS rider.

After Lance found out that Levi had given evidence, he sent a
text to Levi's wife, Odessa, saying: "Run, don't walk . . ."

There have also been moments in all this when I have been worried for my safety. *Have I said too much? Did I go too far? Are the brakes
suddenly going to fail on my car? Will I have a terrible riding accident, a sudden unexplained heart attack?* That is probably paranoia, but it felt real
enough during the investigation.

There were other occasions when Lance tried to undermine me.
We had an agreement with Taylor Phinney to join the team before
he went to the Beijing Olympics in 2008, but after he got back from
China, we couldn't get in touch with him. He wasn't returning my
calls, and his parents wouldn't talk to me, either.

Then I heard that he was up in Aspen, hanging out with Lance.
Finally, I had some contact with Connie, Taylor's mom. She

called up and said, "Oh, we're really sorry but Taylor's going to take up a different opportunity next year..."

Lance had got to him.

At the time, Lance didn't even have a development team, so he just created one through Livestrong, his charity, solely based on stealing Taylor from us (or at least that's how it looked to me). It was his chance to say, "Fuck you, JV."

These days, Lance and I successfully manage not to talk to each other. We avoid each other and almost never speak. The only time I've spoken to him in years was a while back, when I was involved in a talk on anti-doping in Aspen.

Lance showed up, sat down—next to Ashley, my wife at the time—and glared at me.

After 2006, I didn't see Travis again for about three years, until we randomly bumped into each other on a ski lift in Breckenridge, Colorado, in 2009. We were both sitting there in ski gear, in goggles and hats, when he peered at me and said in his Texan accent: "Jonathan, is that you?"

We skied and talked that day and the last thing we said to each other, before we parted ways, was that we wished Floyd had just come clean. Then, a year or so later, in May 2010, Floyd finally did, firing allegations out to the media and the authorities. Even so, I had mixed feelings when he sent the emails detailing his own doping and Lance's.

Floyd could have done all that in 2006, when he had the opportunity, but instead he opted to fight USADA all the way into the ground, to set up his "Fairness Fund" and use millions of dollars of other people's money, to go broke and also nearly break himself. I also knew that he was again in a very dark place, living up in Idyllwild, California.

In May 2010, when nobody would take him back into the sport, he seemed to have decided: "Okay, now I'm going public and I'm going to do as much damage as I possibly can."

Travis and Floyd had very different motivations. Travis was trying to help the sport, to smash a culture of doping, while Floyd was trying to destroy the sport and bring it down to his level. Travis was being progressive and logical, but Floyd was vengeful and angry. I don't blame Floyd for his anger: after all, he had to watch his world burn to the ground, while Lance flew around the world in a Gulfstream.

Once Floyd's allegations over doping at U.S. Postal Service had gone public and the federal investigation opened, Doug and I had a long discussion on how we should respond to the implications. The biggest issue for us was Lance's reaction, which was vitriolic and hateful toward Floyd. He came out and attacked Floyd in the media. Doug and I knew that Floyd was very depressed and possibly suicidal. Lance should have just remained quiet.

When I was bullied in high school, it left a nasty scar. I was a little kid who got hurt and ostracized by "bro culture" and bullying. Bullying is something I hate beyond anything else, because I know how much it sucks to be on the other end of it.

When Lance chose to bully Floyd, it lit my fire. All the years of avoiding direct questions about Lance's doping, of silently absorbing my feelings as I watched Lance bully Frankie and Betsy Andreu, Filippo Simeoni, Greg LeMond—it had gone one step too far. I couldn't hold back anymore.

Doug and I felt Floyd had been hurt enough already without Lance saying what he said. We felt he needed somebody to stand up for him, but nobody was. Pat McQuaid, the UCI President—the entire sport in fact—all they could say was: "Floyd's a scumbag."

Even David Millar called Floyd "a liar and a cheat" who "wants to burn the house down." I was so pissed with David over that statement. Of all people, he should have known better.

Doug and I agreed that our team policy was to say nothing—publicly—but to say everything to those who counted. It was a very odd tack to take, in that we just didn't talk to the media about the issue at all and avoided the topic entirely. Behind the scenes, we were laying it all out there—all of it.

Doug and I both knew that Lance was very good at taking people down when they came forward publicly, so we didn't want to give him the opportunity. It was easy for him, an all-conquering world icon and a cancer hero, to dismiss an individual. One by one, he'd shot down and damaged the Andreus, LeMond, Emma O'Reilly, David Walsh, and now Floyd, because they'd gone against him.

Doug and I knew that wounding Lance was like wounding a tiger—it just made him angrier and more dangerous. We knew we had to be patient and strategic to finally end the mess.

The office of the lead investigators had also sent us a letter stating that it was their strong preference that we did not speak to the media about the investigation at all, as it would interfere with their work. We supported Floyd, but we did it behind the scenes.

A few days after Floyd had gone public with his confession and exposé of Lance, Doug and I composed a press statement with our communications lead, Marya Pongrace.

It didn't seem too explosive at the time, nothing like Floyd's letter to the world. But while not explosive, it explained how we were going to proceed as an organization. If Lance read it closely, he should have known the jig was up. But I imagine he read it and dismissed it. *"Those pussies don't have the balls ..."*

Boy, was he wrong.

"We cannot change what happened in the past, but we believe it is time for transparency," our statement read. "We expect anyone in our organization who is contacted by any cycling, anti-doping, or government authority will be open and honest with that authority. In that context, we expect nothing short of 100 percent truthfulness—whatever that truth is—to the questions they are asked.

"As long as they express the truth about the past to the appropriate parties, they will continue to have a place in our organization and we will support them for living up to the promise we gave the world when we founded Slipstream Sports."

We had maybe seven or eight people in our team who'd worked, either as staff or riders, for Postal Service. I called Travis and asked him for Jeff Novitzky's phone number. I spoke to Novitzky, who was leading the federal investigation, for about an hour. I wanted to understand his motivations and what was really going on.

He laid it all out to me, and I was happy with what he said. So I told him it was the policy of our team that we would support, financially and otherwise, all of our employees who volunteered to come forward on this matter and that were truthful in their testimony.

That's important to remember: they volunteered. We called them, they didn't call us.

They talked to me first, then they talked to Dave Zabriskie and to Tom Danielson. Travis was on the periphery of those talks, but after that we dealt directly with the feds. The interviews with Novitzky's people weren't that confrontational. They just asked us to detail what had happened, which we did.

It wasn't intimidating, it wasn't adversarial, and we weren't coerced. That's another of the Lance-propelled myths, that it was like an episode of *CSI*—that a bunch of badge-wearing, gun-toting FBI agents sat us down and grilled us. It wasn't like that at all. We volunteered and it was very friendly.

Doug and I encouraged everyone in our team who had information to talk to them, because that was our policy as a team and it was what we expected from the people on our team. Yes, there was an "Are you with us?" element of persuasion, but it was still their choice.

Doug was the true hero in this whole saga. He'd done something never done before in cycling. He'd agreed to financially support riders and staff who were about to go in and admit to doping. From paying their salary to helping with attorneys' fees, Doug was in, to the tune of millions.

We weren't going to watch our people burn. The only thing that would trigger us leaving one of ours unaided would be lying, which would have led us to end our relationship. That was the deal we made with them. It went to the very heart of what the team was founded on, which was acknowledging the past and trying to shape a better future.

By that point, I'd become quite evangelical. The anger over doping, over what I'd done and what others had done, too, suppressed when I was younger, had built up in me. But looking back, sometimes I do think I might not have made the call to Novitzky had Lance not attacked Floyd. The bullying sent me over the edge.

When he came out and attacked Floyd, it changed me.

Lance was condemning someone else for his crimes. It crossed a line, because we'd moved into the domain of setting out to ruin people's lives and of hurting people in a very profound and lasting way, just to protect our secrets. It was too much, it was unacceptable.

You have to remember Lance didn't have to make a comeback. He could have stayed away from cycling, played golf, lived his life, kept his trophies, but he chose not to—he came back and then started attacking someone for telling the truth. He was perpetuating the *omertà*, perpetuating the problem. It was untenable to me and I'm lucky that I had a boss in Doug who felt it was untenable, too.

The doping? We all doped. It's inexcusable and it's a fact.

But the bullying? The bullying was the reason Lance paid a higher price than the rest of us.

Doug and I spoke. He knew we couldn't remain silent anymore.

"Okay, it's time to come clean . . ."

GAME OVER

After the federal investigation into Lance Armstrong was dropped in early 2012, there was a sense of a sport left in limbo, wondering what to do next. The one thing that UCI president Pat McQuaid and I seemed to agree on was that the only way forward was through stronger anti-doping measures.

Agreement between us was rare. In our respective roles as president of the UCI and president of the AIGCP, we had not been very kind to each other in the media for the last few years. We seemed to disagree on every major issue in cycling. Every single one.

The use of radios, team sizes, the number of teams, how to deal with ASO, the number of sponsors on jerseys, the three-kilometer rule, turkey or ham, mustard or no mustard, ketchup or mayo . . .

If there was something to disagree about, Pat and I disagreed. At the base of it was just a difference in how we thought of cycling. I thought of cycling as a sport in which the teams should have a strong voice. Teams pulled $500 million in revenues every year into the sport, and employed more than two thousand people. Collectively, we were the largest entity in the sport, and I felt our representation should reflect that.

Pat felt differently. He felt the teams were like little children. They needed to be told when to eat, when to sleep, and when to go to the bathroom. Teams were run by irresponsible miscreants and could not be trusted.

These vastly different views ran into each other at full speed in every meeting we had over the span of my five-year tenure as AIGCP president. In the press, in the boardroom, in the hotel lobby, and at the bar, Pat and I disagreed on everything. Our tussles spilled over into the media often, with both of us using every opportunity to undermine each other. I think the media loved it, really. It was like a Three Stooges skit, poking eyeballs and twisting noses.

In his old-fashioned way, Pat was truly looking to improve cycling via stronger anti-doping measures. To some, this statement raises an eyebrow, I'm sure, but just looking at the facts, Pat authorized action and funding to make cycling the first sport ever to implement the biological passport and to suspend riders based on indirect testing.

It was a huge risk and, credit to Pat, he took it on. Even going back to Pat's more politicized best friend and presidential predecessor, Hein Verbruggen, cycling was the first sport, by many years, to come out with blood testing of any sort. I know these guys were never paragons of transparency, yet they both led an organization that was well ahead of its time in respect to anti-doping. Cycling was far ahead of any other sport. I know, this isn't the narrative that is heard these days, but it's true.

I knew the time had come when I needed to have a real sit-down with Pat over what was coming down the tracks in the aftermath of the federal investigation into Armstrong. Since Pat was visiting Colorado during the USA Pro Cycling Challenge, I figured I would invite him to sit in the team car with me for the longest stage of the race.

I think Pat was pretty thrown by my invitation to ride along. We'd spent so much of the past years trying to publicly strangle each other, so why was

I inviting him to hang out? Maybe he thought it was a secret plot to murder him in a strange car accident or a wheel change gone wrong, or something. Nonetheless, Pat agreed to ride with me.

Pat loved Colorado, which is something I found endearing about him. He just loved the huge mountains and the wide-open spaces. He'd bought his first pair of cowboy boots during the race and wore them proudly to the start. We exchanged pleasantries before packing up and heading off behind the race.

My mechanic that day was Geoff Brown. Geoff was also Lance Armstrong's mechanic at the peak of the USPS days. Geoff had seen it all during his days wrenching bikes. I think he was just a bit nervous to buckle in for a full six hours in a car with no one except Pat and me.

We headed off behind the race in the crisp, early-morning Colorado air. It was a sunny and clear day to start with, but being Colorado, I knew as we hit the afternoon that the clouds would build and the rain would come down.

Pat and I immediately started discussing issues that would be coming up for both of us in the next PCC (Pro Cycling Council) meeting. The PCC is, in theory, the board of directors that decides on the strategic direction of professional cycling, along with more pragmatic issues, like the race calendar, rule changes, and policy direction.

Pat and I started bickering over the last tussle we had had in the Salzburg PCC reunion, which was over the white-hot issue of how many names a team was allowed to have. The PCC was fairly split on this issue. A few teams had asked me if they could add a third name, as it would bring in extra dollars. For me, while I felt that the brand dilution was substantial, I just figured that should be the teams' problem, not something that's in the rules.

The rules shouldn't really care how many names a team has. Some on the PCC, like Stephen Roche, felt that the potential for added revenues and wage increases for riders that could happen by adding a third name would be offset by ugly jerseys with too many icky sponsors' logos. I disagreed and brought this highly contentious issue to a vote, the first actual vote the PCC had ever had in its history.

Previously, rule changes and such had always been done by "consensus," usually over drinks at the bar when a bunch of old dudes would just decide the outcome so that they could get on with their UCI-paid vacation. The concept of a vote, while perfectly legal, brought the room to dead silence.

The old boys' club of UCI nominees all voted against the ugly notion of three names. The riders' union and team representatives voted for the relaxing of the two-name rule. The race organizer's association, represented by Christian Prudhomme, director of the Tour, abstained, saying it was none of their business.

The tie-breaking vote would come down to Pat. Of course, he voted against the measure, saying he didn't like race commentators getting confused. I left the room bitterly disappointed, while Pat basked in the glory of having prevented the unmitigated disaster of allowing teams to have three names.

As Pat and I locked horns again in the two- versus three-names debate, race radio crackled into life.

"Warning—please inform your riders there is a very dangerous cattle grid coming up in a mile!"

I turned to Pat.

"Well, I'd love to tell them about that," I said, "but since rider radios are illegal in this level of a race, I can't!"

Pat muttered something about how the race organizer should have warned us much earlier, which I guess was so that we could "safely" drive our cars into the middle of the peloton and yell out the window that a cattle grid was coming.

When we came to the cattle grid, a widely spaced metal grate built across a road that keeps livestock from crossing, a couple of riders from Steve Bauer's team, SpiderTech, crashed—hard. Both had to be hospitalized with facial injuries. Understandably, Steve was livid. He also knew Pat was in my car.

He drove up alongside us and started berating Pat, saying that he was a fucking idiot for not allowing race radios in smaller races, and that this shit was going to happen until the UCI pulled its head out of its ass. The car went quiet. Sitting in the back, Geoff tried to chew his apple more quietly. Or just swallowed it whole.

Race radios had been the big debate for a year or so. The UCI insisted races were safe enough without radios and that riders relying on them somehow made for boring and predictable racing. Pat had a more nuanced view in private, and one that I actually respected. He felt that riders should think for themselves, know the race course for themselves, and have autonomy in race tactics. I actually agreed with him on all of this.

This debate raged on in public, not just between Pat and me, but teams, riders, UCI, race organizers, the media. Everyone had an opinion. Everyone disagreed. And as is typical in cycling, everyone needed to make sure the media knew about their opinion. It had come to a head the year before with the teams almost boycotting the Tour of Beijing.

I received some incredibly memorable voicemails from Pat's predecessor, Hein Verbruggen, over that one. One morning, as the pre-Beijing standoff continued, I checked my messages. There was one from Verbruggen.

"If it's true that you guys are trying to boycott China," he told me, "then we're finished, you and I. Goddamn it, I've been working my fucking ass off to get that race from [sic] the ground and you guys are gonna do that . . . to me . . . ? Don't ever call me again. You can call me to tell that this is all bullshit—if not, then I'm really extremely disappointed in your leadership."

But I had a very different relationship with Pat. We could laugh in private at how we'd crucified each other in public. We could somehow sit in a car behind a race, sharing a sandwich, and just talk about the issues.

As the race wore on, I finally broached the subject neither of us really wanted to discuss. The USADA investigation into Lance.

"Pat, I think the UCI needs to start considering its position when all of this comes out," I said.

Pat was not having it at all.

"I doubt it's coming out," he said. "You and I both know the federal investigation has been closed, and USADA legally can't get ahold of that testimony. So, it's case closed."

"Yeah, but Pat, what if the witnesses voluntarily testified to USADA?" I replied.

"None of you have the courage to do that," he snapped.

"I don't know, Pat—maybe some people just feel it is the right thing to do . . . ?"

By that I meant me, of course, and some of the riders and personnel on my team.

Over the next few hours I gave Pat my position on the issue. I told him I thought the UCI should call USADA and work together with them on the issue. Pat and I both knew that the whole of the sport was tied up in this mess, one way or another, and that the backlash would be spectacular.

"Maybe it's time to be honest about the past so we can move forward, Pat. I think USADA wants that. They aren't headhunting," I offered.

But the previous battles between UCI and WADA had left deep scars, and USADA was seen as a subsidiary to WADA. There would be no working with USADA. No fucking way.

"Jonathan, this whole thing won't amount to anything," he said. "The federal investigation is over. No one is going to go run to USADA."

"I know your era of riders got away with a fair bit of shenanigans, but I doubt any of you will have the balls to really tell the truth," he said.

*

When the federal investigation into Lance had been closed down, I—like a lot of people—was shocked, but then, when a couple weeks later, Travis Tygart told me that USADA were picking up the reins, I realized it was unfinished business.

"We can't just let this die," Travis said.

But there was a snag.

They couldn't use the original evidence from the federal investigation, so Travis was forced to ask us all to testify again. In theory, the FBI could have subpoenaed us, but USADA have no powers to do that, which meant we could have refused. If we went back in to talk to USADA, it would again be voluntarily.

In truth, we were all pretty weary of the whole thing. Certainly, by then, I was feeling that way, too. We'd already put ourselves on the line, we'd already been through the interviews and now Travis was asking us to do it all over again.

There was a fatigue creeping in, and generally people were starting to feel the moment had gone, so I kicked a little against Travis.

We talked on the phone.

"I don't know," I said. "Maybe it's time to let this go. Lance isn't in the sport anymore. How much are we going to gain by carrying on with this? What's the point anymore?"

Travis listened.

"JV, this is not about Lance," he said. "This is about dismantling a culture that may not be as pervasive now as it was, but it will be again if we do not get people to tell the truth and acknowledge the past."

I knew that, even if we testified voluntarily, our reputations would be permanently damaged. We all realized that. I knew reaction would be split, that there'd be some people thinking "Thank God they're telling the truth" and then others saying, "Who the fuck do they think they are?"

Second time around, I had to be more persuasive, because by then everybody had had enough. I think Lance felt that people wouldn't repeat the allegations to USADA and that it was the threat of the gun-wielding feds that had made them testify the first time. But that, like many of his other ways of justifying people's decisions to give evidence, proved to be untrue.

He also thinks that I sold him down the river, that I ratted on him and that I strategically "took him out," because I viewed him as business competition within American cycling, as if my giving evidence to USADA was some kind of career move, aimed at putting me in a dominant position.

That's not true. In fact, it's complete nonsense, because, of course, the damage to American cycling if he was exposed was huge. If making money was my sole motivation, I'd never have done it. I'd have been in a much better financial position if none of it had ever happened. The sponsorship marketplace in the U.S. was crushed in the aftermath of Lance. There was no financial advantage for us.

Travis acknowledged what giving evidence against Lance would mean for those who came forward. Of course, Travis had been generous with reduced suspensions and such, but most of the athletes who testified were at the end of their career, so that didn't mean much. The damage to reputations was going to be immense, and that was what concerned me.

They had been the few who were willing to voluntarily come forward and expose an entire culture for what it was, yet they would be the ones who would be blamed. There was no way around it. Taking your medicine is just part of the reality of being honest about cheating and the guys accepted that. But was it fair that they were seen as the few who cheated? No, of course not. But then life's not fair. We cheated, it was time to own up to it.

That said, had cycling implemented a proper "truth and reconciliation" program and the full truth been revealed, then I think those who testified to USADA would have been seen as "first through the wall"—not as the bad boys of cycling. But that's the thing, just because you've chosen to be truthful, you can't expect everyone around you to do the same. That was our choice. The others were free to make their own choices, particularly if they had just watched you get publicly burned at the stake on social media.

As I left my interview with Travis, I made one last comment that made me feel a little insane. I told Travis that he needed to offer Lance the same deal that he offered us.

To a degree, he agreed with that, but qualified it by pointing to the level of what he called "egregiousness" on Lance's part. But he was willing to offer Lance something that didn't strip him of all of his titles and that meant he wouldn't be suspended for any longer than a year. I understood the deal to be one year's suspension and the loss of two Tour titles that were still within the statute of limitations.

Hearing that offer scared me. I knew that if Lance took the deal Travis was offering, he'd be waiting for revenge for those twelve months. But I also knew the fair thing was to give Lance the chance to tell the truth. Just like the rest of us.

Lance turned Travis down, cold.

I can remember exactly when Travis's report—the Reasoned Decision—was finally published, because I got married to Ashley on October 7, 2012. The USADA report, condemning Lance for doping, and publishing our affidavits testifying to doping, came out on October 10.

PART 7
2010–2019

CHAPTER 18

MERGERS AND ACQUISITIONS

C ycling attracts dreamers, because since there is no order and no overall strategy to the sport, anyone can just show up and try to reinvent the wheel.

I've always believed that cycling is sustained by, yet suffers from, the extreme independence of the people within the sport. Everyone in cycling wants to build a new team, in a new way, in a new direction, with a new business model.

It's been going on this way for a hundred years—and despite the best efforts of many, most of the teams are functionally about the same as all the other teams. Yet still everyone figures they can do it better and that they must do it all alone. Cycling lends itself to this type of thinking, too, as the only real barrier to entry into the world's biggest race, the Tour de France, is money.

If you can raise $25 million in sponsorship, then you, too, can buy the athletes and directors you'll need to gain entry into the Tour. That's because cycling is one of very few professional sports that you can just buy your way into at the top level. It is also one of the few sports that when you do buy in, you probably displace a team with a longer tradition and greater experience. Often, that team will then go bankrupt as a result of being pushed aside—and then the same will eventually happen to you, too. You'll eventually go down in flames, as you stubbornly refuse to do it any other way than your own.

That is why cycling needs to start pooling resources, as opposed to dividing them. While independence is wonderful, there just aren't enough dollars out there to fund the sport for it to be constantly discarding teams with decade-long histories. Sometimes, compromise and a little bit of working together wouldn't be so bad for this fiercely independent sport.

To that end, I've always been supportive of fewer, but better organized races, and fewer, but better funded teams. Cycling tends to dilute itself way too thinly to make much sense to the newbie or the casual fan. Too many teams are structured and funded at different levels, yet compete in the same races, which sometimes overlap.

Who's the best rider in the world? No one really knows, as the top riders rarely go head to head with each other.

Which is the best team in the world? Depends on who you ask.

And how do all these races relate to the Tour de France? They don't, even though they try to pretend that they do.

Over my decades in the sport, I've watched countless teams, entrepreneurs, and races come in with "an entirely new way of doing things." Usually they make a huge splash for a year and then die, having never really looked at reality.

A classic example of the "I can do it better my way" mentality was the Cervélo TestTeam of 2009–2010. Cervélo figured they would hire a former Tour de France winner and then fund a fully branded Cervélo team. Then, after showing how great and different their team was via very luxurious hospitality programs, they'd sell the title and naming rights to an outside sponsor, yet also maintain the Cervélo identity and ownership of the team.

It would be a coup never achieved before in cycling. A new business model for the sport! The spending was immense in year one. One rider said of his time on the team: "Whatever we asked for, we got . . . it was amazing."

Of course, millions of dollars later, in mid-2010, there was no knight in shining armor stepping in to take on the brunt of the funding. And Cervélo, a middle-sized upscale bike brand, was left holding the entire bill for a very expensive team. They needed a way out, without being saddled with the negative image of having to "fold" a team.

That's how Cervélo came to us. It was the first of three very complex mergers that our team went through over the next five years. The broad stokes of the deal were these: Cervélo was going to bring seven of their male athletes and the entirety of their women's team over to our organization, in return for being the second-name sponsor, the bike sponsor, and for having some loosely defined control over the design and branding of the team. They would pay us a very substantial fee for all this, but the financial backbone of the organization would remain Slipstream's responsibility.

We felt it was a good deal, as the branding of Cervélo was world class at this point. It was the "cool" brand in cycling, and we wanted, unashamedly, to be cool. They were paying enough for us to carry the riders and staff they brought along, so it seemed to be a very positive move on our part. The women's team was ahead of its time, too, and we saw it as an opportunity to get a foothold in women's cycling, which was growing very fast.

However, we still had one more year remaining with our bike sponsor, Felt, and if we wanted to do the deal with Cervélo, we'd need to buy our way out of the Felt contract first. While our head sponsorship guy at Slipstream, Matt Johnson, began to talk terms with Cervélo, Doug Ellis and I started to have the hard discussion with Felt about how much money it would take to let them release us from the contract.

We thought it was reasonable to offer the face value of the contract. So Doug, Matt, and I, along with our attorney, Matthew Pace, saddled up for a conference call with the president of Felt.

This call took an unexpected and hilarious turn.

After about fifteen minutes of discussion, the atmosphere changed when Mister Felt told the call participants that, if we went ahead with Cervélo, he would drive a stake through my heart. The call went very quiet, until finally our attorney Matthew Pace piped up. Was he joking? I assumed so.

"Did you just say you were going to drive a stake through JV's heart...?" Matthew asked.

Luckily, I proved not to be a vampire and we did eventually reach a deal with Felt. Oddly, this would not prove to be the last time I was physically threatened while negotiating my way through the world of cycling sponsorships. In fact, I have come to think that throwing the dismemberment threat around is fairly standard practice.

As Steve Goldstein once told me: "Negotiations will always be fierce when people are negotiating over crumbs." Well, cycling is always about the crumbs.

With that, we were off and running with our first merger. Cervélo insisted on designing the jersey and getting rid of the argyle we'd become quite attached to, which we agreed to, and then they sent us a list of riders that had outstanding contracts with them.

We'd need to get them to sign new contracts, with Slipstream Sports instead of Cervélo. This all went fairly easily, and by mid-September, we'd wrapped up all the details and paperwork. All the riders who got contracts were happy to be joining a new organization; the ones who got left in the cold, a lot less happy.

The train was almost derailed, however, by what you might think would be a huge blessing. Thor Hushovd, perhaps the biggest name among the riders coming across from Cervélo, won the World Championship about a week after he'd signed his new contract with us. Naturally, we were ecstatic about having the world champion on our team, and he was quite happy about being world champion.

But that's where the happiness ended. Within a few hours of Thor winning the world title, I started getting calls from his agent. I phoned Doug and our new partner, Gerard Vroomen. I told them that Thor would want more money. And once again, the line went very quiet.

It was that awkward moment when the bill arrives for an expensive dinner and no one reaches for it. Doug and Gerard waited for the other one to say: "I'll throw in some extra cash" but that moment never came. Doug felt strapped after having to pay off "Stake Through Your Heart" Felt and I think Gerard had pretty much already maxed out the Cervélo credit card.

And so, after an hour of hand-wringing on the phone, it was decided that I should tell Thor's agent that we would be happy to honor the contract that he'd already signed, but that there'd be no pay raise.

On the night after that year's Giro di Lombardia, in an all-too-quiet restaurant outside Milan, I got to deliver the great news to Thor and his agent. Thor sat there, stunned, his face turning red. I was soon turning red, too, as I just kept guzzling wine. After that evening, we were now going to have a team with the world champion in our ranks and he already hated us. To his eternal credit, though, he never allowed any doubts he may have had about his decision to join us to overshadow his performances. He was an excellent rider for us.

ROUBAIX

Roger Hammond had just crashed, hard, on the approach to the cracked cobbles of the Arenberg forest. I pulled alongside, jumped out of the team car and knelt beside him as he screamed in pain at the roadside. This was our whole 2011 Classics season encapsulated, right here. We were broken, battered, and screaming in agony.

Paris—Roubaix was our last chance to make amends in the 2011 spring Classics. The Tour of Flanders had been a disaster, Milan—San Remo a total miss, and Gent—Wevelgem a big fat nothing. We had been billed in preseason media coverage as the Classics team to beat, the only team capable of beating the awesome power of Fabian Cancellara.

But so far, we'd proven to be very far from that. Our best finish was unremarkable, our tactics were being scorned, and our credibility had been lost.

"No surprise, really," tutted the pundits. "Vaughters is a totally inexperienced Classics sports director, who has never actually ridden any of the Classics. Of course the team wasn't performing well . . ."

The whole thing reached its boiling point during Flanders, when I told our four remaining riders in the front group that we weren't going to attempt to pull back a late dangerous breakaway and that we would let the other teams do the work.

Since the radio transmissions were broadcast live that year, the whole world heard me say that. It was seen as a moment of total ineptitude and cowardice. And the thousands of critical Twitter messages I received post-race made that point very clear to me. The team was demoralized and downcast after that moment.

As Roger waited for the medics, it didn't seem that our luck had turned much for us in Paris–Roubaix. He told me to get going with the race and stop trying to play doctor. So I left him, speeding past all the trailing riders and support cars that had been scattered across the road after the crash.

Sitting next to me, in silence, was Peter Van Petegem, Classics legend and former Paris–Roubaix winner. We'd hired him to help me out for the Classics season, because he knew every corner, every section of *pavé*, every change in the wind direction across every empty field. He was a remarkable font of knowledge.

In theory, he was supposed to be directing the team, but Peter wasn't really comfortable with calling the shots. So we ended up being the odd couple, Peter telling me about every pebble in the road, and me having to make the decisions. I think it was a bit confusing for both of us.

We caught back up to the race just as the peloton entered the hated, rutted cobbles of the Arenberg. I figured the Arenberg would be just another mess for us, with riders getting dropped, flatting, crashing, struck down by lightning, whatever. So, I was just waiting for the radio to crackle some horrendous news about our team, just as it had been doing the whole of the last month.

Amazingly, that isn't what happened. Instead, as we came out of the forest, the radio crackled into life and told us something rather gleeful: two of our riders were in a breakaway group that had gone clear just after the Arenberg sector of *pavé* had ended.

Johan Vansummeren and Sep Vanmarcke were both riders that had big potential in the Classics. Sep, as a neo pro, had just been a bit too enthusiastic with his training in February and picked up a nasty case of Achilles tendinitis as a result. He had spent most of March in rehab, doing intervals in a swimming pool.

Johan had, as usual, overcooked his training and come up with a bad knee the week before Flanders. As a Belgian, to not ride Flanders was basically an insult to family honor, but we had to make the call and pull Johan out and send him home to try and recover. He needed to make things right for Paris–Roubaix.

While it was nice to have two riders in the break, it was a little bit uncertain if either one of them would have the condition to make it through the full 265 kilometers of Roubaix.

Up at the front of the race, Thor Hushovd, our disgruntled world champion, was doing a nice job of marking the repeated accelerations of race favorite, Fabian Cancellara, while Andreas Klier, our road captain, was keeping Thor nicely positioned to do so.

Andreas filled an odd yet crucial role in this team of misfits. He was in his last year as a professional rider and was a bit too old to be strong enough to fight during the finales of the great monuments, yet his knowledge of how the races would play out was incredible.

When it came to tactics, he had a genius I'd never seen before. Along with Van Petegem, Andreas had been crucial in helping me make the right choices during the race. I think he reveled in being given a voice in the leadership of the group. Having a rider play an active part in the overall decision-making was very nontraditional in cycling, but Klier loved this role and was a huge asset. While it hadn't worked out that well, at least not yet, results-wise, I felt the three of us had been getting better and better as a unit each day.

Klier's insight during this part of the race was amazing. He would observe what was happening inside the peloton, convey that to me, give a few short snippets of advice for the guys up in the breakaway, and then I would pass that message forward to the riders in the break.

The break containing Vansummeren and Vanmarcke was steadily extending its lead, and Cancellara was having to expend the last of his teammates to keep it in check. Inevitably, the moment was coming when Cancellara would have to try and accelerate away in order to reach the breakaway himself, with no teammates left to help him.

Klier knew that the pivotal moment would come on the cobbled sector at Mons-en-Pévèle. While the cobbles at Arenberg and Carrefour de l'Arbre get all the notoriety, Mons en-Pévèle, Klier had taught me, was the hardest section of all the *pavé* in the race. It would be the best moment for Cancellara to use his superior power to simply ride away from the rest, bridge across to the breakaway, and then sweep up the remnants on his way to victory. The race would turn here, one way or another.

The break approached Mons-en-Pévèle with a bit less than two minutes' advantage over the diminished peloton. Cancellara had his teammates do one last suicide effort before hitting the *pavé*, and then once they had been dropped and Cancellara was left alone, he accelerated away, hard—very hard.

At first it looked like he was away, as we had feared, but then, little by little, Hushovd made his way back to Cancellara's wheel. The two of them were absolutely flying over Mons-en-Pévèle, and reducing the gap of the breakaway very quickly.

I told Thor to just stay firmly planted on the wheel of Cancellara, as we had two teammates in front, and Cancellara had nobody. It was the first moment since we'd started the Classics that I began to feel that our plan was working out a bit. We couldn't have put the world champion in a better spot. Thor was sitting on Cancellara's back wheel with a free ride across to the breakaway.

We exited Mons-en-Pévèle with the breakaway only forty-five seconds in front. As we hit smooth pavement, Cancellara flicked his elbow out, making the pro gesture for the rider to share the pursuit and take a turn in front.

I went on the radio.

"Thor, stay put," I said.

There was a pause, then he radioed back.

"But I should help him . . ."

Again, I told him to stay put.

Up front, the breakaway had split down into a much smaller group, and while Vanmarcke had not made the front part, Vansummeren was clearly the strongest of the remaining five riders. You could see he had fire in him that day and wasn't going to let the opportunity pass him by.

Behind, Cancellara continued to pull to the next section of *pavé*, and then accelerated hard once again. Hushovd held on to his wheel, a bit more easily this time, as Fabian was wearing down from having to do all the work.

We exited that section of cobbles, and the gap was just thirty-five seconds to the front. I figured Fabian would just close the rest of the gap, but instead, he stopped.

Frustrated by Hushovd not working, he threw up his arm asking for his team car and some fresh drinking bottles. I took the chance to drive up alongside and give Thor a bottle, as well. The next thirty seconds proved to be the most crucial of the race.

Thor came alongside the car, clearly upset he wasn't being allowed to work, and knowing his own chances to win were stymied by his teammates ahead. Cancellara, meanwhile, was even more upset that Hushovd wasn't helping him chase.

I had about five seconds to decide. I could let Thor work with Cancellara and then definitely catch the breakaway, or tell him to stay on his wheel, in which case they might still reach the break anyway or maybe, just maybe, Fabian would give up in frustration.

Who did I have faith in, Vansummeren in front, or the sprint finish of Hushovd, the world champion, behind? I could already hear the media and fans the next day if I got this one wrong. My head would be chopped off. The popular choice, of course, would be to let Thor pull.

The world champion versus the great Cancellara would be an ideal scenario for fans watching on TV, for reporters, for everyone. I looked at Van Petegem, and he looked back at me.

"You are the boss, you must decide," he said.

So, in a moment of pure gut instinct and little real knowledge, I made the unpopular choice. I put my bet on Vansummeren. I was choosing to deprive the world champion of his chance of winning Paris–Roubaix. But the team came first, and for better or worse, I made the call. Vansummeren in front was our better chance to win.

I yelled out the car window as loud as I could, so that Cancellara could hear it, too: "No working, Thor! Sit on the wheel! Johan is the strongest in front!"

Thor immediately lost his cool, turning red and throwing a water bottle to the ground.

"Whaat? This is so fucking stupid!" he shouted back at me.

More important, Cancellara lost it, too.

He came totally unwound, yelling abuse and weaving around in the road. In the moments of their collective tantrum, the breakaway gained another forty seconds. That may have been enough to ensure that both Thor and Cancellara lost their chance of winning the race.

I sat quietly in the car, knowing that if I'd made the wrong choice, I would be crucified. Fans, sponsors, the media would pound on me for being the asshole that never let the great battle between Cancellara and Hushovd unfold. Instead I'd made my bet on an unknown rider that might, or might not, be able to beat his fellow breakaway companions to the line.

Even if Vansummeren finished second, it would be viewed as an incredible failure by me. Van Petegem knew the consequences of my decision, too, and sat nervously and very quietly next to me.

Carrefour de l'Arbre, the fourth to last sector of cobbles, was where the race would surely be finally decided. Cancellara had kept the gap amazingly tight, despite his upset, and Vansummeren hit the Carrefour sector with just under a minute in hand and three remaining breakaway partners to deal with. Vansummeren would have to drop his companions here, as, to be blunt, he couldn't sprint for shit.

Rattling across the cobbles in the following team car, I watched, dead quiet, sweat making the armpits of my shirt wet and sticky.

Vansummeren shed the others in the break one by one, distancing them from his rear wheel painstakingly slowly, with sheer power and fortitude. The look of agony on his face was intense, but he kept pushing, harder and harder. Finally, eight hundred meters before the end of the Carrefour pavé, he dropped the last companion.

Now he was alone for the run into Roubaix.

Behind us, Cancellara finally got rid of Thor and was pursuing on his own. A minute seemed too much to overcome in the few remaining kilometers leading to the velodrome in Roubaix, but now that Fabian had no one sitting in his slipstream, he would move very fast.

There was nothing left to do, except hope Johan had just enough left to get him to the line. His face was twisted, dusty, and caked with salty sweat by now, but then a look of panic suddenly appeared in his eyes.

Mind racing, I chewed my nails. "Why does he look like that?"

The gap was closing much faster than expected.

Then I finally saw why Johan was panicking. His rear tire was going flat.

He was riding into the finale of Paris–Roubaix on a flat tire, with Fabian Cancellara chasing some forty seconds behind him. As the race reached its climax, there was no time to change the wheel, just time to watch events unfold, whatever they might be.

Johan rode through the streets of Roubaix and entered the velodrome. He wobbled and weaved his way around the track, hampered by his failing tire. Cancellara shot around the banking like a cheetah after its prey, but Johan held on. He entered the final straight, the closing one hundred meters, arms raised in salute as he took the win.

I screamed. I jumped up and down in glee. I ran around like a child on the infield.

I hugged Johan. I hugged anyone who would come near me. I think I may even have kissed Van Petegem.

I was so happy for Johan. He was a kind and selfless rider who rarely had a chance to race for himself. But today was his moment. He lifted the great stone cobble trophy over his head on the podium, and I could not have been prouder.

As I watched him, I tweeted, "He who laughs last, laughs hardest."

CHAPTER 19

HANGING ON

No matter how awkward it was having a very grumpy world champion on the team, thank goodness we didn't sign a fatter deal with Thor. That said, despite his black moods he was never anything less than professional.

Cervélo, for all their cool style and argyle-less design, struggled to actually make the sponsorship payments. As a team, in 2011 we were having an exceptional season, with yellow jerseys, team time trial wins, and Johan's victory in Paris–Roubaix all part of the equation. But, man, oh man, were the finances tight. I was directing races during the day and then praying we would be able to make payroll at night. Cervélo was clearly struggling to meet their commitment, but we thought it was just a temporary thing, as Cervélo was so cool.

That all changed right before Thanksgiving. We started getting calls from a distressed private equity firm claiming to be the new owners of Cervélo, and also claiming that they were not going to make the sponsorship payments. Cervélo was quite in arrears at this point, and just defaulting on the whole thing would bankrupt the entire team. Doug was pouring in his own cash to plug holes, and asking me to make some hard and fast budget cuts to try and stay afloat.

We managed November payroll, barely, but the news from Cervélo kept getting worse. Even if they were able to pay the 2011 commitment, 2012 was impossible. By December, it was too late for us to find a new bike sponsor and co-title sponsor. There was no way the 2012 budget was going to work. We were going to have to shut the team down, and liquidate the assets, just before Christmas.

I couldn't sleep at all, as I knew the consequences of shutting down a team just before Christmas would be horrible. Very few of the riders would be able to find a new team at such a late date, and almost none of the staff would get another job. We would be throwing more than a hundred people out on the street, jobless. I stopped eating much, stopped leaving the house, and just kept thinking about making those phone calls, over and over again.

Somehow, we were saved. A day or two before Christmas, we got a call from Gerard Vroomen, letting us know that another private equity firm had come in and decided to buy Cervélo. This group didn't want to just throw the team out in the cold among the inevitable budget cuts for Cervélo. They were willing to negotiate with us. It wouldn't be the nirvana of the great merger with Cervélo we'd dreamed of the year before, but with enough hard budget cuts, it would be enough cash, barely, to hold things together for 2012.

So a bullet was dodged, but the budget cuts hurt and, over time, they slowly diminished the performance and influence of the team. From 2010–2017, cycling was in an intense inflationary period. Average team budgets doubled during these years, and rider salaries shot through the roof.

We simply couldn't keep up with the arms race going on between teams that were funded in a much different way than ourselves. We lost riders, staff, and other top talent to teams that were able to offer them twice the salary that we could pay. It was hard to watch many a friend come to me, apologize, and then tell me they had taken a much bigger offer elsewhere. Our team was a tight-knit family, yet slowly but surely the family was being pulled apart by money.

We weren't the only team having this problem, however. Cannondale had taken over the license and ownership of the old Liquigas team at great cost, hoping that they could turn team ownership into not only more bike sales, but also to selling a sponsorship that would cover at least part of the cost of the team. Sponsorship sales are a hard game to win at, especially in this age of Google AdSense and other very targeted and efficient marketing platforms.

Cannondale had not been able to sell any sponsorship, and therefore was having to support the cost of the entire team themselves, just as Cervélo had tried to do. It was just too much, and the team was struggling to keep its talent. It, too, was unable to keep up with the arms race of budgets at the top end of the sport.

The last straw for Cannondale was losing Peter Sagan. They had very wisely signed him to a long-term contract when he was a very young rider, but as that contract ran out, they were unable to match any of the incoming offers. Peter's salary would be equivalent to their entire athlete payroll. To match it would have been impossible for a company Cannondale's size. They needed to look for other options.

As 2015 loomed, we knew that Garmin was planning to cut down their contribution quite a bit, and that Cervélo, in their new ownership format, would be unable to make up the difference. So we were also on the hunt for some additional sponsorship dollars. And we, too, were finding it a very hard game.

The entire sponsorship game had changed very quickly. When the mega-budget teams like Sky, Tinkoff, and BMC moved in, sponsorship became much harder to sell. As these teams bought up all the best talent, smaller teams struggled to perform as well. In 2008, an incoming sponsor worth $10 million would be a game changer in terms of the level of talent a team could pursue on the rider market. However, by 2015, $10 million was just the price of very basic entry. An investment of $10 million wouldn't fund a team that could win the Tour de France; in fact, it wouldn't be able to win that much, period.

This crushed the sponsorship marketplace. As a smaller team, either you were going into the marketplace trying to sell a huge figure, like $25 million, or you were telling a $10 million sponsor they would have no chance at winning the Tour. The marketing metrics of cycling don't support a $25 million investment. Those $10 million are, in truth, better spent elsewhere if you've got no chance of winning the big prize.

Cannondale was doubly affected by this new paradigm for cycling, as Sagan, their star rider and the rider the whole team was built around, had just been scooped up by Russian oligarch Oleg Tinkov for his team. They had nothing to sell anymore in the sponsorship marketplace.

We weren't quite as badly off, as we had just won the Critérium du Dauphiné with Andrew Talansky, who had signed a long-term contract. We also had built an image that wasn't quite as dependent on any single individual star. Our team seemed to have its own personality, spirit, and brand, regardless of which riders we hired. While that was enough to attract Cannondale, in the broader corporate world the same problem existed for us as it did for them. So, like those two lonely kids looking for company, we decided to dance together at the prom.

As was the case with Cervélo, Cannondale brought across athletes and staff into our organization. This was great news for those who made the transfer list, but for those left out of the merger equation, it was hard news to swallow. In both the Cervélo and Cannondale merger, quite a few people ended up disappointed and without work.

Their anger would typically be focused on me, both publicly and privately. It hurt to hear angry and hateful words, when the reality was that we were saving three times as many jobs as we were eliminating. If both teams had just collapsed and disappeared, it would be much worse for the rider employment scene than two teams merging into one awkward organization. But that was little comfort to those left on the sidelines.

The Cannondale merger would be much more challenging, culturally, than the Cervélo one. They were, functionally, a very traditional team, and we were a very culturally American team. Bringing the two organizations together was a challenge. Additionally, we were saddled with very young and inexperienced athletes moving across from Cannondale. They had signed a great crop of young talent to long-term contracts, using the Peter Sagan model.

In the short term, we had to let go of some of our experienced riders to make room for this gang of youngsters. This was a great thing, for the long term. But it also meant we would suddenly become the youngest team in the peloton for 2015. The team was young, inexperienced, and culturally not really sure of its identity.

We put together a bonding camp, sailing around the British Virgin Islands. It truly did pull together a very diverse group of riders into a big family. It was a wonderful week, and by the end of it, all the riders were truly friends—Italian, American, whatever. That was one problem solved, but the other, the sheer inexperience of the team, remained.

Whenever you merge teams together, performance will suffer for a few years. It's not a matter of the team not getting along, or the merger "not working," but rather that a merged team never has a strategically designed roster.

In a typical cycling team, you maybe change 15–20 percent of your roster each year, or maybe four to six riders. Each year, as manager, you carefully look at what weak spots your team has, and then look at who is available in the marketplace to fill those weak spots. Over time, with careful recruitment, the team becomes stronger.

But you can forget about that with a merger. Instead, almost 100 percent of the turnover within the team is a result of the merger. There is no strategic vision and you just take on board whatever athletes you are given, and get rid of whatever athletes are at the end of their contract. The result is a hodgepodge of a roster, based on short-term need, not long-term strategy.

You can sustain performance over one, maybe two mergers, but doing this over and over again erodes the team, and makes any strategic vision impossible. Our merger with Cannondale started to show the cracks in our team as well as the side effects of the mergers. We had a large group of young and talented riders, but they weren't ready to lead a team. We had older and experienced guys, but no one who was a real winner. The roster was too forced together, without real vision or purpose.

This issue only got worse, as Cannondale struggled to carry the load after Garmin had fully departed. To get the books back in the black, we would need to find a partner willing to take the spot left by Garmin. By this point, the ongoing increases in overall team budgets and inflation of rider salaries had spiraled even further, thereby killing potential second-name sponsors in the $4–$6 million range. It was increasingly obvious that teams with limitless budgets were going to win the lion's share of the commercially important events, so unless a sponsor could step in at a very large figure—say $25 million for first name or maybe $10 million for second name—the impact on the performance of the team would be minimal.

Yet $4 million is still a lot of money to spend for something that won't win that much. It was the classic situation of being stuck between a rock and a hard place. We were stuck, and another merger might be the only way forward. We found a willing and enthusiastic partner in property developer Michael Drapac, and we once again merged, but it proved a very difficult task to hold together.

Two thousand and seventeen was the year mergers had to end. I had decided with Doug that we were either going to find a new entrant into the sport that was willing to do things our way, and that was willing to support a true long-term strategic vision, or we were going to end.

Selling our vision wouldn't be easy, as while I'd slowly been able to make a few dark-horse pickups on the rider market, despite the constant mergers, we still didn't have much of a chance, statistically, of pulling off any huge upsets in 2017. On the marketing side, our budget cuts had also been hurting us, as we just didn't have enough people to keep the flow of social media information up where it needed to be. We would need that to show a potential new partner that our organization, our brand, our argyle spirit, was something of value. And we would have to do that on a shoestring and a prayer.

It would be the most stressful, painful, and yet most beautiful year in our team's history; 2017 left me screaming for joy or crying in defeat, constantly. We accomplished so much, and yet I'm not sure I would survive if I had to go through it again.

It was a new feeling going into the start of the year knowing that there were seven, maybe eight months left before you'd need to make the decision to either fold the team or keep going. Doug and I had both decided it just wasn't worth limping along any more. We needed to do it right, or we needed to get the fuck out.

Both of us were worn thin by trying to constantly patchwork together many smaller sponsors, and keep all of them happy. Everyone wanted big publicity, headlines, and top billing for their investment, but yet no one was willing to pay the $45 million a team like Sky had. In some ways, we were a victim of our own success. For many years, mainly prior to all the succession of mergers, we had been able to pull off some spectacular race wins on a meager budget.

The Giro, the Dauphiné, Paris–Roubaix, Il Lombardia, and Liège–Bastogne–Liège were all big races in our wins column. The expectation from sponsors and fans was that this was the underdog team that could pull it off, without a big budget and without star riders. There was also a belief that we would find a way to create more stories and more buzz around our tiny team than teams with twice the budget could manage. All of this was just seen as what we did, as if we were magicians. But as of late, the magic just hadn't been working. Doug and I both knew we had to find a partner to pull us back into the game, or we needed to get out.

That underlying tension was hard to ignore. I can only imagine what those around me felt. I'd come up with a communications timeline and strategy that slowly ratcheted up throughout the season from positive outlook to outright desperation.

The first part was feeding the world the notion of the team as "The Little Engine That Could," a team that would outperform everyone if it just had a little more gas in the tank. There was no hint of panic to this story, because it portrayed us as simply looking for a helping hand.

Business Insider and the *Wall Street Journal* were both intrigued.

The story of how we were a little team that did quite well, but with some more funding could be one of the very best teams, was one that resonated with their business-oriented readerships. We were Apple in the late 1980s. The story had a well-loved and well-worn underdog tone to it.

The guys in the team were helping me out, too, because the team was racing the best it had in years. Those few strategic pickups I'd been able to pull off among all the merger turmoil were coming very close to winning some big races. They were fitting perfectly into the role of underdog, starting with Dylan van Baarle placing fourth in the Tour of Flanders and Sebastian Langeveld taking third in Paris–Roubaix. That was followed up by Pierre Rolland, who won a gorgeous stage in the Giro d'Italia.

Lesser-known riders battling for the win in the world's largest races fit our narrative of "spend money with us; we provide real value." We weren't quite winning, but we were within meters of teams that spent $10–$25 million more than we did. It fed our planned communication onslaught, and the world was aware we needed more sponsorship. What they weren't aware of, though, was that if that sponsorship didn't come through, we would be bankrupt. We would be finished.

As the manager and CEO of a team, this situation is a hard, hard line to walk. It's an unforgiving and slippery tightrope with no safety net underneath. You must exhibit absolute and unshakable confidence that your team is strong and robust, financially. Your staff and riders can't see any flicker of doubt: everything is okay, you tell them—everything is grand. The future could not be brighter.

If the world starts to question this narrative, the team quickly begins to fall apart, as riders and staff sign elsewhere. If a prospective sponsor knows your riders and staff are moving on, you've got no deal.

Surviving in cycling, whether as rider, mechanic, or director, is like being a frog on a fragile lily pad: you must always be ready to jump to the next one. Conversely, if you always bluff and never convey to the broader world how dire your situation is, then you will miss sponsorship opportunities that may have always been there. That's the balancing act. Don't give off too much confidence because prospective sponsors will assume you're just fine.

Like it or not, that was my reality in 2017. Keeping our plight secret and agonizing over the wording of every little thing I said was rotting me from the inside. I had no one apart from Doug that I could really talk to.

Every night, I lay awake spinning the different scenarios around in my head. If I never said a word to our riders and our staff until the last moment, I would hurt them and their opportunities for the future. They would hate me, think of me as dishonest, and never forgive me. Yet if I gave them full disclosure of the situation, it would create a mass panic. The team would fold in on itself in the chaos.

It's a funny thing, but teams who are facing bankruptcy tend to ride very fast. And, indeed, in 2017, we did just that. The Tour de France that year was a dichotomy. It would be our best Tour, and yet I was so buried in my solitary search for a solution to our issues, I never felt anything other than panic throughout the race. Our terrific performances and our drumbeat of publicity surrounding the finances of the team were starting to have an impact, and we were moving a tiny bit closer to finding a solution to our funding gap.

Midway through the Tour, we signed a deal with a company called Oath. Oath was a huge conglomeration of media assets that, in theory, would have provided us with a massive platform to promote the team to a broader audience, in a way no other cycling team ever had. We would be a central component to their content creation.

The behind-the-scenes stories of how a cycling team operates would fuel the plot. Everything, from how the athletes eat, to how we use the cars, to fixing a flat tire, to cleaning out wounds after a crash: all of this would be featured in their huge digital media platforms, like *Huffington Post* and *Engadget*. We thought announcing this partnership and all it would bring would ensure a naming-rights sponsor. Surely that would prove we were worth it?

It was a shot, and a good shot. Meanwhile, Rigoberto Urán winning a stage and pulling himself up to second overall in the Tour was keeping us front and center of the news in July. I had bunkered myself in a little town in the Alps that was close to the race, but not so close that people could overhear my phone calls or see the look of worry on my face.

I didn't want to rain on the parade of a team absolutely kicking ass with my dour attitude, either. But seclusion has always been my default when I'm under pressure. I sequester myself, because I'm not very enjoyable to be around in that situation. So, every day, I'd wake up, ride my bike around gorgeous Lake Annecy and then spend the rest of the day on endless phone calls.

We had agencies, big and small, pounding the streets on our behalf; we had stretched our favors; we had called in every debt owed for the past decade to make contacts with anyone that might be interested. It was a social waltz with interested but skeptical businesses.

People assume that doping always comes up in the course of sponsorship talks. It can, but maybe not in the way you might think. Very proudly, I will say the reputation and passion for anti-doping that Slipstream has had on the anti-doping front has always been very convincing to many sponsors. We happily provide whatever transparency they might like, and if they want to do due diligence with WADA, CADF (Cycling Anti-Doping Foundation), or US-ADA, we happily make the introductions.

No, the worry from sponsors isn't "Is your team going to dope, JV?"

The worry they have is "Can your team win, if you aren't doping, and lots of other people are?"

That is the issue that comes up. That is a much harder question to answer, because you must defend the entire sport, not just your team.

My answer? I just say that I have faith that some of the largest races in the world can be, and have been, won clean. That, having witnessed the change from the inside out, is something I truly believe.

Rigo managed to finish second in the Tour, and our team had done a wonderful job of being the opposite of Sky during the Tour.

We were fun, passionate, open, and friendly. The media coverage we were receiving was flattering and abundant. We were as well positioned as we could possibly be to attract some love from somewhere out there. But time was running out and I couldn't keep the double act of "everything is great" and "help us, please!" going on for that much longer.

I kept up appearances until about a month after the Tour de France was over. We had pulled things so tight, we would be able to make September payroll, and then that would be it; we'd have to shut everything down and sell everything.

The mood was upbeat and jovial as we drank champagne at our post–Tour de France party in the U.S. embassy overlooking the Champs-Élysées. Our sponsors could not have been happier. Our team in 2017 was running on the very lowest budget in the entire World Tour, and yet we'd managed to finish on the podium of the most important race. Cannondale and Drapac executives were as pleased as punch at their wise investment. Yet, when I asked them to commit to the future of the team, and to spend larger dollars, despite the festive mood and the singing of thousands of Rigoberto Urán fans below our balcony, the answer was "No."

They patted me on the back, and told me that with such a wonderful team and brand image, I was not going to have any trouble finding a replacement. None of them had ever raised the finance needed to run a cycling team, so their optimism was based on ignorance, which was hardly encouraging. The reality is that it's incredibly difficult to sell sponsorship at that level in cycling. It doesn't matter how much you win, or how much you grin.

HTC–Highroad, the team with the most wins in the world from 2009–2011, had to close its doors unceremoniously in 2011, after it failed to even come close to nailing down the dollars it needed to continue. They had a great sales force, a great team, and a solid image. And yet . . . nothing.

This isn't the only example of this very common story. A great Tour de France team has high value to a sponsor at a certain price point, but unfortunately, that price point had been driven up (by oil-rich sheikhs, Russian oligarchs, and the Murdoch family), to a point where normal commercial sponsors weren't easy to come by anymore. And no, we definitely weren't going to go try and find some ex-KGB billionaire to fund our team.

The question now was how much longer could we maintain the happy, smiley facade before we went fully public with our predicament? Rigoberto's situation, after his terrific Tour, was problematic. Clearly, after finishing second to Chris Froome, there were a lot of teams interested in him. He was happy to stay with us, at a very increased salary, of course, but crucially, he was happy to stay. But we needed the funding to make that happen, and all we had was a dream and a lot of smoke.

If Rigo agreed terms with another team and it became public knowledge, that would end our hopes right there and then. The team would have lost its star rider and there would be no chance of survival if Rigo left. Yet if we wanted it to seem we were keeping him, I would need to stretch the truth, both publicly and also with Rigo himself. On one hand, if we let him go, it would kill the entire team and the hundred-odd jobs that go with it. On the other hand, I could lie to Rigo and rot my soul.

Stretching the truth with him went against what I knew was right. But I was caught between a rock and a hard place.

Just before I had to make this hard call, we got just enough good news from a prospective sponsor to make us believe our problems might be resolved. They wanted us to send an MOU (memorandum of understanding), graphic designs of kit and uniforms, and a prospective 2018 roster. It was enough progress, especially the request for an MOU, for me to feel comfortable enough to re-sign Rigo. He was with his family in Colorado and so we had them over for dinner at my house.

Rigo and I chatted well into the night. I told him I felt very strongly the team's future was secured. I did truly believe that, but the stretch was that I still had no signed contract. And that was the part I didn't mention. I felt dark and deceptive about it, but I also had to think about how it would be impossible to save the jobs of all the other people who worked for the team if I wasn't able to announce that Rigo was still with us. Our new prospective sponsor needed to see that we had our star Tour podium rider on board, or they would not continue the discussion.

I told Doug that while we could go ahead and make the announcement to the media that Rigo was staying with us for 2018, I could not take another week like this. If the new sponsor had not signed within a week, I needed to let Rigo go ahead and find another team. What we were doing may have been better for the greater good, but it was not fair to Rigo.

That was the week that all hell broke loose. The new prospect backed away, no reason given. That left us dead in the water and without hope. It was time to blow the doors off the act and let panic hit. The ship was sinking and we had to let everyone know.

I sent out an e-mail to everyone, basically stating that while we were hopeful of a resolution, they were all released from their contracts, and should start looking for new opportunities. Within minutes, the media had a copy of the email, which we had anticipated, and within hours the entire organization was panicking. I hated having to let all these people down. I was sure they all hated me.

But then, over the next few days, my heart was warmed in a way it never has since I've been in cycling management. Our team in the Vuelta a España kept racing well and sent me notes of encouragement. All the staff emailed me, saying they trusted me and in my ability to find a solution. It was heartwarming, but also so saddening. I had misled these people and here they were, right behind me, backing me up, entrusting their lives to me.

The most incredible moment came when Rigo announced publicly that he would stay by my side and give me time to find another sponsor. It was unprecedented that a rider of his caliber and value would stand by a broken and struggling organization with a broken and struggling manager. But he did and it's something I will never forget.

We scrambled to find a way forward. By now, all options were on the table. Matt Johnson and Jessi Braverman (our marketing and communications manager) suggested that we try a crowdfunding campaign. It seemed impossible that we could actually raise $10 million to keep the team afloat, and it certainly wasn't the long-term strategic solution Doug and I had been after. But after I thought about it for a while, I thought, maybe—just maybe—it'll create enough buzz that a big sponsor will take notice.

If we raised a million dollars in a few days, it would make a potential sponsor realize that we were valuable, that we were loved. Of course, if the fundraising campaign fell flat on its face, it would prove the exact opposite, but at that point it seemed a risk worth taking.

We went ahead with the campaign. Donations came pouring in. Every time I clicked the link there would be another $30–$40 thousand. It was a rush. But we knew that unless it shook something big out of the trees, we would still be fucked. It was exhilarating though—in a way that being in a plane crash might be.

I went out walking the dog one morning, hoping to find a little peace in playing fetch at the park. My phone rang. It was a UK number and I almost didn't answer, thinking it was probably just another journalist calling to ask me how my blood pressure was doing.

Finally, I picked up.

An American-sounding voice, but with the lilt of someone who's lived abroad quite a bit, introduced himself as Philip Hult, chairman of a company named EF Education First. We ended up chatting for almost four hours, and by the end of our conversation, I'd agreed to fly to Boston the next day to meet his brother, Eddie.

We had shaken the tree hard enough for a big apple to fall.

EDUCATING JV

That falling apple quickly became an opportunity to save the team. In the initial moments of hearing EF Chairman Philip Hult's voice on the other end of the phone, saying that there was a possibility of enough funding to keep the team alive, I was—after months of negativity and anguish—euphoric. Some small miracle had happened.

Founded by Swedish entrepreneur Bertil Hult, EF Education First educates through experience. Instead of sitting in a classroom learning French, EF organizes trips in which you live with French families and soak up French culture. The trips aren't about tourism; they are about learning new cultures and learning language and interaction while in that culture.

Hearing this struck a chord with me, as I also had my share of struggles in school, partially due to my Asperger's—although I didn't know that at the time. I was an experiential learner, not a classroom learner. I had learned Spanish in Spain, and not by failing high school Spanish. It sounded great, but in the back of my head, I began to wonder if a language school could really afford such an expensive venture as a cycling team.

I flew to Boston the day after that first call with Philip to meet his younger brother, Edward. We had precious little time before the team would begin to fall apart, so even though it would be our first meeting, we needed to get down to the business of a real deal, real quick.

It was soon clear that far from being the language school down the street, this was a sophisticated multinational company. EF's offices on the Charles River between Boston and Cambridge are impressive. Gorgeous, full of light, well engineered, and massive.

Edward Hult is a tall, happy, and fit guy who seemed to be genuinely excited to see me and wanting to get down to the details. We were shown into a more private conference room to begin the gritty part of the conversation. Then we called into London, where his brother Philip joined the conversation.

Often in sponsorship deals, you keep your cards pretty close to your chest. Letting a potential sponsor understand the financial situation of your team almost always works against you. If you appear to be financially strapped, they question why they would want to buy into something that not many other people value. If you appear to be financially flush, they question if they are actually needed enough as a new sponsor for you to give them priority and attention.

However, with EF our financial situation was a matter of public record by this point, and our desperation a known quantity, so I had zero bargaining leverage. Well, that's what I thought, at first, anyway . . .

I played the best and only card I had to play, which was pure and simple honesty and transparency. They asked a question about the business of cycling, and I answered it, for better or worse—the good, the bad, and the ugly. When it came to negotiating the price of the sponsorship, I simply opened up the accounts and showed them exactly how significant the hole was.

There was no use in putting lipstick on a pig at this point. The pig was there, in the room, by the watercooler. The pig was part of the conversation.

We went back and forth for hours, trying to figure out how to fill the hole. By the end of the day, we had come to a deal that would save the team for 2019. It was a one-year deal for enough money that allowed me to keep the team together and live to fight another day. While a massive relief, it felt incomplete. It just didn't feel quite right.

On the long flight home, I started thinking. The thought of just a one-year deal gnawed at me. I would be throwing myself right back into the same desperate situation we were in before in just a few short months. I'd have until Christmas to heal up my ulcer and pretend everything was okay, and then we'd be right back into the weeds again, fighting for our lives.

I called Doug the next morning. He too felt a one-year deal wasn't quite right. In the meantime, another party had approached Doug about sponsoring the team. An Italian representative of a Polish shoe company, named CCC, which sponsored a pro Continental team, was going to fly from Italy to meet us in NYC.

Admittedly, Doug and I were both quite skeptical of this new possibility. It seemed like so many deals do in cycling—a lot of bluster and dreams, and not so much reality. All sizzle, no steak. But then, I think we had both felt that way about EF, too, when they originally called. So we went into the meeting with the Italian representative of the Polish shoe company with an open mind, almost.

CCC's representative, Matteo, wanted to know how it would look if the company he represented not only sponsored the team, but actually purchased Slipstream Sports. We worked through various models, ideas, and business plans throughout the day. Matteo impressed both Doug and me, and he seemed to be representing a serious player who wanted a place at the World Tour table. We ended the meeting with a nice dinner, and some positive feelings about this second possibility.

The next day, over lunch in the West Village, Doug and I talked until the restaurant shut down, and then finally made a decision about what we would do. It still makes my heart stop, thinking about how risky this plan was, but we agreed it was the best way forward. We decided to call up Philip and Eddie from EF and basically tell them the only way forward would be a three-year deal, not just one.

Sometimes your best negotiation leverage is just accepting that if it doesn't work, you'll go down in flames and maybe that's preferable to a bad deal. Our new card to play in the negotiation was simply that we were willing to accept the whole thing blowing apart. There was nothing to lose.

The two guys that didn't have a pot to piss in five days ago were now about to demand a tripling of the offer. Most of the time, in the position we were in, this wouldn't work at all. It would end the negotiation and EF would move on to something else. That was the risk we had to take.

Luckily, Philip and Eddie aren't your average corporate stooges. They grew up with risk-taking and entrepreneurship in their blood. They were smart, cultured, and very real. There was no pretense, no bullshit, and they appreciated how straight Doug and I had been playing things. They'd been in positions like we were in before, and knew the score from both sides of the table.

We put forward our new proposal. The phone was quiet for a minute, and then Philip asked if he could speak with Eddie in Swedish for a moment. Doug and I listened to their seemingly happy chat. Finally, after a few moments, Philip spoke up. He said he knew we had other options, and he agreed that to truly build the team, three years would be the best way forward. However, they needed a bit of time to really think about it. We hung up, agreeing that they'd call the next morning.

It was a sleepless and tense night for me. Had we gambled and lost? Was it just a step too far for EF?

The next morning I went out for a long run, wondering when, and even if, they'd call. The anxiety ate me up in a way I can't totally describe. I just felt awful living in the uncertainty.

Doug and I called each other, poring over every last word of our previous conversations to see if we'd misplayed something. I think in fact we just needed a little company, knowing that if this went the wrong way, the consequences would be a fucking dumpster fire.

Finally, they called. They were interested, but they didn't want to do a deal that was sponsorship for only three years. If they were in for three years, they needed more oversight of the inner workings of the team. They wanted to buy the team from Doug and run it as part of EF.

Doug and I were both relieved that they hadn't run for the hills, but selling Slipstream was a tough counterproposal. Our souls were embedded in Slipstream. Doug and I had built it up from the ground. We'd endured many hard moments with Slipstream. We'd felt a lot of joy with Slipstream.

I was better prepared for this than Doug, as I knew that this is the way cycling often works. You have to be ready to adapt, and often that will mean big changes. It's not fun, but we adapt to so much in cycling—to sudden weather changes, terrain, accidents, road hazards. It's a sport that plays out in an uncontrolled environment, so I suppose it's only fitting that the business side can be an uncontrolled environment, too.

I spent the next few days holed up in a Lower East Side hotel. We were on the phone with Eddie and Philip endlessly. We spent even more time with our attorney. We told the Polish shoe folks, "No, thank you," and that felt right. Eddie and Philip were our kind of people. We liked them and they shared the same visions and dreams for the team. Still, selling Slipstream was woeful.

You could see in Doug's eyes that he knew he needed to let go, but that it hurt him. Our baby was now going to transform into something else. Slipstream would survive, but it would grow differently now. Doug and I wouldn't be the only parents anymore.

Signing the final documents and then spreading the good news was a relief and felt good. But there was also a pang of pain. Our child had grown up and left the house. It was time for the next chapter of Slipstream Sports.

CHAPTER 20

BREAKUP

Ironically, as the new relationship with EF got underway, my home life was breaking apart again.

I'm not very proud of my history when it comes to relationships, or of the way I've always put my professional before my personal life. I've been married twice now, and both marriages were failures.

Maybe I've only made a lifelong commitment to a partner once—a partner that hurts you, exhausts you, tortures you, and always forgets your birthday. That partner is bike racing, and we've been together since I was twelve years old.

I have always put training, racing, the team, first. It's my job, after all, but then cycling is not like a normal nine-to-five. It's all-consuming and exclusive, hence all the talk of living like a monk. Perhaps, like religion, it attracts those who have a need to be consumed by it.

As a teenager I had liked a lot of girls, but as a skinny, big-eared, Lycra-wearing kid, no girls had ever liked me. The first was Carrie, a waitress at a local Italian restaurant, and she, too, had big dreams. She was studying to be a chef and wanted to travel the world, to find a way out of being a waitress and to forget her rough childhood.

We quickly fell in love, yet my obsession with training and racing still came first, and I let her know that very clearly.

One day, as I was looking at a new portable lactate monitor in a catalog, Carrie asked me why I was so intent on doing so many things to optimize my training. Was it because I was hell-bent on winning? I thought for a while before I replied.

"I've given up college, I've given up my youth, I've given up a social life, and I've given up ten years of my life, all to be a professional cyclist," I said. "If I don't find a way to ride faster, I will lose that dream. I don't want to lose my dream."

I ordered the lactate monitor and persuaded her to help me by taking the blood samples. I'd get upset and flustered when she didn't take the sample quickly enough to get a good reading. Sometimes, she would cry. I doubt that it was her favorite thing to do, but she did it anyway—and thank you for that, Carrie.

But I wasn't willing to compromise. I wasn't compromising time, I wasn't compromising effort, and I wasn't compromising any emotional intensity. I gave my all to the bike. Hanging out with my girlfriend was a very distant second place. Carrie became the first to decide that she'd had enough of being second place to my dreams.

People sometimes ask me why many professional cyclists get married young, and while I don't know the exact answer, I do have a theory. When you're a bike racer, you give up everything for your sport.

Going out late? No way, need to train. Beer bongs at a frat party? Nope, got to stay sharp and healthy. Make new friends by doing other social activities? Nope—I'll be out on the bike, by myself, for hours on end every day.

Cyclists do live monastic lives—without actually having agreed to being monks and without the celibacy. When someone of the opposite sex comes along that takes an interest, it has a big impact. A steady partner or a spouse doesn't require you to socialize or go to college parties. Spouses are there for you, even when you go to bed at nine every night and are too exhausted to brush your teeth.

Riders, I think, get married early in their lives because it provides an emotional foundation for trying to take on the immense goal of actually succeeding in this brutal, ruthless, and grueling sport. The tricky part, though, is *staying* married.

I've had two divorces, both very painful. One had a happy ending of sorts, as we remain close and have a wonderful son, but the other left a blank absence and a crippling sense of failure.

When Alisa and I were first engaged, we went to Antwerp to pick out the diamond ring together. We spent our days there drinking hot cocoa and envisaging our life together. She was with me all through my racing years, is the mother of my son, and we remain very close friends.

But the strain of my retirement and transitioning out of the sport was just too much for the relationship to handle. I felt it was my first and foremost responsibility to be a breadwinner and I didn't know how I was going to make that happen. I spent long hours alone, brooding anxiously, hoping I could find a way to meet this responsibility.

Alisa wanted to help me, but, isolated by my masculinity, I didn't want her to. I didn't want her to have to worry about anything. I was the hunter-gatherer, the alpha male, the one who would slay the dragon, all by myself.

Alisa stood by me through a tumultuous transition out of cycling and into the business world. She stood by me working endless hours and traveling even more than when I was racing bikes. I figured as long as I paid the bills and kept food on the table, my job in the marriage was done.

By then, I had stopped bringing her flowers or drinking hot cocoa together. Instead I was totally obsessed with the responsibility I had in raising a child, making sure his college account was funded and his private school bills were paid. I just thought of myself as an income producer, not a husband.

As I started to build up the Slipstream team, I became even more obsessed with work. Now I was responsible for the jobs of so many people. I was responsible for millions of dollars to operate such an organization. I was half in Europe, half elsewhere, and very rarely home.

Even when I was home, I was never really there and, understandably, Alisa started to build her own life, without me. She had her own friends, her own social circles, and her own way of doing things without me. I was the absentee husband, and she had found a way to deal with that.

We lived that way for a few years, until the day I got home from the 2008 Tour de France. I was inexperienced at managing a team, and certainly totally inexperienced at managing both a marriage and a team. She picked me up from the airport. On the drive home, she told me she was moving out.

I switched off.

I guess it's my coping mechanism. I'm sure to her it looked like I didn't really care that she was leaving. Yet, on the inside, it felt like I was burning in a fire, and that all I wanted to do was run away, screaming. Outwardly I looked like a dispassionate robot. I just turned off the switch and stared into space.

I took our son to Disneyland for a week while she moved out of the house.

I met Ashley, not ironically, at a wine tasting. Ashley was there as a buyer for a nearby wine shop. I sat straight across from her. Totally entranced, I watched her furiously take notes on each wine that came out.

A shared love of wine is a great place to start any friendship, and within the very first few minutes of seeing her enthusiasm for life, I desperately wanted to know what made her tick. Toward the end of the wine tasting, we exchanged pleasantries but no contact information. I did, however, listen to her very closely when she said she worked at a place called Little's. It was enough information to be able to find her again.

I showed up at Little's a few days later, hoping she'd be there. She was pouring wine for another tasting she was putting on. She really engaged with each and every person who tasted a glass, explaining the history, the grapes, and origins of each wine. You could see she took joy in teaching anyone and everyone about her passion.

I finally had the courage to say hello, unsure if she'd recognize me, or want to recognize me from a few days ago. She remembered me. I didn't linger long, as I came up with some bullshit story as to why I was there in the first place and said I quickly needed to leave to attend to business. But I did get her contact information this time.

We met a week or so later, under the guise of me trying to help her launch a writing career and offering to introduce her to a few editors. We had lunch during an early spring snowstorm in Colorado—it was cold and wet outside, cozy and festive inside the restaurant.

We flirted a little over email until finally, after I'd suggested we travel somewhere together, she wrote back: "I'd love to, but I don't think my boyfriend would approve of that."

My heart missed a beat.

"I'd really like to be your friend, though," she added.

It was a line that at the time I didn't ever want to hear. I could never be just her friend.

"Sorry," I wrote back, "but I can't be your friend. It just would never work."

The polite thing would have been to accept her friendship and respect her relationship with her boyfriend. I did neither. I risked the whole thing with a chirpy and somewhat obnoxious line. And, lo and behold, it worked.

Immediately before that year's Tour de France, Ashley came to visit me in Spain. It was supposed to be a magical little trip for her, introducing her to Europe for the first time. I wanted to show her all my little favorite places around Girona, I wanted to introduce her to the world of bike racing, I wanted to impress her and win her heart.

In hindsight, that was when she first saw how strong cycling's hold was on me. Just before she arrived, tensions within the team spiraled and brought on a black mood during which I didn't want to talk to anyone, see anyone, or have anyone's help. I just wanted to isolate myself, sit in a dark room, and think. Ashley arrived in Spain just as one of those situations was developing, and just as I was falling into a deep, dark hole.

David Millar and Christian Vande Velde had become upset with my way of managing them. So they attempted what was in essence a mutiny, in order to create a team that was more comfortable for them. In behind-my-back phone calls and conversations, they had convinced Doug the time had come to replace me. The morning before Ashley arrived in Barcelona, Doug took me out for a bike ride, during which he informed me of the new structure the team would have, without me.

I was in shock—and in a dark place. The only thing I wanted to do was hide. I didn't want to see anyone, much less the woman I was in love with. When Ashley arrived, I was distant and detached. I almost ignored her entirely.

Amazingly, Ashley hung in there. She stuck around for the first part of the Tour, which was, as always, stressful, but it was made even more so by the saga surrounding my insecure role within the team. This would be her introduction to our relationship, and to a pattern that also characterized the entire span of our time together.

Ashley left after one week of the Tour, and I immersed myself in solving the team's problems. I was so engrossed that I barely communicated with her until a few days before I was coming home. This has also always been a crutch of mine, when I'm traveling or working. I bury myself in work, 100 percent, and forget about everything else. I reasoned that I was just doing my job and that I'd see her soon enough when I got home.

Ten years later, as she was packing up and getting ready to leave me, Ashley told me that I was never really present, that I was never really there. I was always cold and two steps away. She should have known that ten years ago, she said. She had known it on her first trip to visit me, in Girona. Why hadn't she walked away then?

Once again, I just stood there, staring at her, burning on the inside and wondering how she could be doing this, yet appearing to be totally calm and that I couldn't care less.

The inescapable conflict between my professional and personal life was highlighted by our wedding. We were married October 7, 2012, about thirty-six hours before the USADA report on Lance Armstrong was published. I knew the fallout from that report would be devastating, and that my reaction in the first seventy-two hours afterward would set the tone for how I and the team would be remembered for the rest of my professional life.

That was quite a lot to be thinking about on your wedding day.

Our honeymoon was supposed to be a few enjoyable days in Switzerland and Kitzbühel, Austria, before we arrived in Venice. Instead, I was in emergency meetings in Geneva with UCI presidents past and present, Pat McQuaid and Hein Verbruggen. I was also on the phone constantly, with various sponsors, reporters, and attorneys, putting our side of the story, making sure that our ship would stay righted.

Ashley never complained, never told me to get off the phone, never said one word that was negative. In fact, she never said one negative thing our entire marriage. She was the dutiful wife who could stand alone on her own two feet without some coddling husband.

But then one day I think she realized that maybe it was just better to not have a husband at all.

The day after I flew home from Boston, having just finalized the team-saving deal with EF, Ashley and I went out to lunch. I thought it was to celebrate that she had just become a master of wine, and that I had secured the future of my company for the foreseeable future.

But after a few minutes, she welled up with tears and told me she just couldn't do it anymore. She couldn't be married to me. It hurt too much.

Once again, I went cold.

I'm sure the only thing Ashley could see, as I stared off into the distance, was a dispassionate response that made her think I didn't care. The fact was, at that moment, as she told me she wanted a divorce, I didn't want to be alive anymore. I had failed again. It was too much to handle and I shut down.

With one divorce, you blame it on the other party or the relationship or the world or the economy or something. Most people support you in that. They say things like: "It wasn't right," or "It wasn't meant to be."

With a second divorce under my belt, they didn't do that anymore.

I asked myself: "What the hell am I doing wrong?"

And boy, once I asked that question, the floodgates opened.

I never really saw it until Ashley left, but the fact was, I never made room for her. I selfishly focused all my energy on my achievements, as I had done my entire life. I put no energy into my partner, at all.

After our divorce, I went into therapy.

That led to another revelation as I worked through my post-divorce depression. I'm quirky. In fact, I'm diagnosably quirky. I started to explore why, and how this might be affecting my ability to stay partnered with someone. I started looking back at all the hard walls I'd bumped into over my career and how I'd had a very hard time connecting with most people.

Eventually, I was diagnosed with Asperger's syndrome.

Asperger's is a very high functioning type of autism. It can be a great gift at times, and a genuine curse at others. It allows incredible powers of concentration and incredibly creative problem-solving and ideation. Lots of people have it, I guess—like Albert Einstein, who didn't like to be bothered about changing his underwear when he was working on a project.

The downside, however, is that Asperger's has many pitfalls in social situations. The power of concentration can prove very elusive.

"Don't fucking interrupt me, I'm thinking . . . I don't care that the house is fucking burning down!"

So, while a wonderful gift, Asperger's can be a challenge socially. Most people usually do care when the house is burning down.

I'm not sure why it took a second divorce to realize all these things about myself, but I guess sometimes pain is a catalyst. I didn't really love hearing about it, as it was a day late and a dollar short to do anything with that information to save my marriages.

As much as I disliked the diagnosis and the label, it was a start to understanding why personal relationships have always been challenging and why it doesn't bother me at all to shut out the outside world and just focus on my work.

But it also hurt. It was painful to understand how many people I had hurt throughout my life. My cold and aloof demeanor was perhaps effective professionally, but it left many of my friends, coworkers, and colleagues feeling isolated and abandoned.

Asperger's is an asset when there is work to be done, because that work is the quiet solace that brings you peace. I just wish I had known about it a bit earlier in my life, so I knew how to deal with things a bit differently. I'm not using it as an excuse for my behavior in my relationships, either—I didn't talk about the things I should have, I didn't respond to pain or some situations the way I should have, diagnosis or no diagnosis.

It's also been a great gift to me. All the times I'd just had such an intense focus that I made things happen, forced them to happen through sheer will, even when all seemed lost. I'd won races against athletes more talented and stronger than me because I could focus more, especially when left all alone.

Out on the road in a time trial, I used to think it was strange that I could push myself harder when alone than I could with my competition right next to me. I just found other riders to be distracting. It was an odd feeling but I guess that makes more sense now.

Yet it's a burden, too. Maybe I'd still be married if I didn't shut out the rest of the world entirely, and give all of myself to finding a way forward for our team when it was about to die. If only I'd given my spouse a little bit more attention and thought.

But would I have won those tussles if I had given that little bit of myself away to my spouse? Regrettably, I doubt it. Some people may know how to win battles and keep a work/life balance. I haven't found a way to do both. I wish I knew how to balance things better.

There are many people I need to apologize to. And yet, if I'm honest with myself, I'd probably make all the same decisions and errors all over again. Sometimes, I really do wish I was someone more empathetic, someone who made relationships work, who made marriage work.

But I'm not. And that's a hard, hard thing to think about, late at night.

EPILOGUE

I guess I know where to start the end. Colombia. Spring of 2019.

Team time trials usually are uneasy. The margins are tight and the opportunities for error large. Our director that day barked nervously about missed details and sloppy riding when the radio was off, and then faked a calm, encouraging serenity when he pressed the button to speak to the riders. Our six had been fast and powerful, but hardly without error. We unexpectedly lost two riders early on, and so we were forced to play out our best game without any pawns on the table. Sometimes though, losing riders early in a team time trial isn't terrible news. It's because the rest of the team is just moving so fast. The remaining four kept the speed impossibly high. The waning moments of our effort were unskilled and messy, as it often is when all are suffering, yet they found a way forward.

Against a backdrop of enormous and passionate crowds, more than 500,000 on the day, our riders had drawn energy from the people here to cheer on their heroes of the road. The roads were open, and despite our team barreling down the road at 60 kilometers per hour, people still fought for the best view of our riders by bending over each other all the way into the middle of the road. Dangerous, of course, but then what part of cycling isn't dangerous? It's a sport that mimics the realities of life: more can go wrong than right, and no one is going to protect you from that.

We sat in the car staring at the television screen after the finish. It showed our team ahead by just a few seconds. We stopped, looked again, and still couldn't believe it.

We had just won the opening team time trial of the Tour of Colombia 2.1 in downtown Medellin, against all expectations. We won against the massively funded Sky, and we won against the heavily favored Deceuninck–Quick-Step outfit. It was a moment of pure ecstasy. It was a moment that, for me, can only happen with cycling. It was a pure joy that I can only feel when I am with my only true bride of the last thirty-three years: cycling.

This is why I am here.

I wish I could truly describe what it feels like the moment you've found out you've won a race against all odds. I mean, every race win is against all odds. Starting with winning the Buckeye road race when I was only twelve, all the way to winning Paris–Roubaix 2011, the Giro 2012, the team time trial in the Tour de France, Rigo winning with only one gear on stage 9 of the Tour in 2017, and then this team time trial in Colombia, after suffering through a few tough years. The feeling after these wins is something that one cannot experience anywhere else in life. The frustration, the nastiness of disgruntled fans hating you, the constant battle to keep a team alive, and the endless headwind that blows against the sport of pro cycling itself. All of these reasons to simply stop the sport and move on to something else, all these logical facts that stack up against any sane person's thoughts of entering the world of professional cycling . . . all of them, they stop for a moment, and they turn to pure joy. It's a joy that I don't think is possible to experience elsewhere, certainly for me. It just rips through you like lightning, and makes you feel a happiness that is clear and true.

The rareness and beauty of winning in cycling is something I wish the whole world could experience. Cycling is a place where much more can go wrong than right. Crashes, flat tires, illness, and the simple fact that no matter what, the odds are always against you . . . 170 riders start a race. Only one wins. Quite a bit different than a football game where you have a 50 percent chance of winning. So, when you do win in cycling, it's as if you've done the impossible. And that doing the impossible was made possible by a group of people and chain of custody that must be perfect. From the training to the nutrition, to the tire pressure, to the aerodynamics, to the tactics, to the instinct . . . it all must be perfect. There can be no error in that chain.

When it all works, and an organization of a hundred people all working for this magical moment finally breaks through, it is to experience a small kiss from God.

This whole book has been a look back. Back through my life, back through the world of cycling, and back through the lens of an old, grumpy, retired ex–professional athlete. The stories here reveal a romance between a deeply flawed human and a deeply flawed sport. The look back has been hard for me. A harsh reality of things I could have done better and things that I did that were just wrong. But through the process of writing it, and through the process of stumbling my way through this life, I feel like I've made some progress. Progress in being a better person. Progress in building a better team.

So, if I'm so in love with this sport, why spend an entire book writing about how dark it is?

Because it is dark. And it is also beautiful.

I would not trade my journey over the last thirty years. It has left me beaten, broken, and lonely, yet I wouldn't want it any other way. The ever so brief moments where it all works, where a team of individuals becomes one, where you feel the joy of a rider coming across the finish line first. Those tiny moments, those brief seconds in a world of painful hours, those are what keep me here.

I remember seeing Ian MacGregor, an early team rider whom I coached, winning U.S. National Championships in 2004, and feeling the pure joy of this moment. It wasn't professional, it wasn't fueled by doping, it wasn't anything but hard work and a dream come true for him. And I remember thinking that while my experience in cycling was harsh and dark, it was now my job, my responsibility, to make sure that others, like Ian, do not have that experience. And that they can more purely feel the joy of winning. The joy of building a true dream and seeing it come true.

And that is where I am today.

I am in a place where I can proudly look back and say with a true heart, "These riders will not have to face the dark decisions I did. They can build their lives and live their dreams with integrity."

And nothing brings me greater joy than knowing that is true. That's why I am still here.

A question I'm often asked is, "Do you regret the decisions you made?" And the answer to that is an emphatic YES. But, unfortunately, if I take myself back to my twenty-five-year-old Mont Ventoux–winning self, in the same situations, with the same level of maturity that I had, I believe I'd probably make all the same damned decisions again.

I wasn't willing to let my dream fail. And if that meant doping, then so be it.

And if that meant living out the rest of my days spinning in pain and regret, then so be it.

It was my dream.

That's a hard thing to admit. But in that admission, I can see what my purpose has been the last decade. My purpose has been to do everything in my power, use every bit of knowledge and hurt, to prevent the decision between a dream and losing one's soul to never ever be one that is confronted.

A young and ambitious person should never be put in that position.

It is one thing to decide to be greedy and cheat. It is another to finally stumble and fall after your conscience being worn down and your dream slowly being pulled away.

They should never have to encounter the choice of "cheat or leave." That is one of the most blackening experiences a twenty-something just starting in a career could have. My heart is still black because of that choice. It always will be.

And so, I feel that it is my responsibility—deep responsibility— to make sure they never face the hard realities of that choice.

Of course the skeptics will say, "But doping still exists, it's no different now than it was before." That may be a widely held perspective looking from the outside in. A perspective held by former riders unable to fully take responsibility for their actions and looking for others to blame. Or perspective held by people who simply haven't been able to see behind the curtain in pro cycling. But the reality from the inside looking out is much clearer. It is a view that allows me to rest easy at night. It is knowing that while doping may still exist in sport, that the times of the choice being "dope or leave your dream behind . . ." those days are gone.

Why am I so certain?

Well, the biggest reason is that I've been able to watch, up close and firsthand, riders go from teenagers with big dreams to professionals who have succeeded without doping. They've been able to build their lives proudly and without regrets or secrets. This was not possible in my era of racing. Which is hard to look back at and acknowledge in an honest and unpolished way. It is what makes this book dark.

But that darkness is what led me and many others in the sport to try and move things forward.

Is it perfect? No. Have I made mistakes? Yes. But on the whole, I know that now I can watch riders have great and fruitful careers, clean. And knowing that somehow gives me solace that my dark past was not completely in vain. That my efforts to move past it were not wasted breath. That the stinging and painful criticisms I receive for having this very viewpoint were and are worth it.

We are seeing the first generation of riders in pro cycling that many will be able to retire from a long and adventurous career as happy and whole people. People who never succumbed. People who never lost their moral compass.

Maybe I'm too optimistic. But if there is just one rider who has been able to live out a full and successful career without ever seeing doping, being tempted by doping, or having to contemplate the choice, then all of my rose-colored views on cycling will be worth it.

Any amount of pain and humiliation I've felt over the years was worth making that happen.

That's where I am today.

I am broken, but I am proud. I am proud of the many riders who will be able to feel the lightning of winning, without becoming a broken person.

I love this sport.

And I would do it all over again.

ACKNOWLEDGMENTS

There are so very many people that have helped me throughout my life, and so I will forget some. Dammit. My memory just isn't that good anymore. I hope for those of you whom I forget, you'll call me up and give me some shit about it. With that disclaimer, I'm going to try . . .

First off, a big thank-you to Quercus and Penguin for giving me the chance to write and to share my writing with the rest of the world. I missed every deadline, like a true drunken writer, and you guys still stuck by me. Amazing.

Jeremy Whittle . . . You convinced me to do this thing. And almost died with me in a plane that I was flying. Your vision and dedication (and organizational skills) kept this project from going into a ditch. Thank you for seeing it all, well before I could.

Richard Milner . . . The UK editor of the mess of words I sent to him. You turned jumbled ideas and fuzzy memories into a book! For me, that's like watching magic happen. Thank you for giving me some of your magic.

Matthew Klise . . . The U.S. editor. Thank you for actually liking and fighting for some of my more intellectual rants. And thanks for treating me as a true writer and artist from the get-go.

David Luxton and Rebecca Winfield, thank you for holding my hand and guiding me into the world of book publishing.

My parents, Jim and Donna Vaughters. They dedicated their lives to me. I can't express enough gratitude for the effort and pain they went through to help me grow up in this world. I have endless admiration for both of them and hope that someday I can actually live up to the amount of love they poured into me and my growth.

Colby Pearce . . . You are my true brother.

Mark Imboden, Mark Morcus, and Rob Balgley. My thirty-year-old friends when I was fifteen. We trained like we were all going to be pros for all those years. You guys just got old too soon to live out your racing ambitions . . .

Carrie Amos . . . For the first time ever in my life, you made me feel that I was something special, and not something inferior. Thank you.

Julie Clouatre . . . You tried to feed me foie gras before I was ready. I thought it was cat food at seventeen years old. Fond memories. Hope you're well.

Doug Ellis . . . Your friendship and mentorship have been invaluable. I'm so happy we have remained friends all these years, and that even through all the hurt we've been through, somehow we've become even closer. BFF!

Alisa Metcalf . . . The kind and intelligent nature of our son is borne from the fact he was from our very powerful love for each other. I see you and your sparkling green eyes in him every day, and that makes me feel warm and loved to this day.

Ashley Hausman . . . This book would have never happened if not for you. I was so desperate to do something that might impress you enough to win your love back that I decided to write a book! My pain in your stark absence gave me the focus and energy to write. That is something I will always be grateful for. Within these pages is the self-reflection I was gifted because of you. I also listened to Eric Church's "Record Year" about a thousand times. I guess that's been a gift, too. Hope you are well.

Charlie Vaughters . . . Could you please flush the toilet and pick up your dirty socks off the floor?

Alie Hopper . . . I would have lost my way a long, long time ago without you.

Beth Wrenn-Estes . . . Your race, the Bob Cook Memorial Hill Climb, has inspired every day of my entire life. I will forever be in debt to you for organizing it for so many years.

José Luis Nuñez . . . Our dream on Santa Clara ended badly, but you were the reason I pushed onward. What you did for me can never be repaid. I hope you are well.

Matt Koschara . . . Matt, thank you for listening. So many times. You have such a gift in this life with people. I'm glad you shared it with me.

Frankie Yantorno . . . The best friend a kid could have. And the first in a long line of true mentors. You taught me about the beauty of cycling.

Steve Goldstein . . . One of my incredible mentors. So many athletes struggle to transition from their sporting careers to the world of business. You made that possible for me. You also taught me to be tough in this world. To never give up.

Desiree Edwards . . . You taught me how to fly!! Since Leonardo da Vinci, this is the greatest gift any human can give another. I can fly because of you. Thank you!!!

Bill Ramsey . . . Your enthusiasm for life is inspiring. Thank you for dragging me around to so many bike races and making sure I remembered to bring my shoes.

Rigoberto Urán . . . You didn't have to stick by me. But you did. El Presidente de Colombia!

Charly Wegelius and Andreas Klier . . . You are two grumpy old men. Thank you for holding me up so many times when I was going to fall. #WaldorfandStatler

Marya Pongrace . . . You gave me the ability to speak. To communicate. In this book there is so much of you and the lessons I learned from you.

Mark Holowesko . . . Another mentor I admire. Your steady vision and undying love for true ethics is guiding.

John Bucksbaum . . . We've both been there for each other in some pretty rough moments. I'm proud to call you one of my friends, and I'm eternally grateful for all of your support.

Grady Durham . . . Thank you for being my sounding board for so many ideas. Your patience with me and my eccentricities has made you a dear friend.

Jon Cassat . . . We found our way because of you.

Anne Gripper . . . Anne, you are my hero in life. You are, without a doubt, the strongest person I know. I am so lucky I was involved in cycling and the anti-doping movement while you were at the helm. You changed my life, you changed my world, and you remain a great friend.

Juliet Macur . . . You showed me that doing the right thing has value. You allowed me to step away from the fear I had of my own past.

Paul Kimmage . . . Reading *Rough Ride* changed my life. I hope this book will do the same for someone, someday.

Jim Beasley . . . Tell your mother I loved her baking.

Greg Strock . . . The kid nobody knew about from Indiana. Was the OG anti-doper. Kudos.

Roger Legeay . . . You taught me that making the right choice sometimes really sucks. But even if it sucks, it is still right. Thanks, boss. You are forever my boss.

Shane Steffens . . . I would have never had the time to write this book without your help in running this team.

Mike Friedman . . . Meatball . . . Love you, man.

Matt Johnson . . . It was a wild ride. Thank you for your ability to sell ice to someone in a blizzard. Garmin, Transitions, Sharp, Cervélo . . . the list goes on and on. Team never would have happened without you.

Travis Tygart . . . You fought for the rights of athletes. And for the truth to be revealed. To the point that WADA tried to get rid of you. Brave man.

Beth Seliga . . . You were the first in a line of many powerful and strong women that have worked in leadership roles within this team. You were my right arm, and left one, too. Very proud of our time together and all those late nights trying to do something that everyone said wasn't possible.

Louise Donald . . . Your dedication to making the trains run on time allowed us to flourish. Your passion is beyond words of gratitude that I can give.

Matt Beaudin . . . Your style is something I aspire to. Thank you for making so many edits in my life.

Gary Dickinson . . . Thank you for making me understand that the IRS really do want their money.

Clay Young . . . Hopefully I can rescue you someday, instead of you always rescuing me.

Chris Farnum . . . You were the style that launched this whole team. I thank you and all the staff at Adega for the parties that started it all. My liver feels otherwise.

Jaq Poussot . . . You allowed me to feel my heart again. Without that, I could have never written these words.

Kelly Woodridge . . . Thanks for letting me cry on your shoulder— and making me dinner when the house was bare and lonely.

Jessi Braverman . . . When the team was about to fall flat on its face, you stayed at the keyboard, pushing onward. Without you, we never would have had "Save Argyle," and thus, no team . . .

Dan Brogan . . . My first sponsor. You seeded this whole adventure.

Danny Pate . . . The team was about you and your dream. I hope someday you'll see that.

Mike Creed . . . Makes me so happy seeing you building your own path. Best of luck.

Philip and Edward Hult . . . My next mentors in life. I learn so much from you guys, every day.

To all the old-school Slipstreamers I've missed here. We were a pirate ship held together with tape and bubble gum. And I wouldn't change a single part of that. Thank you for believing in me, in the idea of the team, and in a better way forward.

And to all the folks that threw themselves and their money into #SaveArgyle. I'll never get to know all of you, and I'll never get to say thank you to everyone. But you are the people that made this happen. I will never forget that.

And finally, Lance Armstrong . . . For better or worse, you've impacted this book in a big way. Maybe someday we will let it all go. Maybe.